A SYNOPSIS OF THE BOOKS
OF ADAM AND EVE

Second Revised Edition

SOCIETY OF BIBLICAL LITERATURE

EARLY JUDAISM AND ITS LITERATURE

Series Editor
John C. Reeves

Editorial Board

Steven D. Fraade, Yale University
David Frankfurter, University of New Hampshire
Sarah J. Tanzer, McCormick Theological Seminary

Number 17

A SYNOPSIS OF THE BOOKS
OF ADAM AND EVE
Second Revised Edition

edited by
Gary A. Anderson
Michael E. Stone

A SYNOPSIS OF THE BOOKS OF ADAM AND EVE
Second Revised Edition

edited by
Gary A. Anderson
Michael E. Stone

Scholars Press
Atlanta, Georgia

A SYNOPSIS OF THE BOOKS OF ADAM AND EVE
Second Revised Edition

edited by
Gary A. Anderson
Michael E. Stone

Copyright © 1999 by the Society of Biblical Literature

All rights reserved. No part of this work may be reproduced or transmitted in any form or by any means, electronic or mechanical, including photocopying and recording, or by means of any information storage or retrieval system, except as may be expressly permitted by the 1976 Copyright Act or in writing from the publisher. Requests for permission should be addressed in writing to the Rights and Permissions Office, Scholars Press, P.O. Box 15399, Atlanta, GA 30333-0399, USA.

Library of Congress Cataloging-in-Publication Data

Life of Adam and Eve. Polyglot.
   A synopsis of the books of Adam and Eve / edited by Gary A. Anderson, Michael E. Stone. — 2nd rev. ed.
      p.   cm. — (Early Judaism and its literature ; no. 17)
   Text in English, Armenian, Georgian, Greek, Latin, and Slavonic.
   Includes bibliographical references (p.   ) and index.
   ISBN 0-7885-0566-1 (cloth : alk. paper)
   1. Life of Adam and Eve—Criticism, Textual. I. Anderson, Gary A., 1955– . II. Stone, Michael E., 1938–   III. Title. IV. Series.
BS1830.A25A1   1999
229'.911—dc21   99-28348
                                                     CIP
ISBN 978-1-58983-458-3 (paper : alk. paper)

Printed in the United States of America
on acid-free paper

TABLE OF CONTENTS

Introduction... vii
I. Text Versions... vii
Addendum: Notes On The Translation Of The Georgian Prepared By J.-P. Mahé............ xii
II. Principles Of Versification.. xvii
Bibliography... xvii
Acknowledgements..xix
Sigla.. xx

Pericope Number and Title

1. Authority over Animals *[Slavonic only]*................................... 1

2-6 Penitence of Adam and Eve (Greek Omits)

2. **PENITENCE:** Expulsion 2
3. **PENITENCE:** Cheirograph *[Slavonic only]*............................... 6
4. **PENITENCE:** Penitence and Second Temptation 7
5. **PENITENCE:** Fall of the Satan 15
6. **PENITENCE:** Separation of Adam and Eve 19

7. Cain and Abel 26
8. Adam's Vision *[Latin only]*... 32
9. Illness of Adam.. 33
10. Adam's Story of the Fall 36
11. Command to Retrieve the Oil 39

12-15 Quest of Eve and Seth for the Oil

12. **QUEST:** Encounter with Beast 41
13. **QUEST:** Arrival at Paradise... 44
14. **QUEST:** Michael's Reply... 45
15. **QUEST:** Return to Adam 46
16. **QUEST:** Adam's Rebuke of Eve 47

17-27 Eve's Tale (Latin Omits)

17. EVE'S TALE: The Portions of Adam and Eve in Paradise 48
18. EVE'S TALE: Satan's Encounter with the Serpent (Gen 3:1a) 49
19. EVE'S TALE: Serpent's Approach to Paradise (Gen 3:1b-3).......... 51
20. EVE'S TALE: Temptation of Eve (Gen 3:4-6a) 54
21. EVE'S TALE: Eve's Oath 56
22. EVE'S TALE: Eve's Sin (Gen 3:7a) 58
23. EVE'S TALE: Temptation of Adam (Gen 3:6b-7) 60
24. EVE'S TALE: Entry of God into Paradise (Gen 3:8-13) 62
25. EVE'S TALE: Judgment of Adam, Eve, and the Serpent (3:14-19) .. 65
26. EVE'S TALE: Adam's Plea for Mercy (Gen 3:22-24) 69
27. EVE'S TALE: Expulsion (Gen 3:22-24) 72

28. Death of Adam 74
29. Eve's Confession 76
30. Angelic Liturgy 78
31. Assumption of Adam to Paradise 82
32. Adam and Abel's Funerary Rites 84
33. Two Stelae Legends *[Latin only]*................................... 91
34. Eve's Prayer to join Adam 92
35. Eve's Funeral and Epilogue 94

Addenda to the Latin Version

36. History of Stelae 96
37. Octipartite Adam.. 96
38. Place of Adam's Creation 96
39: Adam's Name 96

INDEX OF PROPER NAMES.. 97

Introduction

This book is a substantial revision of the synopsis we first published in 1994. In this revised synopsis we have provided fresh English translations of each of the versions and we have provided the original language of each version in a facing column. In spite of this considerable advance, this book must still be considered "a tentative document." Text-critical problems still remain and the Greek, Latin and Slavonic versions are especially problematic from this perspective.

Here we will not discuss the text-critical problems that attend the individual language traditions. A very detailed and up-to-date discussion of these issues can be found in Stone's recent publication on the Adam literature (1992). However, some background information is required about the origin of the texts provided in this volume and the conventions of formatting used to present them.

I. Text Versions

The Greek Version
The text used in this edition was produced by Nagel just shortly before his death and printed in the concordance of Denis (1987). The English translation has been provided by Gary Anderson.

Nagel did not produce a critical text for Denis' concordance. Rather, it appears that he chose manuscript S from Family I as a base text and supplemented it with additional material from an important subgroup of Family I: ATLC. In his dissertation, Nagel was of the opinion that this subgroup was secondary, though its importance stemmed from the fact that it closely resembled the Georgian version (Nagel only spoke of and knew the similarities to the Georgian; the parallels to the Armenian became clear only after the publication of Stone's edition).

It has not yet been determined finally whether the Armenian and Georgian versions stem from an existing sub-family within the Greek textual tradition or whether, as seems more likely,

Introduction

represent a witness to an independent form of the Greek text that has been lost. The text Nagel bequeathed us leaves this question open for further study.

A thorough review of the Greek material in light of the publication of the Georgian and Armenian editions is now being undertaken by J. Tromp (Leiden).

Nagel divided the Greek manuscripts into three families:

I	II	III
1. DSV	RM	1. NI(J)K
2. KPB		2. QZ
3. B		3. HEWXF
4. ATLC		

The manuscript group DSV in Family I appears to be the least corrupted. Manuscript D (11th century) is the oldest of these three witnesses, but it lacks chapters 18-35. Perhaps for this reason, Nagel favored S over D and most of his text conforms to this manuscript.

In the present edition we have set all the additions to S from ATLC within square brackets. Longer additions that stretch over several verses, such as those found in chapters 13 and 29, have been put in italics. The long addition found in 29:7 (the so-called "Penitence" narrative) is found in Family II only and is, therefore, in a different category. It is also put in italics.

The Latin Version

The Latin text printed here was supplied by Wilfried Lechner-Schmidt. He is currently finishing a dissertation in Germany on the topic under the direction of K. Berger. The English translation was prepared by Gary Anderson.

The textual condition of the Latin version presents the most text-critical difficulties. For this reason it is important to say something more about it. Meyer (1878) divided the manuscripts which he knew into 4 groups or families, which he numbered from I to IV in Roman numerals. These Roman numerals are also used in this synopsis as abbreviations for the different forms of the text.

Introduction

I Group I of Meyer
II Group II of Meyer
III Group III of Meyer
IV Group IV of Meyer

The text presented in the Latin column is normally that of Meyer's Group I.

Those parts of the Latin column which do not present the text of Group I are enclosed within square brackets ([]). For example: "*Quando expulsi sunt* [II,III=*Cum expulsi (fuissent? essent?) Adam et Eva*]II,III *de paradiso...*" means that Groups II and III read "*Cum expulsi ... Adam et Eva*" whereas Group I reads "*Quando expulsi sunt Adam et Eva.*" The question marks after "*fuissent*" and "*essent*" indicate that some manuscripts read "*fuissent*" whereas others, "*essent.*" If there are variant readings within Group I, readings other than the text are put in round brackets () and a question mark is put at the end. Consider the example of 29:4, ex ore maiestatis suae dabit omnibus mandata et paecepta (*ex ore eius exiet gladius ex utraque parte acutus?*). If there is more than one variant, then the different readings are separated by a comma. Compare Et iterum (*die tertio?, septimo?*) in 29:6.

Occasionally, additional narrative material was woven into the Latin text. Group III includes the Holy Rood legend in chapters 43, 44, and 48. Meyer chose not print this supplementary material in his edition. The present edition of the *Vita* has marked such material as follows: "*[III+***legenda de ligno crucis***]III*" At one point material from the *Gospel of Nicodemus* is introduced. This is marked by the abbreviation: *Nic.*

In addition the following symbols are used:
  +   additional word / words
  -   missing word / words
  =   other variant / variants

The Armenian Version

The Armenian text that is published here is based on the printed edition of the Armenian published in 1981. That edition was in turn based on three manuscripts, all the copies known so far. These are the following:

A Jerusalem, Armenian Patriarchate, No. 1458, pp. 380-431, 17th century.

Introduction

B   Jerusalem, Armenian Patriarchate, No. 1370, pp. 127-150, 17th century.

C   Erevan, Matenadaran, No. 3461, fols. 66r-87v, dated 1662 C.E.

The questions of the intrinsic value of the Armenian version as a witness to the *Life of Adam and Eve* and of its relationship to the other versions have been debated. The work is closely related to the Georgian *Book of Adam*, which was translated and published after the publication of the Armenian version. J.-P. Mahé made a comparative study of the two and concluded that, together with Latin, they go back to a single recension, related to Greek manuscripts A, C and L. Moreover, he concludes correctly that Armenian and Georgian are closer to each other than either is to any other version.

The special readings of the Armenian version were discussed first by Stone, *Penitence of Adam* (1981) and his conclusion that Armenian preserves certain readings preferable to any other version is supported by G.A. Anderson. We see no reason to change this conclusion today (*pace* de Jonge and Tromp). Our study so far has uncovered no special relationship between the Armenian *Penitence of Adam* and any of the other numerous Armenian Adam books.

Due to the editorial policy of the series in which the *editio princeps* was published, readings of only one manuscript were given in the text and other readings, even if they were considered preferable, were put in the apparatus and marked *lege*. Such readings are now included in the text in square brackets and equally in the translation. The text and translation thus contain the best readings available. Variants are not noted. In a number of places small errors of the previous editions have been corrected and the translation has been revised to accord with the translations of the other versions, as far as is practicable.

Chapters had been marked already in the *editio princeps*. In the present text and translation, verses are also marked, which are coordinated with those of the other versions. Capitalization has been introduced and the punctuation normalized.

The Georgian Version

The Georgian text provided in this synopsis is that of C. K'urc'ikidze. We have not noted emendations, corruptions, etc. in the text we have printed. The English translation was made

Introduction

for this synopsis by J.-P. Mahé. C. K'urc'ikidze's edition is based on the following manuscripts:

Recension alpha

A	A153, pp. 1-54, 17th century	
Q	K'ut'aisi 128, pp. 1-23, 17th century	
B	H443, fols. 1r-23r, 19th century	
C	H881, fols. 1r-16r, 19th century	

In addition Museum of Literature, no. 186, pp. 1-10, 19th century, belongs to this recension but it was not utilized by K'urc'ikidze.

Recension beta

S   S5157, 8 leaves with fragments, 17th century. This manuscript was written by the copyist of the famous Queen Mariam's Collection of Georgian Chronicles, known as *K'art'lis Cxovreba* "The Life of Georgia."

In Mahé's French translation of the Georgian he followed, in the main, the text of redaction *alpha*. Readings that were taken from *beta* were chosen because they were thought to provide a better text and were printed in italics. Here we have attempted to standardize the way in which variants have been presented.

The Slavonic Version

This version still requires a fair amount of work. We have published the Slavonic text prepared by Jagič in 1893. It is discussed in Stone (1992) where the known manuscripts and editions are listed.

Introduction

Addendum: Notes on the Translation of the Georgian prepared by J.-P. Mahé

1:1 "to live in": Thus QBC; A has a synonym.

2:2 "till we find out – who knows – (perhaps) the Lord": This is better, on contextual grounds, than "testing (the food), etc." They are attempting to see whether God will take them back.

4:3 "do penance": Georgian has, literally, "let us repent in penitence," meaning "let us do penance." The construction resembles "to die a death" in 3:1 *supra*.

6:1a "stay and be": Thus K'urc'ikidze, using the imperative and following AC; QB have "do."

8:2 "for me": Thus QB; "for us" K'urc'ikidze, following AC.

15:1 "heard": The enclitic particle *ya* here means "still," stressing the simultaneity of the action. Alternatively translate: "while the six ...that, then my speech..."

16:2 "by your power": Thus B; "before you" K'urc'ikidze, following AQC.

20:1c "lamb": Perhaps "little ewe"; if *t'arigi* means *k'ravi*. It means, most likely, "small female lamb" (like French "agnelle").

20:2a "[[luminaries]]": or "[[lights]]." The manuscripts have *natesavta* "generations" which we emend to *mnatobta* "luminaries": see 44(32):2. One might also emend to *nateli* "light": see 44(34):1.

21:2 "because of Adam, (the) elect (one)": We use a different word division to K'urc'ikidze, reading *adamis gamo, rčeulisa* in place of her *adamis, gamorčeulisa* which might be translated "...of Adam, the elect ..."

"you are sure to have conceived": In fact, the power says, "you have conceived," not using an aorist, which would mean an objective, real fact, but a perfect with some sort of dubitative nuance. Alternatively render, "it seems you have conceived."

21:3d "I have taught": Thus QAC which read *ray vasc'ave*: B has *rayta asc'ave*, followed by K'urc'ikidze, "so that you teach."

Introduction

23(3):2a "[[Tell Adam]]": This is an emendation by K'urc'ikidze, with no manuscript support. Note, however, that Armenian reads *asa Adamay* "Tell (or: say to) Adam."

23(3):2b "[[he]] will teach you": This is an emendation of the text of QAC from *gasc'ao šen* "I will teach you" to *gasc'aos šen* "he will teach you." This would accord with Armenian Ms B which has *c'uc'c'ē k'ez* "he will teach you."

23(3):3a This verse is given according to recension *alpha*. Recension *beta* reads: "[[God told Gabr]]iel; the angel came and told Adam and Adam kept these words in his heart. And they were both sad, Adam and Eve."

23(3):3a This verse occurs only in recension *alpha*.

23(3):3d "hand(s)": It is impossible to distinguish the singular from the plural in Georgian at this point.

24(4):2 "before me" *alpha*; "before you (sing.)" *beta*.

30(5):4-5 Recension *alpha* reads: "And his sons told him: What is this, Father Adam? or how will a man become ill?" Recension *beta* reads: "And his sons told him: What is (this), Father? And he told them: I am sick my sons. And they told him the …"

32(7):1 "to eat its fruit": Thus recension *beta*; *alpha* omits and adds, "But there was one of the plants, beautiful, in the garden."

32(7):3b "to ascend": Thus recension *beta*; *alpha* omits.

32(7):4 "the garden": This word, not found in the text of *alpha* is introduced into it by K'urc'ikidze from recension *beta*.

35(9):2 "Eve" is an addition in *alpha* supported by *beta*.

36 (9):4 This occurs only in *alpha*.

37(10):1 This passage occurs only in *alpha* with no variants.

37(10):3 "Did you dare": This reading presumes a different word division.

Introduction

38(11):2 "You [[on account]] of whom": Here the text reads *romlisa gamoy* which is emended into *romlisa <gamo>*. The unemended text would mean "whose taste the form of everything is changed." The syntax is unclear and it does not really make sense.

42(13):3b [[resurrect]]": There is a corruption in Georgian of *aǧsrulobad* "to finish, accomplish" for *aǧdginebad* "to resurrect." K'urc'ikidze keeps the mistake, but marks it with an exclamation mark.

43(13):4 "that unction": This, rather than oil, seems to be the meaning. For "oil" Georgian uses the word *zet* "(olive) oil". Here, however, there is the word *sacxdeli* which derives from *cxebay* "to anoint," and therefore the translation "unction" has been chosen here.

44(16):2a "I [[hear]] that": Recension *alpha* reads, "the Devil told the serpent: You are wiser"; recension *beta* reads: "the Devil thirdly told the serpent: You are wiser." The text must be corrupted and we emend *mesamed vitarmed* into *<vitarmed> mes<mis> vitarmed. mes<mis>* is exactly equivalent to Armenian *lsem* here.

44(16):3 "inferior": From this point on, we follow recension *beta*. The remaining text of recension *alpha* is: "why do you eat (something) inferior and contemptible, and not the good fruit of the garden? But came and hearken to me, so that I (thus QAC; we B) may have him expelled outside the wall of the Garden." The word "wall" (*alpha*) seems better than "enclosure" (*beta*) since Armenian reads *orm* "wall." The Georgian *zǧade* may have both meanings.

44(17):2c The text of recension *alpha* resumes here and is used in the translation.

44(17):5 "Yes, we eat": Thus *beta*; "I eat" *alpha*.

44(18):4 "you would become": Thus B; "you were" AQC K'urc'ikidze *alpha*; "you would be" *beta*.

44(18):5 "Go to": Thus B K'urc'ikidze; "look at" *beta*; "take" QAC.

44(21):2 We propose reading *raymetu* instead of *rametu* accepted by K'urc'ikidze.

44(21):4a "[[she told me]]": An addition by the translator.

Introduction

44(21): 5 Recension *alpha* reads: "Then I gave (it to) your father and we learned that we were naked. And it happened when God came to the garden, we hid from the face of the Lord, because both of us had covered ourselves with a leaf of a fig tree."

44(23):1 Recension *alpha* reads: "And God summoned Adam: Adam, Adam where were you? And he told him: I am here, Lord, because I was naked and I hid from you."

44(24):1 "[[Because]]": So we have emended the text to *rametu*, cf. Armenian *p'oxanak zi*. Recension *beta* has *rata* and K'urc'ikidze proposed the emendation *raysa* "why (do)."

44(24):3 All the negatives were added by K'urc'ikidze into the text of the one manuscript extant for this section. "have [[no]] rest" is confirmed by the Armenian *mi lic'i k'ez hangist*. There is no support "[[not]] be sated" and "[[not]] taste" in Armenian. The second occurrence of "[[not]] be sated" (following "bitterness") might well be a dittography in Georgian.

"fle[[e to soak yourselves]] with water": Only the first four letters of "fle[[e]]" survive and the instrumental of "water." The rest is conjecture.

44(26):1 The translation here combines readings of *alpha* and *beta*. *Alpha* has "and God (AQC: he B) told the serpent: You too perish..." *Beta* has "When he had said all this to me, he became very angry with the serpent: Be cursed ..."

44(26):3 "exhausted and broken": Thus *beta*; *alpha* has "thin and [unknown word]."

44(28):4 The translation follows *beta*. *Alpha* reads: "... from every evil, and you say: I shall die. And [[after]] death, I will arise in the future, then I will give you of the tree ..."

44(29):1 Thus *beta*: *alpha* reads: "When the Lord had said that in the garden."

44(31):3 "alone": Thus *beta*: *alpha* omits.

"do not move": Thus *beta*: *alpha* has a third person.

44(32):2 The text of *beta* reads: "I have sinned against you before your angels and I have sinned before the Cherubs, and I have sinned before your altar, and I have sinned before the

Introduction

holy light, and I have sinned against the winged birds of the heavens and the beasts of the earth."

44(32):3 "on her [[knees]]": So *alpha* emended: *beta* reads "while Eve was praying that …" The text is emended from "feet" to "[[knees]]" since the next phrase says that she arose. Does kneeling down to pray indicate something about the original context of the text?

44(33):2 "[[winds]]": This is an addition by K'urc'ikidze.

44(33):4 "cups": This occurs only in *beta*.

"three angels": This occurs only in *alpha*. Both these readings are confirmed by the following words.

44(34):1 "before God": Thus *beta*; "before him" *alpha*.

44(35):4 "the blood of my spouse": Thus *beta*; *alpha* has "the deeds of blood" K'urc'ikidze; "the deed of blood" QABC.

47(37):2 Thus *beta*; *alpha* reads: "Blessed are you, Lord, who have pardoned the protoplast."

47(38):4 That is to say that they had fallen into a deep sleep, like Adam before the birth of Eve. See below 48(42):3.

48(40):2 Emend *sindisani* into *sindnisani* or *sindonisani* "of [[cloth]]."

48(41):1 "Here I am, [[Lord]]." Emending here to *upalo*. The manuscripts have *parao* "Pharaoh" or *para* "he hid" or "he said."

48(42):3 "[[when]] she saw all [[that]]": We read *ese ray* instead of *esera*.

"…": There is a lacuna here and K'urc'ikidze's reconstruction is unacceptable.

Introduction

II. Principles of Versification

1. The chapters correspond to the chapters of the Latin as found in Charles.

2. Where the Greek also exists, its numbers are given in parentheses.

3. When one Latin chapter corresponds to numerous Greek chapters, the Latin chapter number is repeated at the start of each "Greek" chapter.

4. Where Armenian and Greek are longer than Latin, the Latin number is repeated in square brackets.

5. The versification is taken from Charles from chapter 1 to chapter 22 who follows the Latin, thereafter it follows the Greek. From time to time we have altered the versification slightly so that the various versions can be brought into proper alignment.

6. If a verse is exceptionally long, we have subdivided it by adding the markers: "a," "b," "c," etc.

Bibliography

D.A. Bertrand, *La vie grecque d'Adam et Eve* (Recherches intertestamentaires 1) Paris: Maisonneuve, 1987.

A.-M. Denis, *Concordance grecque des pseudépigraphes d'Ancien Testament: Concordance, corpus des textes, indices*. Louvain-la-Neuve: Université Catholique de Louvain, 1987.

V. Jagič, "Slavische Beiträge zu den biblischen Apocryphen, I, Die altkirchenslavischen Texte des Adamsbuche," *Denkschr. kais. Akademie der Wissenschaften, philos.-hist. Klasse* (Vienna, 1893) 42, 1-104.

Introduction

M. de Jonge and J. Tromp, *The Life of Adam and Eve and Related Literature*. Sheffield: Sheffield Academic Press, 1997.

C. K'urc'ikidze, "Adamis Apokrip'uli C'xovrebis K'art'uli Versia," *P'ilologiuri Dziebani* 1 (1964), 97-136.

J.-P. Mahé, "Le Livre d'Adam géorgien," *Studies in Gnosticism and Hellenistic Religions*. ed. R. van den Broek and M.J. Vermaseren, Leiden: Brill, 1981, 227-260.

W. Meyer, "Vita Adae et Evae," *Abhandlungen der königlichen Bayerischen Akademie der Wissenschaften, philosoph.-philologische Klasse* (Munich, 1878) 14.3, 185-250.

J.H. Mozley, "The Vitae Adae," *Journal of Theological Studies* 30 (1929), 121-49.

M.E. Stone, *The Penitence of Adam* (CSCO, 429-30; Scriptores Armeniaci 13-14) Leuven: Peeters, 1981.

M.E. Stone, *A History of the Literature of Adam and Eve* (Early Judaism and its Literature 3) Atlanta: Scholars Press, 1992.

L.S.A. Wells, "The Books of Adam and Eve," *The Apocrypha and Pseudepigrapha of the Old Testament*, ed. R. H. Charles (Oxford: Clarendon, 1913) 2, 123-54.

Introduction

Acknowledgements

The English translation of the Armenian is cited from M.E. Stone, *Penitence of Adam* (CSCO, 429-30; Scriptores Armeniaci 13-14; ed. R. Draguet; Leuven: Peeters, 1981) by permission of Peeters Press in Leuven, Belgium. The Greek text printed here is that prepared by M. Nagel for A.-M. Denis (ed.), *Concordance grecque des pseudépigraphes d'Ancien Testament* (Louvain-la-Neuve: Université Catholique de Louvain, 1987) pp. 815-818. It is reprinted by permission of the Publications de l'Institut Orientaliste, Université Catholique de Louvain, à Louvain-la-Neuve.

There are many to thank for their gracious help in bringing this work to completion. The National Endowment for the Humanities supported the project. M.E. Stone put final touches on his contribution while a Fellow-in-Residence of the Netherlands Institute of Advanced Studies in Wassenaar, Netherlands. Appreciation is expressed to both these institutions which do much to nurture studies in the humanities.

Thanks are due to J.-P. Mahé for his meticulous work on the Georgian edition and the English translation he provided. Many thanks are also extended to: Mr. W. Lechner-Schimidt who graciously supplied us with a text of the Latin version; the members of the Intertestamental Literature seminar of the Society for New Testament Studies which reviewed the production of the Synopsis at several stages (special thanks being due to M. de Jonge who provided many helpful criticisms of the work in progress); Richard Layton and Sergio Laporta who provided very able editorial help in the final stages of the assembling of this volume; and, finally, the members of the 1993 and 1996 NEH summer seminars on the Adam literature held at the University of Virginia and the Hebrew University of Jerusalem respectively.

Gary A. Anderson
Michael E. Stone   April 1998

Introduction

Sigla

(XXX)   addition provided to English for sense

[XXX]   addition to base manuscript from another supporting manuscript; correction of orthography

{XXX}   corruption

[[XXX]]   editor's conjectural emendation

Pericope 1 *Authority over the Animals*

INTRODUCTION IN THE GREEK
0.1 διήγησις καὶ πολιτεία Ἀδὰμ καὶ Εὔας τῶν πρωτοπλάστων ἀποκαλυφθεῖσα παρὰ θεοῦ Μωϋσῇ τῷ θεράποντι αὐτοῦ ὅτε τὰς πλάκας τοῦ νόμου ἐκ χειρὸς αὐτοῦ ἐδέξατο διδαχθεὶς παρὰ τοῦ ἀρχαγγέλου Μιχαήλ. κύριε εὐλόγησον.

SLAVONIC 1.1 Бѣше Адамь вь раи прѣжде сьгрѣшения и вьса имѣаше вь хотѣниѥ своѥ и вьса вь хотѣниѥ ѥго ходѣхѹ· 1.2 звѣриѥ и скоти и вьсе птице перьнатыѥ, и вьса же повелѣниѥмь ѥго хранѣхѹ се и ходѣхѹ и лѣтахѹ. 1.3 не повелѣвьшѹ Адамѹ кь вещемь не смѣахѹ ни ходити ни лещи ни сьнѣсти чьто, доньдеже не повелить имь Адамь. 1.4 такожде и Ѥвьга.

Pericope 1 *Authority over the Animals* 1E

INTRODUCTION IN THE GREEK
0.1 The story and the history of Adam and Eve the first-created, revealed by God to Moses his servant, when he received the tablets of the law from His hand, having been instructed by the Archangel Michael. O Lord pronounce a blessing.

SLAVONIC
1.1 Before the trespass, Adam was in Paradise and had everything he wanted and everything happened according to his will: 1.2 the wild animals and the domestic animals and all the feathered birds--all drew near, left and fled at his command. 1.3 Apart from Adam's command nothing was allowed to move around, or land, or eat anything before Adam permitted it. 1.4 It was the same with Eve.

Pericope 2 *Expulsion*

GREEK	LATIN	ARMENIAN	GEORGIAN	SLAVONIC
29:7a [Ἐγένετο δὲ ἡμᾶς πενθῆσαι ἡμέρας ἑπτὰ	1:1 Quando expulsi sunt [II,III=Cum expulsi (fuissent? essent?) Adam et Eva]II,III de paradiso, fecerunt sibi tabernaculum et fuerunt VII dies lugentes et lamentantes in magna tristitia.	1.1 եւ իբրեւ յելանելն Ադամայ ի դրախտէն աստի, հանդերձ կնաւն իւրով, ի դուրս ի կողմ արեւելից դրախտին, եւ արարին իւրեանց տաղաւար բնակութեան, եւ մտին անդ, եւ իջանէին արտասուք իւրեանց աննպար, եւ եղեն զաւուրս իւրեանց սգաւոր սալով եւ տրտմութեամբ, եւ ասէն զմիմեանս եթէ հրաւցար ի կենաց։	1:1 და იყო ოდეს გამოვიდა ადამ და ევა, ცოლი მისი, სამოთხით, გამოვიდეს სამოთხეს აღმოსავალით კერძო. ქმნა ადამ ტალავარი საყუდელად თვისა. და შევიდეს ორნივე და დაყვეს მუნ შვიდი დღე. ტიროდეს ორნივე ტირილითა დიდითა, რამეთუ ჴყოდეს საყოფელთა მათვის სასუფეველისათა, რომელთა განშორნეს.	28-29.1 и сѣдохомь прѣдь двєрьми раискыми .
29:7b [καὶ μετὰ ἑπτὰ ἡμέρας ἐπεινάσαμεν	2:1 Post VII autem dies coeperunt esurire et quaerebant escam, ut manducarent et non inveniebant.	2.1 եւ ապա յետ ՛սւտից եթէ քաղցեան եւ խնդրէին կերակուր.	2:1 და შემდგომად შვიდისა დღისა შექშია და ეძიებდეს საჭმელსა.	28-29.2 Адамь прилєгь къ зємли и плака сє за .з. дьни и .з. ноши и ничьто сьньдьно нє имѣхомь и възалькахомь вєлико .
29:7c [καὶ εἶπον τῷ Ἀδάμ· ἀνάστα καὶ φρόντισον ἡμῖν βρώματα ἵνα φάγωμεν καὶ ζήσωμεν ἵνα μὴ ἀποθάνωμεν, ἐγερθῶμεν καὶ κυκλώσωμεν τὴν γῆν εἰ οὕτως εἰσακούσῃ ἡμῖν ὁ θεός.	2:2 Tunc dixit Eva ad Adam: domine mi, esurio. vade, quaere nobis, quod manducemus. forsitan respiciet et miserebitur nobis dominus deus et revocabit nos in locum, quo prius eramus.	2.2 եւ ասէ եւա ցԱդամ. Տէր իմ քաղցեայ. արի խնդրեա կերակուր զի ապրեցուք, եւ գիտասցուք եթէ գայցէ է Աստուած եւ տանիցի զմեզ ի դրախտն, ի տեղի մեր։	2:2 ჰრქუა ევა ადამს:" უფალო ჩემო, ადამ, აღდეგ და მოძიე მე საჭმელი, რაითა ვჭამოთ ვიდრე განცოცხლდე, ვინ უწყის, შემიწყალოს ჩუენ უფალ- მან და შემიყვანნეს ჩუენ მასვე ადგილსა სამოთხისასა".	28-29.3 азь же къвга възъпихь гласомь вєликѣмь помилоуи мє, творьчє, мєнє ради Адамь сико патить . 28-29.4 и глаголахь Адамоу . въстани, госп одинє мои, да поишєвѣ храноу сєбѣ . ѹжє бо дѹхь мои омалѣ въ мьнѣ и срьдьцє моє олєдєнѣло ѥсть въ мьнѣ.

Pericope 2 *Expulsion*

GREEK	LATIN	ARMENIAN	GEORGIAN	SLAVONIC
29:7a *[And we grieved for seven days*	1:1 When Adam and Eve were expelled from paradise they made for themselves a tent and spent seven days mourning and lamenting in great sadness.	1:1 It came to pass, when Adam went forth from the Garden with his wife, outside, to the east of the Garden, they made themselves a hut to live in and went inside. Their tears fell ceaselessly and they spent their days in unison of mind, weeping and saddened, and they said to one another, "We are far from life."	1:1 It came to pass, when Adam went out from the Garden with his wife Eve, they went out at the eastern part of the Garden. And Adam made a hut to live in. They both entered (it) and resided there for seven days. They both wept with abundant tears, for they regretted the residences of the kingdom from which they had been expelled.	28-29.1 And we sat ourselves down before the gates of Paradise.
29:7b *[and after seven days we grew hungry*	2:1 But after 7 days they began to be hungry and sought food to eat and did not find any.	2:1 Then, after seven days, they grew hungry and looked for food.	2:1 And after seven days, they were hungry and looked for something to eat.	28-29.2 Adam lay down on the ground and cried for seven days and nights, and we had nothing to eat and felt horrible hunger.
29:7c *[and I said to Adam: "Rise and give some thought to food that we might eat and live and so that we do not die. Let us get up and circle the earth perhaps God will hear us."*	2:2 Then Eve said to Adam:"My lord, I am hungry. Go, seek for us something to eat. Perhaps the Lord God will look upon us and have mercy on us and will call us back to the place where we were previously."	2:2 Eve said to Adam. "My lord, I am hungry. Arise, seek food so that we may live and know that God is going to come and bring us to the Garden, to our place."	2:2 Eve told Adam: "Adam, my lord, arise and (go) search for food for me that we may eat, until we find out-- who knows -- (perhaps) the Lord will accept us and take us back to the same place in the Garden.	28-29.3 I, Eve, cried out with a loud voice, "Have pity on me, O Creator, for on my account Adam suffers so severely." 28-29.4 And I said to Adam, "Get up, my husband, that we may seek nourishment; for my spirit is already diminishing in me and my heart is going numb within me."

Pericope 2 *Expulsion*

GREEK	LATIN	ARMENIAN	GEORGIAN	SLAVONIC
29:7d [Καὶ ἀνέστημεν καὶ διωδεύσαμεν πᾶσαν τὴν γῆν ἐκείνην καὶ οὐχ εὕρομεν.	3:1 Et surrexit Adam et ambulavit VII dies omnem terram illam et non invenit escam, qualem habebant in paradiso.	3.1 Յարեաւ եւ զրեցաւ ի վերայ երկրի, եւ ոչ գտին կերակուր նման կերակրոյն որով կերակրէին ի [դրախտին]։	3:1 და აღდგა ადამ შემდგომად შვიდისა დღისა და იქცეოდა პირსა ზედა ქუეყანისასა. და არა პოვა საზრდელი მსგავსად მისა, რომლისა-იგი ჭამდეს სამოთხესა მას შინა. მიფგო ადამ ევას და ჰრქუა: "სიჴუდი ლითა მოსიაჴუდიდ ვართ.	
	3:2 Et dixit Eva ad Adam: domine mi, putas fac me utinam moriar. et forte introducat te dominus deus denuo in paradisum, quoniam propter me iratus est tibi dominus deus.	3.2a եւ ասէ եւա զԱդամ. Մեռանիմք ի սովոյ ասաբիկ. երասի էր եթէ ես մեռայն էի. տէր իմ, քերևաս տանէին զ[եզդ] ի դրախտն, զի վասն իմ իցէ բարկացեալ Աստուած։	3:2a ჰრქუა ევა ადამს: "ნეტარ თუმცა მე მოვკუდი და შენ ხოლო შეგიყვანა სამოთხედ".	
		3.2b Ասէ Ադամ. Մեծ ցասումն Հասեալ է ի վերայ մեր, ոչ գիտեմ վասն քո եթէ վասն իմ։	3:2b მიფგო ადამ ევას და ჰრქუა: "დიდი რისხვაი არს ჩუენ გამო ყოველ- თა ზედა დაბადებულთა. ესე არა ფწყი, ანფ თუ ჩემ გამო, ანფ თუ შენ გამო".	

Pericope 2 *Expulsion*

GREEK	LATIN	ARMENIAN	GEORGIAN	SLAVONIC
29:7d *[We arose and went about the entire earth but we did not find food.*	3:1 And Adam arose and walked for seven days over all that land but did not find food such as they had in paradise.	3:1 They arose and went about upon the earth, and they did not find food like the food by which they had been nourished in [the Garden].	3:1 And Adam arose after seven days and went about upon the face of the earth and he did not find any food like that which they used to eat in the Garden. Adam replied to Eve and told her, "We are going to die a death."	
	3:2 Eve said to Adam: "My lord, would that I might die. Perhaps then the Lord God would bring you back into the Garden, for it was because of me that the Lord God grew angry with you.	3:2a Eve said to Adam, "I am dying of this hunger. It would be better if I were dead, my lord; perhaps (then) they would bring [you] into the Garden, for because of me God is angry."	3:2a Eve told Adam, "Oh, if only I were dead then God would have accepted you in the Garden!"	
		3:2b Adam said, "Great wrath has come upon us, I know not whether because of you or because of me."	3:2b Adam replied to Eve and said to her, "Because of us a great anger lies upon all creatures. (However) I do not know this: whether it is because of me or because of you."	

3E

Pericope 2 *Expulsion*

GREEK	LATIN	ARMENIAN	GEORGIAN	SLAVONIC
29:8 [Καὶ ἀποκριθεῖσα εἶπον τῷ Ἀδάμ· ἀνάστα κύριε καὶ ἀνάλωσόν με ἵνα ἀναπαύσωμαι ἀπὸ προσώπου σοῦ καὶ ἀπὸ προσώπου τοῦ θεοῦ καὶ ἀπὸ προσώπου τῶν ἀγγέλων ὅπως παύσωνται τοῦ ὀργίζεσθαί σοι δι᾽ ἐμοῦ.	vis interficere me, ut moriar? et forte introducet te dominus deus in paradisum, quia propter meam causam expulsus es inde.	3.2c Ասէ զն[ա] նմա. եթէ կամիս, սպան զիս. զի դադարեսցէ լատանն եւ բարկութիւն տերնասց ընդ. զի վասն իմ եղեւ այդ, եւ տանիցեն զբաց ի դրախտէ անտի:	3:2c მოუგო ევა ადამს: "უფალო ჩემო, უკეთეს ჯერ-გიჩნს, მომაკუდინე მე, რათა მოვისპო პირისაგან ღმრთისა და ანგელოზთაგან მისთა, რათა დასცხრეს რისხვაი ღმრთისაი შენ ზედა, რომელ არს ჩემ გამო და შევუყვა-ნოს მუხვე სამოთხე".	28-29.5a тогда Адамъ къ мьнѣ рече · Евьго, приходить ми на срьдьце,
29:9a [Τότε ἀποκριθεὶς ὁ Ἀδὰμ εἶπέν μοι διὰ τί ἐμνήσθης τῆς κακίας ταύτης ἵνα φόνον ποιήσω καὶ ἐνέγκω θάνατον τῇ ἐμῇ πλευρᾷ; ἢ πῶς ἐπενέγκω χεῖρα τῇ εἰκόνι τοῦ θεοῦ ἣν ἔπλασεν;	3:3 Respondit Adam: noli, Eva, talia dicere, ne forte aliquam iterum maledictionem inducat in nos dominus deus. quomodo potest fieri, ut mittam manum meam in carnem meam?	3.3 Ասէ ցնա Ադամ. Մի՛ եա մրցեսցես զայդ բան, զուցէ ածիցէ Աստուած ի վերայ մեր այլ եւս չարիս լլկումանս, եւ իբրեւ այպանող լինիցիմ. իսկ զիա՞րդ կարիցեմ չարի ինչ առնել բեզ զի մարմին իմ ես դու:	3:3 მოუგო ადამ და ჰრქუა:" ნუვე, ნუცა მოიხსენებ მაგას საქმესა, რათა არა ღმერთმან სხუაი სასჯელი მოავლინოს ჩუენ ზედა კულვისათვის, ვითარ-მე ადვილ ხელი ჩემი ვჰყო ხორცთავე თვისთა ზედა?" მაშინ ჰრქუა ევა:	28-29.5b, 6 да съмрьти прѣдамь тебе, нь бою сѧ, понѥже образъ твои богъ сътвориль ѥсть. того ради не могѹ сьзданиѥ госп одьнѥ разорити, нь понѥже каѥши сѧ и въпиѥши къ богѹ, того ради срьдьце моѥ не отлѫчаѥть сѧ отъ тебе.
	3:4 sed surgamus et quaeramus nobis, unde vivamus, ut non deficiamus.	3.4 Ասէ նմա. Արի զի խնդրեսցուք կերակուր բանձարոյ.	3:4 "აღდეგ, ვიდოთ ორთავე მხალო".	
	4:1 Et ambulantes quaesierunt novem dies et non invenerunt sicut habebant in paradiso, sed hoc tantum inveniebant, quod animalia edebant.	4.1 [խնդրեցին] եւ ոչ գտին կերակուր [ճաշակ բանձարոյ նման որ ի դրախտին էր]	4:1 და არა პოვეს ცხემი მცავისად ცხორისა მის, რომელი იყო სამოთხე-სა მას შინა.	30-32.1 И въста Адамь и обидоховѣ вьсю землю и не обрѣтоховѣ сьнѣсти ничесоже, тькмо цволь травѫ сельнѫ

Pericope 2 *Expulsion* 4E

GREEK	LATIN	ARMENIAN	GEORGIAN	SLAVONIC
29.8 *[And I answered and said to Adam: "Rise, O Lord and destroy me that I might cease from before you and from before God and the angels (and) so that they might cease their anger toward you on my account."*	Do you wish to kill me, that I might die? Perhaps the Lord God will bring you back into the Garden, since on account of my action you were expelled from there."	3:2c Eve said, to h[im], "Kill me if you wish, so that the wrath and anger may abate from before you—for this has come about because of me— and they will bring you into the Garden."	3:2c Eve replied to Adam, "My lord, if you think it wise, kill me so that I will be exterminated from the sight of God and his angels, so that God's anger against you may cease, which came about because of me: and he will bring you back into the Garden."	28-29.5a Then Adam said to me, "Eve, I have half a mind to give you over to death,
29:9a *[Then Adam answered and said to me, "For what reason do you call to mind this evil that I could commit murder and impose death upon my rib. How could I lift a hand against the image of God which he made?*	3:3 Adam responded: "Don't say such things Eve lest the Lord God bring upon us some other curse. How could it be that I should raise my hand against my own flesh?	3:3 Adam said to her. "Eve, do not (even) mention this matter; lest God bring upon us even greater evils and we become contemptible. How, indeed, can I do you any evil, for you are my body?"	3:3 Adam replied and told her, "No, no! Do not mention this matter, lest God send another judgment upon us because of (this) killing. How could I raise my hand and cause my own flesh to suffer?"	28-29.5b, 6 but I am afraid to do so, because God created your countenance. Thus, I cannot destroy the creation of God, on the contrary, because you now are filled with remorse and pray to God, my heart can never part from you."
	3:4 Let us arise and seek for ourselves something by which we might live so that we might not perish."	3:4 Eve said "Arise, so that we may seek vegetable food."	3:4 Then Eve told him, "Arise, let us both seek vegetables."	
	4:1 Walking about, they searched for nine days but did not find anything like they had in the Garden. They only found what animals eat.	4:1 [They sought] and they did not find [vegetable] food [like that which was in the Garden].	4:1 And they did not find (anything) tasting like the fruit of the tree which was in the Garden.	30-32.1 And Adam stood up and we traveled about the whole earth but found nothing to eat, except thorns, a wild grass.

Pericope 2 *Expulsion*

GREEK	LATIN	ARMENIAN	GEORGIAN	SLAVONIC
	4:2 Et dixit Adam ad Evam: haec tribuit dominus animalibus et bestiis, ut edant; nobis autem esca angelica erat.	4.2 ꜳանդի դայս կերակուր բաշխարդյ Հաստատւհաց Աստուած կերակուր դադանաց դի կերիցեն լերկրի. այլ մեր կերակուր այն է դոր Հրեշտակքն կերակրին:	4:2 და ჰრქუა ევა:" ესე დაბადა უფერთმან მხეცთათვის, რაითა იზარდებოდიან, ხოლო ჩუენდა საზრდელად იყო ანგელოზთა იგი ცხორებაი.	
	4:3 Sed iuste et digne plangimus ante conspectum dei, qui fecit nos. peniteamus penitentiam magnam; forsitan indulgeat et miserebitur nostri dominus deus et disponet nobis, unde vivamus.	4.3 Արդ ապաշխարեսցուք ատուրա քաասաան, թերևս գթասցի Աստուած ի մեղ և տացէ [մեզ] կերակուր որ լսպայն իցէ քան զդադանացն, դի մի նմանեսցուք նոցա:	4:3 აწ მოვედ და შევინანოთ სინანულითა დიდითა ფრიად ომეოც დღე, რაითა წყალობა ყოს უფერთმან ჩუენ ზედა და მომცეს ჩუენ საზრდელი ფერხობლი პიროუტყუეთასა, რაითა არა მსგავსად მათსა ვიყვენით".	30-32.2 и пакы възвратившемъ се намъ въ Едемь (ed. къ дверемь раискымь) кединогласьно възьпихомъ, молеще се · помилоуи, владыко, творьче, тварь свою · господи, прип оусти намъ сьнѣдь .

Pericope 2 *Expulsion*

GREEK	LATIN	ARMENIAN	GEORGIAN	SLAVONIC
	4:2 Adam said to Eve: "The Lord gave these things to animals and beasts to eat. Ours, however was the angelic food.	4:2 {Eve said "…} because God established this vegetable food as food for the beasts that they might eat on the earth, but our food is that which the angels eat.	4:2 And Eve told him, "God created that for the beasts to get (as) their food; but our food was that by which the angels live.	
4:3 But justly and worthily do we lament before the face of God who made us. Let us perform a great penitence. Perhaps the Lord God will yield and have mercy on us and give us something by which we might live."	4:3 Arise, let us repent for forty days; perhaps God will pity us and give [us] food which is better than that of the beasts so that we should not become like them."	4:3 Now, come and let us do penance for forty days, so that God may pity us and then give us better food than that of the animals, lest we should become like them."	30-32.2 And when we returned to Eden (ed. to the gates of Paradise), we cried together praying, "Have pity, O Master and Creator, on your creatures; furnish us with nourishment."	

Pericope 3 *Cheirograph*

SLAVONIC

30-32.3 непрѣстаньно молещемь се намь .єі. дьнєи, тогда слышахомь архаггела Иоила (ed. Михаила Иѡила), молеща се о нась.
30-32.4 и повелѣ господь Иоилѹ, и вьземь .з. чьсть оть рая и даде намь.
30-32.5 Тогда рече господь · трьниє и влъчьць изь дланіи твоихь да изидеть и оть пота твоєго сьнѣси . и да зьрить жена твоя тебѣ и да трепещеть .
30-32.6 рхаггель Иоиль рече · тако глаголеть господь кь Адамѹ · женѹ твою не сьтворихь да єсть тебѣ на повелѣниє, нь да єсть тебѣ на послѹшаниє . по чьто ты женѹ свою послѹшаєши;
30-32.7 Пакы архаггель Иоиль повѣда Адамѹ · отлѹчи скоты и все вещи оть летещихь и оть ходещихь и сьтвори дивиє и питомы, и нареци вьсѣкои вещи имена .
30-32.8 такожде вьзеть Адамь воловы и вьзора, да сьтворить себѣ хранѹ.

33-34.1 Тогда дияволь прииде и ста прѣдь вольми и не дасть Адамѹ землю работати
33-34.2 и рече дияволь кь Адамѹ · моя єсть землѣ а божія сѹть небесьная (и раи) .
33-34.3 да аще хощеши мои быти, тогда землю работаи ·
33-34.4 аще ли хощеши божіи быти, поиди себе вь раи .
33-34.5 Адамь рече · божіа сѹть небеса и божіи раи, божія землѣ и море и вьса вьселенньная .
33-34.6 дияволь рече · не дамь ти землю работати, аще не запишеши рѹкописаниє своє, да (є)си мои .
33-34.7 Адамь рече · кьто землѣ господинь, томѹ єсмь азь и чеда моя . диаволь вьзрадова се ·
33-34.8 Адам бо знааше, яко господь хощеть сьнити на землю о облѣщи се хощеть вь чловѣчь образь и попрати хощеть диявола .
33-34.9 и рече диявол · запиши мьнѣ рѹкописаниє своє .
33-34.10 и записа ємѹ и рече · кьто землѣ господинь, томѹ азь и чеда моя
35-37.1 Диаволь приєть рѹкописаниє Адамлє .

Pericope 3 *Cheirograph*

SLAVONIC
30-32.3 And as we prayed unceasingly for fifteen days, we heard the archangel Joel (ed Michael Joel) praying for us.
30-32.4 And the Lord commanded the archangel Joel and he took a one-seventh portion from Paradise and gave it to us.
30-32.5 Then the Lord spoke,'Thorns and thistles shall come forth from your hands and from your sweat you will have nourishment, and your wife will look on you in trembling.'
30-32.6 And the archangel Joel said, 'Thus says the Lord to Adam, I have not created your wife to command you, but to obey you; why do you obey your wife?'
30-32.7 Moreover, the archangel Joel told Adam, that he was to make a separation between farm animals and every sort of flying and creeping creature, namely, the wild and the tame, and to give to each creature a name.
30-32.8 Accordingly, Adam took oxen and began to till, that he might obtain nourishment.

33-34.1 Then the Devil appeared and stood steadfastly in front of the oxen and wouldn't allow Adam to till the earth.
33-34.2 And the Devil said to Adam, 'the earth is mine, God owns Heaven (and the Garden).
33-34.3 If you want to become mine, then, by all means, till the earth.
33-34.4 If, however, you want to belong to God then go only into Paradise.'
33-34.5 Adam said, 'God owns Heaven and Paradise, but God also owns the earth and the sea and the entire world.'
33-34.6 The Devil said, 'I will not permit you to till the earth, unless you sign a *cheirograph*, pledging that you belong to me.'
33-34.7 Adam said, 'Whoever is Lord of the earth, to him both I and my children belong.'
33-34.8 Adam knew of course that the Lord would come down to the earth and take on himself the form of a man and trample down the Devil.
33-34.9 The Devil said, 'Write for me your *cheirograph*.'
33-34.10 And Adam wrote and said, 'Whoever is Lord of the earth, both I and my children belong to him.'
35-37.1 The Devil took the *cheirograph* for himself.

Pericope 4 *Penitence and Second Temptation*

GREEK	LATIN	ARMENIAN	GEORGIAN	SLAVONIC
	5:1 Et dixit Eva ad Adam: domine mi, dic mihi, quid est penitentia et qualiter peniteam, ne forte laborem nobis inponamus, quem non possumus sustinere, et non exaudiat preces nostras.	5.1 Ասէ Արամ եւա. զի՞ր արինակ ապաշխարհս դու, կամ բան՞ի ար կարես համբերել վշտութակոց. գուցէ սկսանիս եւ ոչ կարես ապաշխարել, եւ ոչ լուիցէ Աստուած.	5:1 ვჰკო ადამ ევას და ჰრქუა: "მითხარ-რა მე აწ, რაბამითა სინანულ-ლითა ობანი, ანუ რაოდენთა დღეთა შეუდლო სინანულად სინანულისა შენისა, ნუუკუე აღუტკუათ ღმერთისა	35-37.2 и азь, чеда моя, рѣхь кь отьцоу вашемоу Адамоу, вьстани, госп одине, и помоли се господоу о семь, да избавить насъ оть диявола сего, понеже сико патиши мене ради.
	5:2 Et avertat dominus faciem suam a nobis, quia sicut promisimus non adimplevimus.	5.2 զի զոր ի սկզբանէ ստացաք եւ ոչ կարացաք պահել.	5:2 და ვერ აღუსრულოთ აღთქმაი იგი მისი, რომელი აღუტკუათ".	35-37.3 Адамъ же рече къ мьнѣ о Еввго, понеже сико каеши сео злобѣ свои, и срьдьце мое оуслышить те, понеже сьзда тебе господь оть рѣбрь моихь.
	5:3 Domine mi, quantum cogitasti penitere, quod ego tibi induxi laborem et tribulationem.	5.3 Ասէ եւա. Տուր ինձ գիտել տուրցի զոր խորհեցայց ապաշխարել, գուցէ երկայնիցէն տուրբն. բանցի իս [աժ] ի վերայ քո գապաշխարութիւն դ գալր.	5:3 ვჰკო ადამს ევა და ჰრქუა: "მითხარ-რა ნიცხუნი იგი დღეთანი, რაოდენ ქაქ ევულების სინანული, ვინ იცის, შე-ცა-ჟმატო მას, რამეთუ მე შეგამთხვიენ ჭირნი ეს".	35-37.4 да постимь се .м. дьнии, еда како оумилосрьдить се господь о насъ и припоустить намь разоумь и животь (ed. разоумь животьныи).

Pericope 4 *Penitence and Second Temptation*

GREEK	LATIN	ARMENIAN	GEORGIAN	SLAVONIC
	5:1 Eve said to Adam: "My lord, tell me what is penitence and how long should I perform it, lest we place on ourselves a labor which we cannot endure, and he hears not our prayers,	5:1 Adam said to Eve, "In what fashion will you repent? How many days can you endure toils? Perhaps you will begin and be unable to repent, and God will not hearken,	5:1 Adam replied to Eve and told her, "Explain to me now by what penitence you (wish to) repent, or for how many days will you be able to repent in your penitence, lest, perchance, we make a promise to God,	35-37.2 But I, my children, said to your father Adam, 'Arise, my husband, pray to God, that he deliver us from the Devil, for you suffer so on my account.'
	5:2 and the Lord turn his face from us because we did not fulfill what we promised.	5:2 so that we will not be able to keep that which we originally received."	5:2 and be unable to fulfill the promise which we will have made to him."	35-37.3 But Adam said to me, 'Eve, now you feel such remorse over your error, that you will listen to my heart, for God created you from my rib.
	5:3 My lord, how much penitence are you thinking of doing since I brought labor and tribulation upon you."	5:3 Eve said, "Set me the number of days which I might think to repent; perhaps the days will be too long—for I brought this penitence upon you."	5:3 Eve replied to Adam and she told him, "Tell me about the number of days, then; for what period of time will you consider doing penitence? Who knows, (perhaps) I will add more to that—for it is I who have brought these tribulations upon you."	35-37.4 We will fast for forty days, perhaps the Lord will pity us and leave for us understanding and a portion of life (ed. life's understanding).'

Pericope 4 *Penitence and Second Temptation*

GREEK	LATIN	ARMENIAN	GEORGIAN	SLAVONIC
29:9b [ἀλλὰ μετανοήσωμεν ἡμέρας τεσσαράκοντα ὅπως σπλαγχνισθῇ ἡμῖν ὁ θεὸς καὶ δώσῃ ἡμῖν τροφὴν κρείσσονα τῆς τῶν θηρίων. 29·10a Ἐγὼ μὲν ποιήσω ἡμέρας τεσσαράκοντα σὺ δὲ ἡμέρας τριάκοντα τέσσαρας ὅτι σὺ οὐκ ἐπλάσθης τῇ ἡμέρᾳ τῇ ἕκτῃ ἐν ᾗ ἐτέλεσεν ὁ θεὸς τὴν κτίσιν αὐτοῦ.	6:1a Et dixit Adam ad Evam: non potes tantum facere quantum ego, sed tantum fac ut salveris. ego enim faciam quadraginta diebus ieiunans.	6.1a Ասէ Ադամ. Ոչ կարես համբերել քառսնից աւուրց պահոց եւ ես, այլ արա դու զոր ինչ ասացից քեզ եւ կաց ի [ս]մին րահնի. Ասէ Ադամ. Ես լինիմ աւուրս քառասունս, սակայն քան զքեզ վեց աւր, քանզի դու ստեղծար աւուրս վեցերորդի զոր ստացաւ զարարածս իւր.	6:1a მოუგო ადამ და ჰრქუა ევას:" ვერ შეუდგო შემატებად, გარნა რაოდენი გრქუა, ეგოდენ დაადგენ და ყავ. და მე შევიქმო ორმეოც დღე და შენ შეინანე ოცდაათობდღე დღე. ექუსნი იგი დღენი მე მომიჭვენ, რამეთუ შენ არა ლაბადე დღესა მას მეექუსესა, რომელსა შექმნა უფალმან ყოველი დაბადებული?	35-37.5 азь рѣхь · госп одине, ты пости се . м. дьнеи, и азь да пощѹ се . мд.
29:10b [Ἀλλ' ἀνάστα καὶ πορεύου εἰς τὸν Τίγριν ποταμὸν καὶ λάβε λίθον καὶ θὲς ὑπὸ τοὺς πόδας σου καὶ στῆθι ἐνδεδυμένη ἐν τῷ ὕδατι ἕως τοῦ τραχήλου, καὶ μὴ ἐξέλθῃ λόγος ἐκ τοῦ στόματός σου · ἀνάξιοι γάρ ἔσμεν καὶ τὰ χείλη ἡμῶν οὐκ ἔστι καθαρά.	6:1b tu autem surge et vade ad Tigris fluvium et tolle lapidem et sta super eum in aqua usque ad collum in altitudine fluminis. et non exiet sermo de ore tuo, quia indigni sumus rogare dominum, quia labia nostra inmunda sunt de ligno inlicito et contradicto.	6.1b արդ՛ արի այսուհետեւ, գնա դու ի Տիգրիս գետն. եւ առ քար մի եւ դիր ի ներքոյ ոտից քոց. եւ կաց դու ի ջուր ամն համանրդամ քո մինչեւ ցպարանոցն քո. եւ մի ելցէ բան ի բերանոյ քումմէ աղաչել զՏէառնէն, քանզի անարժան անձամբք եւ պիղծ են շրթունք մեր եւ չեն սուրբ, վասն յանցանացին զոր արարաք ի դրախտին լսուել մեր ի ծառոյ անտի.	6:1b აწ შენ ადეგ და მოვედ მდინარესა ტიგროსისა და მოიღე ქვაი ერთი ქვეშე ქუეშე შენთა და შთადეგ წყალსა და ვიდრე ყელადმდე. და ვიდრე ოლოცვიდე, ნუ გამოვალნ ხმაი პირით შენით, რამეთუ არა ღირს ვართ ლოცვად პირითა ჩუენითა, რამეთუ ბაგენი ჩუენნი არაწმიდა არიან გარდასლვითა მათ მცნებათათვის ჭამადისა მისგან სამოთხისა, რომელისა-იგი არა გვიბრძანა უფალმან,	35-37.6 и рече Адамь кь мьнѣ · прииди вь рѣкѹ, рекомѹю Тигрь, и поими камыкь великь и подложи подь носѣ свои и вьниди вь водѹ, и одежди се водою яко свитою до выѣ своеѣ и моли бога вь срьдьци своемь и да не изидеть рѣчь изь ѹсть твоихь .

Pericope 4 *Penitence and Second Temptation* 8E

GREEK	LATIN	ARMENIAN	GEORGIAN	SLAVONIC
29:9b *[Rather let us repent for forty days so that God may have mercy on us and give to us better food than the animals. 29:10a I will do forty days of penitence whereas you shall do 34 days for you were not made on the sixth day when God made his creation.*	6:1a Adam said to Eve: "You cannot do as much as I, but do as much so that you might be saved. For I will do forty days of fasting.	6:1a Adam said, "You cannot endure the same number of days as I, but do what I tell you and abide by [this] instruction."—Adam said, "I shall be (in penitence) for forty days, six days more than you, because you were created on the sixth day (of those upon which) he accepted his works.	6:1a Adam replied and said to Eve, "You will not be able to add (anything to it). On the contrary, as many (days) as I will tell you, that many (days, you should) stay and do. And I will do penitence for forty days, and you, do penitence for thirty-four days. Leave me these six days, since were you not created upon the sixth day, when God completed the creation of all creatures?	35-37.5 I said, 'My husband, you fast forty days, and I will fast forty-four days.'
29:10b *[Arise and go to the Tigris river and take a stone and put it under your feet and stand there covered in the water up to your neck and let not a word come from your mouth for we are not worthy and our lips are unclean."*	6:1b You, however, arise and go to the Tigris River and take a stone and stand upon it in the water up to your neck in the depth of the river. Let not a word go forth from your mouth since we are unworthy to ask of the Lord for our lips are unclean from the illicit and forbidden tree.	6:1b Now, therefore, arise, go to the T[i]gris river and take a stone and place it under your feet and stand in the water up to your neck, in your clothes. Let no word of supplication to God escape your mouth, for we are unworthy of [soul] and our lips are impure and unclean, because of the transgressions which we committed in the Garden when we ate of the tree.	6:1b Now, you, arise and go to the river Tigris; and put a stone under your feet and stay in the water and clothe yourself (with it) up to your neck. While you pray, let no sound come from your mouth, for we are not worthy to open our mouths, for our lips are impure because we transgressed the commandments, so as to eat from (the tree) of the Garden which God had forbidden us.	35-37.6 And Adam said to me, 'Come to the river called Tigris, take a stone and place it under your feet, stand up in the water and cover yourself with water, as with a coat up to the neck, and pray to God in your heart, but no word should come out across your lips.'

Pericope 4 *Penitence and Second Temptation*

GREEK	LATIN	ARMENIAN	GEORGIAN	SLAVONIC
	6:2 Et sta in aqua fluminis XXXVII dies. ego autem faciam in aqua Jordanis XL dies. forsitan miserebitur nostri dominus deus.	6.2 լռեալ կացցես անդ ի մէջ ջրոյն մինչեւ ապաշխարեսցէ[ս] զամուրս երեսուն եւ չորս. եւ ես ինքն ի Յորդանան գետ մինչեւ գլուխացուք եթէ աշա լուաւ մեզ Աստուած, եւ տացէ մեզ զկերակուրն մեր:	6:2 არამე დადუმენ, ხოლო წყალსა მას შინა ობანდე : ლ' ე : დღე ყოვლითა გულითა შენითა და მე ევედრო ყუ იორდანესა მდინარესა შინა, ვიდრემდე არა ოსმინოს ჩუენი ღმერთმან და მოგუცეს ჩუენ საზრდელო'.	35-37.7 и азь рѣхь · госп одинє, азь възовоу къ богоу вьсѣмь срьдьцємь моимь. 35-37.8 и рєчє кь мнѣ Адамь · вєлико сьблюди сєбє. аще не видиши мене и вьсє бѣлєгы моѥ, не изиди изь рѣкы ни вѣроую глаголомь, да не пакы сьблажнєна боудеши.
	7:1 Et ambulavit Eva ad Tigris flumen et fecit sicut dixit ei Adam.	7.1 Գնաց այլուհետեւ եսա ի Շիքրիս եւ արար որպէս հրամայեաց նմա Արամ.	7:1 წარვიდა ევა მდინარესა მას ტიგროსასა და ყო ევზრ. ვითარცა ამ-ცნო მას ადამ.	
29:11a [Ἐπορεύθη δὲ Ἀδὰμ εἰς τὸν Ἰορδάνην ποταμὸν καὶ ἡ θρὶξ τῆς κεφαλῆς αὐτοῦ ἤπλοῦτο εὐχομένου αὐτοῦ ἐν τῷ ὕδατι.	7:2 Similiter ambulavit Adam ad flumen Jordanis et stetit super lapidem usque ad collum in aqua.	7.2 եւ Արամ [գնաց] ի Յորդանան. եւ Հեր գլուխ նորա մեղկեալ էր:	7:2 ხოლო ადამ დადგრა იორდანესა მდინარესა და თანა თავისა მო- სისანი გარდაემატებნს.	35-37.9 и идє Адамь кь Иорданоу и вьниде вь водоу иорданьскоую и погроузи сє вьсь вь водѣ и вьсє власы главы своѥ погроузи.
29:11b [καὶ ἔκραξε φωνῇ μεγάλῃ λέγων σοι λέγω τῷ ὕδατι τοῦ Ἰορδάνου· Στῆθι καὶ εὔχου ὁμοῦ καὶ πάντα τὰ θηρία καὶ πάντα τὰ πετεινὰ καὶ πάντα τὰ ἑρπετὰ ἐν τῇ γῇ καὶ θαλάσσῃ.	8:1 Et dixit Adam: tibi dico, aqua Jordanis, condole mihi et segrega mihi omnia natantia, quae in te sunt et circumdent me ac lugeant pariter mecum.	8.1 եւ ապացեաց ասէր. Քեզ ասեմ Յորդանանու կշտասկեզ լերուք ինձ եւ ժողովեա զամենայն կայտառս[ս] որ ի քեզ են, եւ շրջեսցին զինեւ եւ լացցեն զիս.	8:1 და თქუა ადამ:" შენ გეტყუ. იორდანო, ოჳკუეთუ ჰნე თანავე და შე-კრიბენ ყოველნი ცხოველნი, რომელნი არიან გარდმოს შენსა ჰიროტყუნე, რაითა გარე- მოვადგენ და მტიროდიან მე,	35-37.10a молєщоу же сє богоу, молитвы высылающоу,

Pericope 4 *Penitence and Second Temptation* 9E

GREEK	LATIN	ARMENIAN	GEORGIAN	SLAVONIC
	6:2 Stand in the water of the river for thirty-seven days. I however, will do forty days in the water of the Jordan. Perhaps the Lord will have mercy on us."	6:2 Stand silent there in the middle of the water until [you] have done penitence for thirty-four days, and I will be in the Jordan river, until we learn that, behold, God has hearkened to us and will give us our food."	6:2 Rather, be silent, only do penitence in the water for thirty-four days with all your heart and I will do the same in the Jordan river, until God hearkens and gives us food."	35-37.7 And I said, 'My husband, I will call out to God with my whole heart.' 35-37.8 And Adam said to me, 'Guard yourself carefully; if you don't see me and all my features, don't climb up out of the water, give no credence to words, so that you won't get into any more trouble.'
	7:1 Eve walked to the Tigris River and did just as Adam told her.	7:1 Then Eve went to the Tigris and did as Adam had instructed her,	7:1 Eve went off to the Tigris river and she did as Adam had ordered her.	
29:11a *[Adam went to the Jordan river and the hair of his head was spread out as he prayed in the water.*	7:2 Likewise, Adam walked to the Jordan River and stood upon a rock up to his neck in the water.	7:2 and Adam [went] to the Jordan. And the hair of his head was uncovered.	7:2 But, as for Adam, he remained in the Jordan river and the hair of his head spread out.	35-37.9 And Adam went to the Jordan and stood up in the water and immersed himself in water and also dampened the hair on his head.
29:11b *[And he cried in a loud voice saying: "I say to the waters of the Jordan stand still and pray with me even all the beasts, all the birds, and all which creeps on the land and the sea."*	8:1 Adam said: "I say to you, water of the Jordan, mourn with me and separate from me all swimming creatures which are in you. Let them surround me and mourn with me.	8:1 He prayed and said, "I say to you, waters of Jordan, be fellow sufferers for me and assemble all the moving thing\<s\> which are in you, and let them surround me and bewail me,	8:1 And Adam said, "I tell you, O Jordan, suffer with me and assemble all the animals which are around you, so that they (may come) to surround you and bewail me,	35-37.10a While he prayed to God and his prayers went up,

Pericope 4 *Penitence and Second Temptation*

GREEK	LATIN	ARMENIAN	GEORGIAN	SLAVONIC
	8:2 Non se plangant, sed me, quia ipsi non peccaverunt, sed ego.	8.2 ոչ եթէ վասն անձանց լրեանց, այլ վասն իմ. զի ի նոցանէ ոչ արդել Աստուած զկերակուր լրեանց զոր Հրամայեաց Աստուած ի սկզբանէ, իսկ ես արդելայ ի կերակրոյն իմոյ ես ի կենացն:	8:2 არა თუ მათთვის, არამედ ჩემთვის, რამეთუ მათ არა მოაკლო უფერ- თმან საჭმარი, რომელი მისცა უფერთმან დასაბამითვან, ხოლო მე მოვაკ- დო ცხორებისა ჩემისაგან და საზრდელისა".	
29:11c [Καὶ πάντες οἱ ἄγγελοι καὶ πάντα τὰ ποιήματα τοῦ θεοῦ ἐκύκλωσαν τὸν Ἀδὰμ ὡς τεῖχος κύκλῳ αὐτοῦ κλαίοντες καὶ προσευχό- μενοι τῷ θεῷ ὑπὲρ τοῦ Ἀδὰμ ὅπως εἰσακού- σηται αὐτοῦ ὁ θεός.	8:3 Statim omnia animantia venerunt et circumdederunt eum et aqua Jordanis stetit ab illa hora non agens cursum suum.	8.3 դայն իրրեւ ասաց Ադամ, ժողովեցան առ նա ամենայն կալուածք որ էին ի Յորդանան, եւ կացին չորք զլովալ իրրեւ զպարիսպ. եւ դադարեցին չորք Յորդանանու ի ժամուն յայնմիկ, եւ զտեղի առին ի գնացելց լրեանց: Արամ աղաղակեաց առ Աստուած եւ մեկնեաց ի նոցանէ դաս մեց Հարիր ի ձայն աղաչանաց կարդալ առ Աստուած զամենայն աաուրա:	8:3 ესე რა თქვა ადამ ტირილითა მწარითა, შეკრბეს ყოველნი საცხო- ვარნი მის თანა და გარე- მოადგეს მას ვითარცა ზღუდებნი. მას ქალსა, ვი- თარცა წყალმან იორდანემან დააცადა სლვა თვისი, მაშინ აღუტევა ადამ ხმაი ლმრთისა მიმართ და იქცია მტხრელნი ხმისა თვისისაი ექვსად ანგავსად ხმისა მის ყოველთა ანგელოზთასა ყოველსა ქამსა.	35-37.10b и тоу сънидоше сє аггели и вьсє вєщи летєщєє, звєриє и скоти, и вьсє пьтицє перьнатыє, ставьше яко и стѣна о крьсть Адама, молеще сє кь богоу за Адама.

Pericope 4 *Penitence and Second Temptation* 10E

GREEK	LATIN	ARMENIAN	GEORGIAN	SLAVONIC
	8:2 Let them not lament for themselves, but for me, for they have not sinned, but I."	8:2 not for their own sakes, but for mine. Because God did not withhold their food from them, which God appointed from the beginning, but I have been withheld from my food and from life."	8:2 not for their own sakes, but for me. Because God did not withhold their fodder from them, which God gave them from the beginning, but I have been withheld from my means of life and from my food."	
29:11c *[And all the angels and all things made by God circled Adam like a wall around him and cried while praying to God on behalf of Adam so that God might hearken to him.*	8:3 Immediately, all living things came and surrounded him and the water of the Jordan stood from that hour not flowing in its course.	8:3 When Adam said that, all moving things which were in the Jordan gathered to him and stood around him like a wall. And the waters of the Jordan stopped at that time and became stationary from their flow. Adam cried to God and he set apart six hundred orders of them to call to God in prayers all the days.	8:3 When Adam had said that with bitter tears, all the cattle gathered close to him and stood around him like walls. At the moment when the water (of) the Jordan had restrained its flow, then Adam raised his voice towards God and he varied his tone of voice six times, like the voices of all the angels in all times.	35-37.10b the angels assembled themselves and every flying creature, the wild and the domestic and every winged bird, and they stood as a wall around Adam, praying to God for him.

Pericope 4 *Penitence and Second Temptation*

GREEK	LATIN	ARMENIAN	GEORGIAN	SLAVONIC
29:12a [Ὁ δὲ διάβολος μὴ εὑρὼν τόπον εἰς τὸν Ἀδὰμ ἐπορεύθη εἰς τὸν Τίγριν ποταμὸν πρός με. καὶ λαβὼν σχῆμα ἀγγέλου ἔστη ἐνώπιόν μου	9:1 Et transierunt dies XVIII. tunc iratus est Satanas et transfiguravit se in claritatem angelorum et abiit ad Tigrem flumen ad Evam.	9.1 Ընդ այս կատարեցան աւուրք ութ եւ տասն. յայնժամ բարկացաւ Սատանայ ի ձեռ թիւրեքի ի զարդ պայծառութեան եւ գնաց ի Տիգրիս գետ խաբել զեւա.	9:1 ოცდა ათერთმეტსა დღესა იგი აღურმეტსა ტიროლსა მას შინა მისსა ფერიცვალა ეშმაკი და იქცია ხატად მისა და სამოსელი მისი სიტრფოითა მით ხელოვანებისა მისისათა და მიუდა იგი ევას თანა მდინარესა მას ტიგრისასასა და დადგა იგი გარემე.	38-39.1a дияволь прииде кь мнѣ аггельскымь образомь и свѣтлостию,
29:12b [κλαίων καὶ τὰ δάκρυα αὐτοῦ ἔρρεεν ἐπὶ τὴν γῆν. καὶ λέγει μοι· ἔξελθε ἐκ τοῦ ὕδατος καὶ παῦσαι τοῦ κλαυθμοῦ	9:2 Et invenit eam flentem. et ipse diabolus quasi condolens ei coepit flere et dixit ad eam: egredere de flumine [II,III+et repausa]II,III et de cetero non plores. iam cessa de tristitia et gemitu. quid sollicita es tu et Adam vir tuus?	9.2 եւ արտասուք նորայ իջանէին ի վերայ զարդու նորա մկիչք. եւ սուտ ի լրդ այլ եւ հանդերձ զի լուաս Սատանայ ապաշխարութեան ձեր, թէզ եւ Ադամայ այր քո.	9:2 და ტიროდა და დასწთობდა საცრელსა ცრემლთა მისთა ზედა სამოსელსა მისსა და სამოსელი ჰქუებოდა. და ჰრქუა ევას: "გამოვედ მაგიერ წყლით და დასცხერ ჭირთა მაგათგან, რამეთუ ისმინა უფალმან სინანული შენი და ადამის, ქმრისა შენისა".	38-39.1b идеже стояхь вь водѣ, слъзы велики ронещи по земли, и глагола кь мнѣ · изиди Євго изь воды,
29:12c [ἤκουσε γὰρ ὁ θεὸς τῆς δεήσεώς σου ὅτι καὶ ἡμεῖς οἱ ἄγγελοι καὶ πάντα τὰ ποιήματα αὐτοῦ παρεκαλέσαμεν τὸν θεὸν ὑπὲρ ὑμῶν.	9:3 Audivit dominus deus gemitum vestrum et suscepit penitentiam vestram; et nos omnes angeli rogavimus pro vobis deprecantes dominum,	9.3 վասն զի մեք աղաչեցաք զՍատանայ.	9:3 და ჩვენცა ვევედრებით უფალსა თქუენთავის, რომელი ვიხილეთ.	38-39.2a услыша богь молитву твою, и нась аггелы услыша госп одь, молещихь сє за вась,
	9:4 et misit me, ut educerem vos de aqua et darem vobis alimentum, quod habuistis in paradiso et pro quo planxistis.	9.4 եւ Սատանայ աատրեաց զ[իս] հանել զձեզ այտի եւ տալ ձեզ զկերակուրն ձեր վասն որոյ ապաշխարեցէք:	9:4 და მომავლინა მე უფალმან გამოყვანებად თქუენდა და მიცემად საჭმელი, რომლისათვისცა ინანით".	38-39.2b и посъла менє господь кь тебѣ, да изидеши оть воды сєє.

Pericope 4 *Penitence and Second Temptation* 11E

GREEK	LATIN	ARMENIAN	GEORGIAN	SLAVONIC
29:12a *[But the Devil, not finding a place with respect to Adam, came to the Tigris river to me. And assuming the form of an angel he stood before me*	9:1 Eighteen days passed. Then Satan grew angry and transfigured himself into the brilliance of an angel and went off to the Tigris River to Eve.	9:1 When eighteen days of their weeping were completed, then Satan took on the form of a Cherub with splendid attire, and went to the Tigris river to deceive Eve.	9:1 When the twelve days of his weeping were completed, the Devil trembled and changed his shape and his clothes by his artful deceit. He drew close to Eve, on the Tigris river, and stood beside the bank.	38-39.1a The Devil came to me in the form and radiance of an angel,
29:12b *[weeping and his tears flowed upon the ground. And he said to me, "Come forth from the water and cease your crying, for God has heard your request*	9:2 He found her weeping, and then, the Devil himself, as if mourning with her began to weep and said to her: "Come out of the water [II,III+ and rest] II,III and weep no longer. Cease now from your sadness and lamenting. Why are you uneasy, you and your husband Adam? The Lord God has heard your lamenting and accepted your penitence.	9:2 Her tears were falling on her attire, down to the ground. Satan said to Eve, "Come forth from the water and rest, for God has hearkened to your penitence, to you and Adam your husband,	9:2 He was weeping and had his false tears dripping down on his garment and from his garment down to the ground. Then he told Eve, "Come out of that water (where you are) and stop your tribulations, for God has hearkened to your penitence, to you and to Adam, your husband.	38-39.1b there where I stood in the water, letting passionate tears fall to the ground, he said to me, 'Come forth, Eve, out of the water.
29:12c *[because even we, the angels, and all things made by him, have beseeched God on your behalf.*	9:3 All of us angels have pleaded for you, praying to the Lord.	9:3 because we beseeched God.	9:3 Moreover, we too have prayed because of your misfortunes which we have seen.	38-39.2a God has heard your prayer and also we angels, we who prayed for you,
	9:4 And he sent me to lead you forth from the water and to give you the nourishment which you had in the Garden and for which you have grieved.	9:4 And God sent [me] to lead you forth from there and to give you your food, on account of which you repented.	9:4 Thus God sent me to have you (pl.) come forth and to give you the food on account of which you repented.	38-39.2b and the Lord has sent me to you, that you should emerge from this water.'

Pericope 4 *Penitence and Second Temptation*

GREEK	LATIN	ARMENIAN	GEORGIAN	SLAVONIC
29:13 *[Καὶ ταῦτα εἰπὼν δεύτερον ἠπάτησέν με ὁ ἐχθρός· καὶ ἐξέβην ἀπὸ τοῦ ὕδατος.]*	9:5 Nunc ergo egredere de aqua et perducam vos in locum, ubi paratus est victus vester.	9.5 [Armenian text]	9:5 აწ ადამზედ მაგიერ, რამეთუ მისრულ ვარ ადამისა და მომავლინა და მრქუა მე: "მივედ და უთხარ ცოლსა ჩემსა ევას და მოიყვანე იგი ჩემდა". აწ მოვედ და მიგიყვანო შენ ადამისა, ადგილსა მას, სადა არს იგი და სადა- ცა-იგი არს საზრდელი თქუენი".	
	10:1 Haec audiens autem Eva credidit et exivit de aqua fluminis et caro eius erat sicut herba de frigore aquae.	10.1 [Armenian text]	10:1 და ადამზედა ევა მიერ წყლით გა ოუვნეს ხორცნი მისნი ვითარცა მხალნი დამჭნარ განთოშვითა წყლისაითა. გარდაქცეულ იყო ყოველი იგი ხატი ქმნულკეთილობ ისა მისისა.	38-39.3 азъ же познахь, яко диаволь ксть и ничєсожє юмоу нє отвѣщахь.
	10:2 Et cum egressa esset cecidit in terram et erexit eam diabolus et perduxit eam ad Adam.	10.2 [Armenian text]	10:2 და ოდეს ადამზედა იგი მიერ წყლით, დაეცა პირსა ზედა ქუეყანისა- სა მრავლითა მით უძლურებითა და ითქვა იგი შეუძველად ორ დღე. და შემდგომად ორისა დღისა აღდგა და მიუძღვა მას ეშმაკი, სადაცა იყო ადამ.	38-39.4 И по .м. дьнии грєдоущоу Адамоу отъ Иордана и обрѣтє слѣдь диѩволовь и ѹбоѩ сє ѕѣло, ѥда како прѣльстиль мє ксть.

Pericope 4 *Penitence and Second Temptation*

GREEK	LATIN	ARMENIAN	GEORGIAN	SLAVONIC
29:13 *[And when he said these things, the enemy deceived me a second time. And I came out of the water.]*	9:5 Now, therefore, come out of the water and I will lead you to the place where your food is prepared."	9:5 Since just now I went to Adam and he sent me to you and said, 'Go, son, summon my wife,' now come, let us go to Adam and I will lead you to the place where your food is."	9:5 Now, come up from there, for I have gone to Adam and he sent me and told me, 'Go and speak with Eve, my spouse; bring her back to me.' Come, now, and I will lead you to Adam, to the place where he is and where your food also is."	
	10:1 Hearing this, Eve believed him and went out of the water of the river. Her flesh was like grass from the waters coldness.	10:1. When Eve came forth from the water, her flesh was like withered grass, for her flesh had been changed from the water, but the form of her glory remained brilliant.	10:1 And Eve came up out of the water and her flesh was withered like rotten vegetables because of the coldness of the water. All the form of her beauty had been destroyed.	38-39.3 And I discerned that he was the Devil, and answered him nothing at all.
	10:2 When she had come out, she fell to the ground, but the Devil stood her up and led her to Adam.	10:2 [When she came forth from the water] she fell down and remained upon the ground in great distress for two days, for she was quite unable to move from the spot. Then she arose and Satan also led her to where Adam was.	10:2 And when she had come up out of the water, she fell on the face of the earth in great weakness and remained lying (on the ground) without moving for two days. And after two days she arose and the Devil led her to where Adam was.	38-39.4 But when after forty days, Adam emerged from the Jordan, he noticed the footprints of the Devil and was very afraid lest the Devil had duped me.

Pericope 4 *Penitence and Second Temptation*

GREEK	LATIN	ARMENIAN	GEORGIAN	SLAVONIC
	10:3 Cum autem vidisset eam Adam et diabolum cum ea, exclamavit cum fletu dicens: O Eva, O Eva, ubi est opus penitentiae tuae? quomodo iterum seducta es ab adversario nostro, per quem alienati sumus de habitatione paradisi et laetitia spiritali.	10.3 *Ի իբրև տեսև Ադամ զՍատանայ և զնա գալր գշան նորա, բլաց լալիս մեծ և աղաղակեաց բարբառով և ասէ գևա. ո՞ւր է ապուշէտ իմ ապաշխարութեան զոր խոսէ քեզ. զիա՞րդ մոլորեցար դու գշան դորա գալ, որով ատարացաք ի բնակութենէ մերմէ*։	10:3 და ვითარცა იხილა ადამმან ევა, ვითარ-იგი მისდევდა ეშმაკსა მას, იტყო ტირილითა მწარითა და ხმა-ყო ხმითა მაღლითა და ჰრქუა: "სადა არიან მცნებანი სინანულისანი, რომელი გამცვე, ვითარ კუალად შესცევ მაგის მიერ, რომლისაგანცა უცხო ვართ საყოფელთაგან ჩუენთა".	38-39.5 ЕГДА ЖЕ ВИДѢ МЕНЕ ВЬ ВОДѢ СТОЮЩѼ, ВЬЗРАДОВА СЕ ВЕЛИКО, И ПОЮМЬ МЕНЕ И ИЗВЕДЕ МЕ ИЗЬ ВОДЫ.
	11:1 Haec cum audisset Eva cognovit quod diabolus suasit exire de flumine et cecidit super faciem suam in terram et duplicatus est dolor et gemitus et planctus ab ea.	11.1 *Զայս իբրև լուաւ Եւա գիտաց եթէ Սատանայ է որ խաբեաց գնա, անկաւ առաջի Ադամայ այնուհետև կրկին ցաւք Ադամայ լալման իբրև տեսև զտառապանս կնոջ իւրոյ, զի լբաւ և անկաւ իբրև գմեռեալ*։	11:1 ესე რა ესმა ევას, რამეთუ ეშმაკი არს, რომელმანცა აცთუნა იგი, დავარდა იგი წინაშე მისსა, ხოლო ადამს ორ წილ ექმნა სალმობაი იგი ევაი-სი, რამეთუ ხედვიდა იგი მას დავრდომილსა ქუეყანასა ზედა ვითარცა მკუდარსა.	
	11:2 Et exclamavit dicens: ve tibi, diabole, quid nos expugnas gratis? quid tibi apud nos? aut quid tibi fecimus, quoniam dolose nos persequeris? aut quid pertinet ad nos malitia tua?	11.2 *տրտմեցաւ և աղաղակեաց ճճութեամբ մեծաւ և ասէ գՍատանայ. զիա՞րդ ալեցար մարտ դնել ընդ մեզ, կամ գի՞նչ մեղանք են մեր առ քեզ, զի հանես գմեզ ի տեղոյէս մերմէ*։	11:2 შეჭუენა და თქუა დიდითა კუნესითა, ხმა-ყო: "ვა შენდა, მბრძოლსა მაგას ჩუენთასა, რაი ბოროტი გიყავთ შენ, რამეთუ შენითა შეტყუვილითა იყო გამოხდაი ჩუენი სამოთხით. უკუეთუ ჩუენ განგაგდეთ შენდა ჩუენდა მომართ არს მდურვაი შენი?	

Pericope 4 *Penitence and Second Temptation* 13E

GREEK	LATIN	ARMENIAN	GEORGIAN	SLAVONIC
	10:3 When Adam saw her and the Devil with her, he cried out with tears, saying: "O Eve, O Eve, where is the work of your penitence? How have you again been seduced by our adversary, through whom we were alienated from the dwelling of the Garden and spiritual happiness?	10:3 When Adam saw Satan and Eve who was following him, he wept loudly and called out with a great voice and said to Eve, "Where is my command of repentance, which I gave you? How did you go astray, to follow him by whom we were alienated from our dwelling?"	10:3 And as soon as Adam saw Eve (and) how she was following the Devil, he started to weep with burning tears and called out with a great voice and told her,"Where are the commands of repentance which I gave you? How have you been deceived again by him, because of whom we are aliens to our dwellings?"	38-39.5 But when he saw me standing in the water, he was very happy, and he took me and led me out of the water."
	11:1 When Eve heard this, she knew that it was the Devil who had persuaded her to go out from the river and she fell on her face on the ground and her grief was double, as was her wailing and lamentation.	11:1 When Eve heard this, she knew that he who dec[ei]ved her was Satan; she fell down before Adam. From that time Adam's distress increased twofold when he saw the sufferings of his wife, for she was overcome and fell like one dead.	11:1 When Eve heard that it was the Devil who had deceived her, she fell down before him and Adam's distress for Eve increased twofold for he saw her lying on the earth like one dead.	
	11:2 He cried out, saying: "Woe to you, Devil. For what reason do you fight against us? What concern do you have with us? What have we done to you that you should persecute us so grievously? Why does your malice extend to us?	11:2 He was sad and called out great lamentation and said to Satan, "Why have you engaged in such a great conflict with us? What are our sins against you, that you have brought us out of our place?"	11:2 He was sad and called out with great groaning, "Woe to you who fight against us! What evil have we done to you? For it is because of your calumnies that we went out from the Garden. Is it because we have caused you to be expelled that you are angry against us?	

Pericope 4 *Penitence and Second Temptation*

GREEK	LATIN	ARMENIAN	GEORGIAN	SLAVONIC
	11:3 Numquid nos abstulimus gloriam tuam et fecimus te sine honore esse? quid persequeris nos, inimice, usque ad mortem impie et invidiose?	11.3 մի թէ գկարսն քո հանաք մեք ի քէն. մի թէ մերժեցաք զքեզ լինել մեզ տտացուած. զի մարտնչիս ընդ մեզ ի տարապարտուց:	11:3 ანუ ჩუენ მიერ მოგედრცყუა დიდებაი შენი? ანუ სადამდე ჩუენითა შექმნითა ევრეთ ნაკლულევან ხარ, ანუ ჩუენ ხოლო ვართ დაბადებულნი ღმრთისანი, რამეთუ ჩუენ გუბრძავთ?	

Pericope 4 *Penitence and Second Temptation* 14E

GREEK	LATIN	ARMENIAN	GEORGIAN	SLAVONIC
	11:3 Did we ever take your glory from you or cause you to be without honor? Why do you persecute us, O enemy, impiously and jealously unto death?"	11:3 Did we take your glory from you? Did we reject you from being our possession, that you fight against us unnecessarily?"	11:3 Or is it because of us that you were despoiled of your glory? Or is it, in some way, by our action that you are in such deficiency? Or are we the only creatures of God that you fight against us alone?"	

Pericope 5 *Fall of Satan*

GREEK	LATIN	ARMENIAN	GEORGIAN	SLAVONIC
	12:1 Et ingemescens diabolus dixit: O Adam, tota inimicitia mea et invidia et dolor ad te est, quoniam propter te expulsus sum et alienatus de gloria mea, quam habui in caelis in medio angelorum, et propter te eiectus sum in terram.	12.1 *[Armenian text]*	12:1 ტირილად იწყო ეშმაკმან ტირილითა იმწუხარისათა, და ჰრქუა ადამს ეშმაკმან:" შო ადამ, ყოველივე ანგარებაი და მრუდეაი, და ყოველი ვე ჭუელი გულისა ჩემისაი შენდა მომართ არს, რამეთუ შენ გამო გამოვარდი მე საყოფელთაგან ჩემთა, შენ გამო უცხო ვიქმენ მე საყდრისაგან ჩემისა. ქერობინთაგან უფრო ფრთენი ჩემნი ზედა გარდამატებულ იყვნეს და დაეარულ ვიყავ მე მათ ქუეშე, აწ ვლენას ფერხნი ჩემნი ქუეყანასა ზედა, რომელ არა მრწმენა".	
	12:2 Respondit Adam: quid tibi feci?	12.2 *[Armenian text]*	12:2 მიუგო ადამ ეშმაკსა და ჰრქუა:	
	12:3 Aut quae est culpa mea in te? cum non sis a nobis nocitus nec laesus, quid nos persequeris?	12.3 *[Armenian text]*	12:3 "რომელი არს ბრალი ჩემი, რომლი- თა -ესე გიყავ შენ?"	
	13:1 Respondit diabolus: Adam, tu quid dicis mihi? propter tuam causam projectus sum inde.	13.1 *[Armenian text]*	13:1 მიუგო ეშმაკმან და ჰრქუა :" შენ არაი მიყავ მე, არამედ შენ გამო გამოვარდი მე ქუეყანად.	

Pericope 5 *Fall of Satan* 15E

GREEK	LATIN	ARMENIAN	GEORGIAN	SLAVONIC
	12:1 Groaning, the Devil said: "O Adam, all my enmity, jealousy, and resentment is towards you, since on account of you I was expelled and alienated from my glory, which I had in heaven in the midst of the angels. On account of you I was cast out upon the earth."	12:1 Satan also wept loudly and said to Adam. "All my arrogance and sorrow came to pass because of you; for, because of you I went forth from my dwelling; and because of you I was alienated from the throne of the Cherubim who, having spread out a shelter, used to enclose me; because of you my feet have trodden the earth."	12:1 The Devil began to cry with forced tears and the Devil told Adam, "O Adam, all the greed and the anger and all the grief of my heart are directed against you because (it was) through you that I fell from my dwellings; (it was) by you that I was alienated from my own throne. My wings were more numerous than those of the Cherubim, and I concealed myself under them. Because of you, now my feet walk on the earth, which I would never have believed."	
	12:2 Adam answered: "What have I done to you? 12:3 What fault do I have against you? Since you have not been harmed nor injured by us, why do you persecute us?"	12:2 Adam replied and said to him, 12:3 "What are our [[sins]] against you, that you did all this to us?"	12:2 Adam replied to the Devil and told him, 12:3 "What is my fault, by which I have done all that to you?"	
	13:1 The Devil answered: "Adam what are you saying to me? On account of you I was cast out from heaven.	13:1 Satan replied and said, "You did nothing to me, but I came to this measure because of you, on the day on which you were created, for I went forth on that day.	13:1 The Devil replied to him and told him, "You did nothing to me, but it is because of you that I have fallen upon the earth.	

Pericope 5 *Fall of Satan*

GREEK	LATIN	ARMENIAN	GEORGIAN	SLAVONIC
	13:2 Quando tu plasmatus es, ego proiectus sum a facie dei et foras a societate angelorum missus sum. quando insufflavit deus spiritum vitae in te et factus est vultus et similitudo tua ad imaginem dei, et adduxit te Michahel et fecit te adorare in conspectu dei, et dixit dominus deus: ecce Adam, feci te ad imaginem et similitudinem nostram.	13.2 Իբրեւ փչեաց Աստուած գոգին քո ի ձեզ առեր դու զանձնութիւն պատկերի նորա. իսկ այսուհետեւ Միքայէլ եւ ոտ քեզ երկիր պագանել առաջի Աստուծոյ: եւ ասէ Աստուած զՄիքայէլ. Աճա, արարի զԱդամ ի նմանութիւն պատկերի իմում:	13:2 რომელსაცა დღესა შეიქმენ შენ, მასცა დღესა გამოვარდი პირისა-გან ღმრთისა, რამეთუ ოდეს შთაბერა შენ პირსა შენსა სულნი ღმერთმან, გაქუნდა შენ ხატი და მსგავსებაი ღმრთეებისაი. და მოვიდა მიქაელ, წარ-მოგადგინა შენ და თაყუანი-გაცემინა შენ ღმრთისა. და ჰრქუა ღმერთმან მიქაელს:" შევქმენ ადამ მსგავსად ხატისა და ღმრთეებისა ჩემისა".	
	14:1 Et egressus Michahel vocavit omnes angelos dicens: adorate imaginem domini dei, sicut praecepit dominus deus.	14.1 Եւ ելեալ Միքայէլ կոչեաց զամենայն հրեշտակն, եւ ասէ. երկիր պագէք Աստուծոյ որ արարի:	14:1 მაშინ მოვიდა მიქაელ და მოუწოდა ყოველთა ერთა ანგელოზთასა და ჰრქუა მათ:" თაყუანის-ეცით მსგავსსა და ხატსა ღმრთეებისასა".	
	14:2 Et ipse Michahel primus adoravit, et vocavit me et dixit: adora imaginem dei Jehova.	14.2 Եպաց երկիր նախ Միքայէլ. կոչեաց զիս եւ ասէ. երկիր պագ եւ դու Ադամայ:	14:2 და ოდეს მოუწოდა მიქაელ და ყოველთა თაყუანის-გცეს შენ, და მეცა მომიწოდა.	

Pericope 5 *Fall of Satan* 16E

GREEK	LATIN	ARMENIAN	GEORGIAN	SLAVONIC
	13.2 When you were formed, I was cast out from the face of God and was sent forth from the company of the angels. When God blew into you the breath of life and your countenance and likeness were made in the image of God, Michael led you and made you worship in the sight of God. The Lord God then said: 'Behold, Adam, I have made you in our image and likeness.'	13:2 When God breathed his spirit into you, you received the likeness of his image. Thereupon, Michael came and made you bow down before God. God said to Michael, 'Behold I have made Adam in the likeness of my image.'	13:2 The very day when you were created, on that day I fell from before the face of God, because when God breathed a spirit onto your face, you had the image and likeness of divinity. And Michael came; he presented you and made you bow down before God. And God told Michael, 'I have created Adam according to (my) image and my divinity.'	
	14:1 Having gone forth Michael called all the angels saying: 'Worship the image of the Lord God, just as the Lord God has commanded.'	14:1 Then Michael summoned all the angels, and God said to them, 'Come, bow down to god whom I made.'	14:1 Then Michael came; he summoned all the troops of angels and told them, 'Bow down before the likeness and the image of the divinity.'	
	14:2 Michael himself worshipped first then he called me and said: 'Worship the image of God Jehovah.'	14:2 Michael bowed first. He called me and said. 'You too, bow down to Adam.'	14:2 And then, when Michael summoned them and all had bowed down to you, he summoned me also.	

Pericope 5 *Fall of Satan*

GREEK	LATIN	ARMENIAN	GEORGIAN	SLAVONIC
	14:3 Et respondi ego: non habeo ego adorare Adam. et cum compelleret me Michahel adorare, dixi ad eum: quid me compellis? non adorabo deteriorem et posteriorem meum. in creatura illius prius sum. antequam ille fieret, ego iam factus eram. ille me debet adorare.	14.3 Պատասխանի ետու. իմ բայց ասէ որս Մրայէլ, ոչ պատասն[ե]մ ես [երկիր] իւանող իմոյ, զի առաջ ես իմ. զի՞ նա արժան է [իմձ] ինձ երկիր պատանել:	14:3 და მე ვარქუ:" განეშორე ჩემგან, რამეთუ უმრწემესსა ჩემსა არა თაყუანის-ვსცემ, რამეთუ უწინა მაგისა მე ყოფალ ვარ და მაგის ღირს ჩემდა თაყუანის-ცემად".	
	15:1 Hoc audientes ceteri qui sub me erant angeli noluerunt adorare eum.	15.1 Լուան եւ [այլ] հրեշտակքն որ ընդ իս էին եւ հանձն թուցաւ բանք իմ եւ ոչ պատիւս քեզ երկրպագութիւն Ադամ:	15:1 ესე-და ესმა სხუათა ანგელოზთა ექუსთა დასთა და სონდა სიტყუაი ესე ჩემი და არა თაყუანის-გცეს შენ.	
	15:2 Et ait Michahel: adora imaginem dei. si autem non adoraveris, irascetur tibi dominus deus.			
	15:3 Et ego dixi: si irascitur mihi, ponam sedem meam super sidera caeli et ero similis altissimo.			
	16:1 Et iratus est mihi dominus deus et misit me cum angelis meis foras de gloria nostra, et per tuam causam in hunc mundum expulsi sumus de habitationibus nostris et proiecti sumus in terram.	16.1 Բարկացաւ աստուծուն Աստուած ի վերայ իմ, եւ հրամայաց հանել զմեզ ի պսակութենէն մերմէ եւ ընկենուլ երկիր զիս եւ զհրեշտակս իմ որ ընդ իս հասանեցան, եւ որ էիր անդրէն ի դրախտին:	16:1 მაშინ განრისხნა ღმერთი ჩუენ ზედა და უბრძანა გარდამოგდებაი ჩემი და მათიცა ქუეყნად საყოფლით ჩუენით, ხოლო შენი ბრძანა ყოფაი სამოთხესა მას შინა.	

Pericope 5 *Fall of Satan*

GREEK	LATIN	ARMENIAN	GEORGIAN	SLAVONIC
	14:3 I answered: 'I do not have it within me to worship Adam.' When Michael compelled me to worship, I said to him: 'Why do you compel me? I will not worship him who is lower and later than me. I am prior to that creature. Before he was made, I had already been made. He ought to worship me.'	14:3 I said, 'Go away, Michael! I shall not bow [down] to him who is posterior to me, for I am former. Why is it proper [for me] to bow down to him?'	14:3 And I told him, 'Go away from me, for I shall not bow down to him who is younger than me; indeed, I was master before him and it is proper for him to bow down to me.'	
	15:1 Hearing this, other angels who were under me were unwilling to worship him.	15:1 The other angels, too, who were with me, heard this, and my words seemed pleasing to them and they did not prostrate themselves to you, Adam.	15:1 When the six classes of other angels heard that, then my speech pleased them and they did not bow down to you.	
	15:2 Michael said: 'Worship the image of God. If you do not worship, the Lord God will grow angry with you.' 15:3 I said: 'If he grows angry with me, I will place my seat above the stars of heaven and I will be like the Most High.'			
	16:1 Then the Lord God grew angry with me and sent me forth with my angels from our glory. On account of you we were expelled from our dwelling into this world and cast out upon the earth.	16:1 Thereupon, God became angry with me and commanded to expel us from our dwelling and to cast me and my angels, who were in agreement with me, to the earth; and you were at the same time in the Garden.	16:1 Then God became angry with us and ordered us, them and me, to be cast down from our dwellings to the earth. As for you, he ordered you to dwell in the Garden.	

Pericope 5 *Fall of Satan*

GREEK	LATIN	ARMENIAN	GEORGIAN	SLAVONIC
	16:2 Et statim facti sumus in dolore, quoniam expoliati sumus tanta gloria, et te in tanta laetitia delitiarum videre dolebamus.	16.2 իբրեւ զխոացի եթէ վասն քո եմք ի լիսակութենէ լոյսոյս եւ եղէ ի վասատակս եւ ի ցաւս.	16:2 ოდეს გულისხმა-ვყავ, რამეთუ შენ ძლით გარდამოვარდი, და მე ვიყავ ჭირსა შინა და შენ განსვენებასა,	
	16:3 Et dolo circumveniebam mulierem tuam et feci te expelli per eam de delitiis laetitiae tuae, sicut ego expulsus sum de gloria mea.	16.3 յախժամ պատրաստեցի քեզ որոգայթ զի ատարացուցի[ց] զքեզ լուրախութենէ քումմէ, որպէս եւ ես վասն քո ատարացայ:	16:3 და მოგიადირე, რაითა უცხო გქმნა შენცა სამოთხისა მისგან საშუებელისაისა, ვითარცა მე უცხო ვიქმენ შენითა.	
	17:1 Haec audiens Adam a diabolo exclamavit cum magno fletu et dixit: domine deus meus, in manibus tuis est vita mea. fac ut iste adversarius meus longe sit a me, qui quaerit animam meam perdere, et da mihi gloriam eius, quam ipse perdidit.	17.1 զայս իբրեւ լուաւ Ադամ աաէառ Տէր. [Տէր աստուծ իմ ի ձեռս քո]. ի բաց արա լցէս գիշնասիիս իմ որ կամի մոլորեցուցանել զիս որ ի խնդիրս եմ եղեալ լոյսոյն զոր կորուսի:	17:1 ესე რა ესმა ადამს, ღაღადყო ხმითა მაღლითა და თქუა: "უფალო, ცხორებაი ჩემი ხელთა შენთა არს, განმაშორე ჩემგან მტერი ესე, რომელსა უნებს ცთუნებაი ჩემი და რომელი ედიებს წარწყმედასა ნათესავისა ჩემი - სასა, რომლისაგან წარწყმედილ არს ევა".	
	17:2 Et statim non apparuit diabolus ei.	17.2 ի ժամու այնմիկ ելյալ Սատանայ ի նմանէ.	17:2 მას ქამსა ჩრისნ იქმნა ბელიარი.	
	17:3 Adam vero perseveravit XL diebus stans in poenitentia in aqua Jordanis.	17.3 եւ Ադամ այլուէեղւ եկաց ի ջուրս ապաշխարութեան. եւ նա կեցալ եկաց ի վերայ երկրի անկեալ ասույա երիս իբրեւ գնեալյալ. եւ ապա չու երից ասույյ յարեաւ յերկրէ.	17:3 ხოლო ადამ დაადგრა წყალსა მას შინა და ინანდა, ხოლო ევა დავრდომილ იყო ქუეყანასა ზედა ვითარცა მკუდარი. და შემდგომად ალ-დგა იგი ქუეყანით	

Pericope 5 *Fall of Satan* 18E

GREEK	LATIN	ARMENIAN	GEORGIAN	SLAVONIC
	16:2 Immediately we were in grief, since we had been despoiled of so much glory, and we grieved to see you in such a great happiness of delights.	16:2 When I realized that because of you I had gone forth from the dwelling of light and was in sorrows and pains,	16:2 When I had realized that I had fallen by your power, that I was in distress and you were in rest,	
	16:3 By a trick I cheated your wife and caused you to be expelled through her from the delights of your happiness, just as I had been expelled from my glory."	16:3 then I prepared a trap for you, so that I [might] alienate you from your happiness just as I, too, had been alienated because of you.'	16:3 then I aimed at hunting you so that I might alienate you from the Garden of delights, just as I had been alienated because of you."	
	17:1 Hearing this, Adam cried out with a great shout because of the Devil, and said: "O Lord my God, in your hands is my life. Make this adversary of mine be far from me, who seeks to ruin my soul. Give me his glory which he himself lost."	17:1. When Adam heard this, he said to the Lord, "[Lord, my soul is in your hand.] Make this enemy of mine distant from me, who desires to lead me astray, I who am searching for the light that I have lost."	17:1 When Adam heard that, he cried in a loud voice and said, "Lord, my life is in your hands. Make this enemy distant from me, who desires to lead me astray and seeks to destroy my race. It is by him that Eve has been lost."	
	17:2 Immediately the Devil no longer appeared to him. 17:3 Adam truly persevered for forty days standing in penitence in the waters of the Jordan.	17:2 At that time Satan passed away from him. 17:3 Adam stood from then on in the waters of repentance, and Eve remained fallen upon the ground for three days, like one dead. Then, after three days, she arose from the earth,	17:2 At that moment, Beliar became invisible. 17:3 As for Adam, he remained in the water and did penitence. But Eve had fallen upon the ground like one dead. Then she stood up from the ground.	

Pericope 6 Separation of Adam and Eve

GREEK	LATIN	ARMENIAN	GEORGIAN	SLAVONIC
	18:1 Et dixit Eva ad Adam: vive tu, domine mi. tibi concessa est vita, quoniam tu nec primam nec secundam praevaricationem fecisti, sed ego praevaricata et seducta sum, quia non custodivi mandatum dei. et nunc separa me a lumine vitae istius, et vadam ad occasum solis et ero ibi usque dum moriar.	18.1 եւ ասէ գԱդամ. Դու ապաւուր ես կառաջին յանցանացն եւ երկրորդուս, բայց միայն ինձ յաղթեաց Սատանայ ի պատճառս բանին Աստուծոյ եւ քո. եւ ասէ դարձեալ եւս գԱդամ. Աշա երթամ ես ի մուտս արեւու եւ լինիմ անդ եւ կերակուր իմ խոտ մինչեւ մեռանիմ. զի ալյաւշեսցէ ասարժան իմ կերակրոցն կենդանութեան։	18:1 და პრქუა ადამს:" ცხონდი ადამ, რამეთუ შენ არა მიერთე გარდა-სლვასა მცნებათასა არცა პირველსა, არცა მეორესა. მძლოს მე სიტყუამან უმრთისამან". და პრქუა ევა:" აპა ესერა, მე წარვიდე მზისა დასავალით კერძო და ვჭამდე თივასა ვითარცა პირუტყვი, ვიდრემდე მოვკუდე, რამეთუ რაითურთით არა ღირს ვარ ჭამადისა მისგან ცხოველთაისა".	
	18:2 Et coepit ambulare contra partes occidentales et coepit lugere et amare flere cum gemitu magno.	18.2 Գնաց նա ի մուտս արեւու, եւ եղեւ նա ի սուգ եւ ի տրտմութիւն.	18:2 და წარვიდა ევა მზისა დასავალით კერძო და იყოფებოდა მუნ გლოვით და კუნესით.	
	18:3 Et fecit ibi habitaculum habens in utero foetum trium mensium.	18.3 եւ ապա արար իւր տաղաւար ի մուտս արեւու. եւ ձանձալ էր ամսաց, եւ ուներ ի արդանդի զկալխս անասրէնն.	18:3 და შემდგომად ღელთა მათ იქმნა მზისა დასავალით ტალავარი. ოდეს მიდგომილ იყო სამი თვით და მუცელსა ედვა კაენი.	
	19:1a Et cum adpropinquasset tempus partus eius coepit conturbari doloribus et exclamavit ad dominum dicens:	19.1 իբրեւ ետին ժամանակք ծննդեան նորա, սկսաւ ապաղակել ի ձայն մեծ եւ ասէ.	19:1 ოდეს მოეწივნეს ღელენი შობისა მისისანი, და შეძრწუნდა და ხმა- ყო ხმითა მაღლითა უმრთისა მიმართ და თქუა:	

Pericope 6 *Separation of Adam and Eve* 19E

GREEK	LATIN	ARMENIAN	GEORGIAN	SLAVONIC
	18:1 Eve said to Adam: "Long may you live, my lord to you is my life submitted, since you did not take part in either the first or second collusion. But I conspired and was seduced, because I did not keep the commandment of God. Now separate me from the light of this life. I will go to the west and I will be there until I die.	18:1 and she said to Adam, "You are innocent of the first sin and of this second one. Only me alone did Satan overcome, as a result of God's word and yours." Again Eve said to Adam, "Behold, I shall go to the west and I shall be there and my food (will be) grass until I die; for henceforth I am unworthy of the foods of life."	18:1 and told Adam, "Be saved, Adam, for you did not join me in the transgression of the commandments, neither in the first (instance) nor in the second. (But) the word of God will prevail against me." And Eve told him, "Behold, I shall go in the direction of the setting sun and I will eat grass like an animal until I die, for by no means am I worthy of (having a part in) the food of the living."	
	18:2 She then began to walk toward the western regions and began to wail and weep bitterly with great moaning.	18:2 Eve went to the west and she mourned and was sad;	18:2 Then Eve went away in the direction of the setting sun and she remained there in mourning and moaning.	
	18:3 She made there a dwelling, being three months pregnant.	18:3 and then she made a hut for herself in the west, and she was advanced in her pregnancy and she had Cain, the lawless one, [in] her womb.	18:3 And after these days, she made for herself a hut in the direction of the setting sun. She had conceived three months before, and Cain was in her womb,	
	19:1a When the time of her delivery approached, she began to be distressed with pains, and she cried out to the Lord, saying:	19:1 When the times of her parturition came, she began to cry out in a loud voice and said,	19:1 and when the days of her parturition arrived, then she started to tremble; she wailed towards God in a loud voice and said:	

Pericope 6 *Separation of Adam and Eve*

GREEK	LATIN	ARMENIAN	GEORGIAN	SLAVONIC
	19:1b miserere mei, domine, adiuva me. Et non exaudiebatur nec erat misericordia dei circa eam.			
	19:2 Et dixit ipsa in se: quis nuntiabit domino meo Adae? deprecor vos luminaria caeli, dum revertimini ad orientem, nuntiate domino meo Adam.	19.2 Ո՞ր է Արամ զի տեսցէ զգաա իմ գայս. Իսկ ո՞ պատմեսցէ գտարապանս իմ Արամայ. եթէ իցէ Տոդմ ի ներքոյ երկնից զի երթեալ պատմեսցէ Արամայ. եթէ եկ ածասկան լեր եաժի. եւ ասէ. Աղաչեմ զձեզ ամենայն լուասաւոր լորժամ երթաք(ս)ք դուք յարեւել պատմեսջք տեառն իմում Արամայ վասն ցաւոց իմոց:	19:2 " სადა-მე არს ადამი, რაითა მილხინოს მე ჭირთა ამათ შინა ჩემთა ანუ ვინ ფუხრნეს სალმობანი ესე ჩემნი? არავინ არს მტრინველთაგან ი, მი-მცა-ვიდა და ვრქუა: მოვედ და ეშიე ევას, ცოლსა შენსა, გევედრები თქუენ, ყოველთავე ნათესავთა ცისათა, და ოდეს მიხვიდეთ აღმოსავალით, უთხრენით უფალსა ჩემსა სალმობანი ესე ჩემნი".	
	20:1 In illa autem hora dixit Adam: planctus Evae venit ad me;	20.1a Յայնման ժաա Արամ ի զետ Որդասան անդր. գբարբառ եսայի եւ գյալիս նորա:	20:1a და ესმა ადამს მტინარესა შინა თირდანისასა ხმაი ტირილისაი და ტრვათა მისთაო.	

Pericope 6 *Separation of Adam and Eve* 20E

GREEK	LATIN	ARMENIAN	GEORGIAN	SLAVONIC
	19:1b "Have mercy on me, O Lord, help me." She was not heard, nor was the mercy of God toward her.			
	19:2 She said to herself: "Who will tell my lord Adam? I beseech you, lights of the heavens, when you turn again to the east, tell my lord Adam."	19:2 "Where is Adam, that he might see this pain of mine? Who, indeed, will relate my afflictions to Adam? Is there a wind under the heavens that will go and tell Adam, 'Come and help Eve?!" And she said, "I implore you, all luminaries, when you come to the east, tell my lord Adam about my pains."	19:2 "Where is Adam so that he can console me in my present pain, or who will tell him about my sufferings? Is there none among the birds, who would go to him and tell him, 'Come, help Eve, your spouse.' I beg of you, all you races of heaven, when you go to the east, tell my lord about my present sufferings."	
	20:1 In that very hour Adam said: "The lament of Eve has come to me;	20:1a Then Adam, in the river Jordan, heard Eve's cry and her weeping.	20:1a Then Adam, in the river Jordan, heard her tearful crying and misfortunes.	

Pericope 6 *Separation of Adam and Eve*

GREEK	LATIN	ARMENIAN	GEORGIAN	SLAVONIC
		20.1b իբրև լուաւ Աստուած ձայնի աղաչարութեան Ադամայ	20:1b მაშინ ისმინა ღმერთმან ლოცვაი იგი ადამისი და მიუვლინა მი- ქაელ ანგელოზი და მოართუა მას	
		և ուրցք նմա գկարել և գՆմբէս և գեկեալ նմա և գսասկի սորա։	თესლი შებეჭდული ბეჭდითა საღმრ- თოთა მორთუმად ადამისსა. და ასწავა მათ თესვაი და საქმე მისი, რაითა ცხოვნდენ იგინი მით და ყოველნი ნათესავნი მისნი.	
	forte iterum serpens pugnavit cum ea.	20.1c և ապա լուաւ Ադամ գձայն աղաչանացն ևագի ի մոսա արհու և ասէ Ադամ ի սիրտ իւր. Զայնս այն մարմնոյ իմոյ է և ոսկիսն. յարեայց և գնացից առ նա և տեսից թէ վասն որոյ աղաղակէ. գուցէ դարձեալ գազանն մարտեաւ ընդ նմա։	20:1c და ვითარცა ესმა ადამ ლოცვაი ევაისი და დაადებაი იგი ტი- რილისა მისისაი დასავალით კერძო, იცნა ხმაი მისი და თქუა ადამ გულსა შინა თვისსა:" ხმაი გუერდისა ჩემისაი არს, ხმაი ტანიგისა ჩემისაი არს, აღვდგე და ვიხილო, რაისათვის ხმობს, ანუ-მე კუალად გუელი იგი ბრძავს?"	

Pericope 6 *Separation of Adam and Eve* · 21E

GREEK	LATIN	ARMENIAN	GEORGIAN	SLAVONIC
		20:1b When God hearkened to the sound of Adam's penitence,	20:1b Then God hearkened to Adam's prayer and sent him the angel Michael who brought him seeds, sealed with the divine seal, destined to be brought to Adam.	
		he taught him sowing and reaping and that which was to come upon him and his seed.	Then he taught him sowing and the work related to it, so that thus they might be saved, (they) and all their descendants.	
		20:1c Then Adam heard the sound of Eve's entreaty in the west, and Adam said to himself, "That voice and weeping are of my flesh. Let me arise and go to her and see why she is crying out. Perhaps the beast is fighting with her once more!"	20:1c And when Adam (had) heard the prayer of Eve and the wailing of her tears from the west, Adam recognized her voice and said in his heart, "This is the voice of my rib, the voice of my lamb; I will arise and I will see why she cries. Perhaps the serpent is attacking her once more?"	
	Perhaps the serpent has fought with her again."			

Pericope 6 *Separation of Adam and Eve*

GREEK	LATIN	ARMENIAN	GEORGIAN	SLAVONIC
	20:2a Et ambulans invenit eam in luctu magno; et dixit Eva: ex quo vidi te, domine mi, refrigeravit anima mea in doloribus posita.	20.2a Եւրհա Արաս եւ գնաց գՃետ բարբառոյն որ եաս էր։ Իբրեւ տեսու եաս խասեցաւ եւ ասէ զԱդամ. Լուա՞ր իմացուցի՞ս քեզ Հոդմք յորում ադադակեց[ի] ւաան քո, եթէ իմացուցիս քեզ լաաաորք երկնից որ կայիս ի կողմանս յար[եւ]ելից այր ըստ այրէ ի գնացից խրեանց. կամ թէ իմացուցիս քեզ թոյումք երկնից կամ գազանք երկրի զոր կոչեցի եւ ատարեցի առ քեզ, զի պատմեցես քեզ։	20:2a ადგა ადამ და მისდევდა კუალსა მას მისსა, და ვითარცა მოვიდა მისა დასავლით კერძო, სადაცა იყო ევა, და ვითარცა იხილა ადამი ევამან, ტიროდა ტირილითა დიდითა და თქუა:" უფალო ჩემო, ადამ, არა გესმა ხმაი ტირილისა ჩემისა? რამეთუ დღეს ცხრა დღე არს და დღით და ღამით არს ლაღადება ესე ჩემი შენდა მომართ, არა გაუწყესა შენ ნათესავთა ადმოსა- ვალისათა ადმოსლვასა მათსა, ანუ არა გაუწყესა შენ მფრინველთა ცისა-თა და მხეცთა ქუეყანისათა, რამეთუ ვევედრებოდე მათ ყოველთა, რაითამ -ცა გითხრეს შენ!	

Pericope 6 *Separation of Adam and Eve* 22E

GREEK	LATIN	ARMENIAN	GEORGIAN	SLAVONIC
	20:2a Walking, he found her in great distress. Eve said: "How is it that I see you, my Lord. My soul has grown cold being in such pains.	20:2a Adam arose and followed the noise (to) where Eve was. When Eve saw him, she spoke and said to Adam, "Did you hear the sound of my crying? Did the winds inform you, whom [I] entreated concerning you? Did the luminaries of heaven inform you, who are in the [east]ern regions every day, in their courses? Did the birds of the heavens inform you, or the beasts of the earth whom I summoned and dispatched to you, to tell you?	20:2a Adam arose and followed her footsteps. When he had come close to her, in the part of the west where Eve was, and when Eve saw Adam, she was crying with abundant tears and said, "My lord, Adam, did you not hear the sound of my tears? For, today, it is nine days, day and night, that there has been this crying of mine towards you. Is it that the [[luminaries]] of the east have not informed you when they arose? And have not the birds of the heavens and the beasts of the earth informed you, for I begged them all that they tell you about it.	

Pericope 6 *Separation of Adam and Eve*

GREEK	LATIN	ARMENIAN	GEORGIAN	SLAVONIC
	20:2b et nunc deprecare dominum deum pro me ut exaudiat te et respiciat ad me et liberet me de doloribus meis pessimis.	20.2b Արդ արի աղաչեա զտէրըն քո, զի վրկեսցէ զիս ի ցաւոց աստի:	20:2b აწვე და ევედრე შემქმედსა შენსა, რაითა წყალობა ყოს და ისმინოს შენი ღმერთმან და მოხსნეს მე სალმობათაგან ჩემთა, ანუ თუ ჯერ--ჩნდეს, მოავლინოს ჩემ ზედა სიკუდილი, ანუ ყრვათა ჩემთაგან განმარი-ნოს ლოცვითა შენითა".	
	20:3 Et deprecatus est Adam dominum pro Eva.	20.3 եւաց Ադամ եւ աղաչէր եկաց վասն նորա առ Աստուած:	20:3 ილოცვიდა და იტყოდა ადამ მისთვის ვედრებასა წინაშე ღმრთი-სა. და ისმინა მისი უფალმან.	
	21:1 Et ecce venerunt XII angeli et duo virtutes stantes a dextris et a sinistris Evae.	21.1 եւ ահա իջին հրկետց երկու հրեշտակք եւ երկու զաւրութիւնք, եկին առ եւա եւ կացին առաջի երեսաց նորա.	21:1 და აჰა ესერა მოვიდეს ზეცით ათორმეტნი ანგელოზნი და ორნი ძალნი. და მოვიდეს ადგილსა მას ევაისსა.	

Pericope 6 *Separation of Adam and Eve* 23E

GREEK	LATIN	ARMENIAN	GEORGIAN	SLAVONIC
	20:2b Now pray to the Lord God on my behalf that he might hear you and look down upon me and free me from my very bad pains.	20:2b Now arise, entreat your Creator to deliver me from these pains."	20:2b Arise, entreat your Creator to have pity, so that God may answer your prayer and deliver me from my sufferings or, if it seems fitting to Him, send death to me or, by your prayers, liberate me from my torments."	
	20:3 Adam then prayed to the Lord for Eve.	20:3 Adam wept and prayed to God on her behalf.	20:3 Adam prayed and spoke a plea to God on her behalf and the Lord hearkened to him.	
	21:1 And behold, twelve angels came and two Virtues, standing to the right and to the left of Eve.	21:1 And behold, two angels and two powers descended from heaven, came to Eve and stood before her.	21:1 And behold, twelve angels and two powers came from heaven. And they came to the place (where) Eve (was).	

Pericope 6 *Separation of Adam and Eve*

GREEK	LATIN	ARMENIAN	GEORGIAN	SLAVONIC
	21:2 Et Michahel erat stans a dextris et tetigit faciem eius usque ad pectus et dixit ad Evam: beata es, Eva, propter Adam. quoniam preces eius magnae sunt et orationes, missus sum ad te, ut accipias adiutorium nostrum. exsurge nunc et para te ad partum	21.2 եւ սահն գնա զայրութիւբ. Երանի է քեզ եւա վասն Ադամայ բնորհելոյ Աստուծոյ, զի մեծ են խնդրուածք նորա, եւ նովաւ եղբ[ւ] ազնակաձութիւն քեզ լԱստուծոյ. բայց [ի սասնէն] ի ձննդենէդ քո լայլմանէ ոչ կարէիր սպրել: եւ ասէ Նեեշտակն գնա. Կագմեա զանձն քո եւ եւ լիսիմ քեզ դայեակ:	21:2 ერთი იგი ძალთაგანი მოვიდა და შეეხო პირსა ევაისსა და მკერ- სა მისსა და ჰრქუა ევას:" ნეტარ ხარ შენ, ევა, ადამის გამორჩეულისა და მონისა ღმრთისა, რამეთუ დიდ არიან ლოცვანი მისნი წინაშე ღმრთისა და მის გამო გიხსნეს შენ ღმერთმან. ჰკუეოფდცა მის გამო არა ყოფილ იყო შეწევნაი შენი, ეგევითარი ეკალი მტცულად- გილებიეს, ვერცა განერე სალ- მობათაგან შენთა. აღდეგ აწ და განეწესე შობად ყრმისა".	
	21:3a Et peperit filium et erat lucidus.	21.3a Ապա իբր ձնաւ գմանուկն էր զոյս մարմնոյ նորա իբրեւ գգոյն աստեղաց.	21:3a აღდგა ევა, ვითარცა ასწავა მას ანგელოზმან, და შვა ყრმაი და იყო ფერი მისი ვითარცა ვარსკულავთაი.	
	21:3b et continuo infans ex surgens cucurrit et manibus suis tulit herbam et dedit matri suae. et vocatum est nomen eius Cain.	21.3b ի ժամուն իբրեւ մանուկն ի ձեռա դայեակին անկաւ, ի վեր վազեաց եւ ձեռալն փետէր գխոտ երկրին առ տատասաի մաւր իւրոյ եւ անապուութիւբ բազում լինէին ի տեղոչն:	21:3b და ხელთა ზედა ამქუმელისათა გარდაამოვარდა და იწყო ფხურად თივისა, რამეთუ ტალავრისა ღელისა მისისასა და მცენარე თივისაი.	

Pericope 6 *Separation of Adam and Eve* 24E

GREEK	LATIN	ARMENIAN	GEORGIAN	SLAVONIC
	21:2 Michael was standing to her right and touched his face to her chest and said to Eve: "Blessed are you, Eve, on account of Adam, for his prayers and supplications are great. I was sent to you that you might receive our help. Arise now and prepare yourself for birth."	21:2 The powers said to her, "Eve, you are blessed because of Adam, God's elect one, for his prayers are mighty and through him help from God has come to you. Apart [from him], you would not be able to survive this birth." The angel said to Eve, "Prepare yourself, and I will be a midwife for you."	21:2 One of the powers came, touched Eve's face and her breast, and told Eve, "Blessed are you, Eve, because of Adam, the elect one and servant of God, for his prayers are great before God and, because of him, God will deliver you. If you had not been brought help because of him, you are sure to have conceived such a thorn (i.e., Cain the killer) that you could not have rescued yourself from your sufferings. Rise up now and prepare yourself to give birth to a child."	
	21:3a She brought forth a son who shone brilliantly.	21:3a Then, when she bore the child, the colour of his body was like the colour of stars.	21:3a Eve arose as the angel had instructed her: she gave birth to an infant and his color was like that of the stars.	
	21:3b At once the infant stood up and ran out and brought some grass with his own hands and gave it to his mother. His name was called Cain.	21:3b At the hour when the child fell into the hands of the mid-wife, he leaped up and, with his hands, plucked up the grass of the earth near his mother's hut; and infertilities became numerous in that place.	21:3b He fell into the hands of the midwife and (at once) he began to pluck up the grass, for in his mother's hut grass was planted.	

Pericope 6 *Separation of Adam and Eve*

GREEK	LATIN	ARMENIAN	GEORGIAN	SLAVONIC
		21.3c եւ ասէ Հեշտակն զնա. Արդար է Աստուած զի ոչ խոտեց զանկանել ի ճետս իմ, զի եւ կալէն անաւրէնն որ բարոյդ եւ.{...} եւ կեեղանողն [տեսող] լիցիս եւ կործանիչ եւ շնութիւն, դատումիթիւն եւ ոչ քաղցրութիւն:	21:3c მიუგო ამქუმელმან მან და ჰრქუა:"მართალ არს უფერთი, რამეთუ არასადა დაგიტევა შენ ხელთა ჩემთა, რამეთუ შენ ხარ კაცნი, გულარძნილი და მკულელი კეთილისაი, რამეთუ ნაყოფიერისა ხისა აღმომყხურელი ხარ და არა დამწრგუელი, განმამწარებელი ხარ და არა დამატკბობელი".	
		21.3d եւ ասէ Հեշտակն դարձեալ գնդամ. կաց եւ մեա աո ենա զի արասցէ նա զոր ինչ Հրամայեցի:	21:3d და ჰრქუა ადამს ძალმან:"დაადგერ ევას თანა ვიდრე ყოფადმდე მისა ყრმისა მისთვის, რაი ვასწავე".	

Pericope 6 *Separation of Adam and Eve* 25E

GREEK	LATIN	ARMENIAN	GEORGIAN	SLAVONIC
		21:3c The angel said to him, "God is just, that he did not make you fall into my hand, for you are Cain, the lawless one, who will be destroyer of the good and {...} and living [p]lant and adultery, bitterness and not sweetness." 21:3d And again the angel said to Adam, "Remain by Eve, so that she will do what I commanded."	21:3c The midwife replied to him and told him, "God is just that he did not at all leave you in my hands. For, you are Cain, the perverse one, killer of the good, for you are the one who plucks up the fruit-bearing tree, and not he who plants it. You are the bearer of bitterness and not of sweetness." 21:3d And the power told Adam, "Remain by Eve until she has done with the infant what I have taught her."	

Pericope 7 *Cain and Abel*

GREEK	LATIN	ARMENIAN	GEORGIAN	SLAVONIC
1:1 Αὕτη ἡ διήγησις Ἀδὰμ καὶ Εὔας. Μετὰ τὸ ἐξελθεῖν αὐτοὺς ἐκ τοῦ παραδείσου,				2.1 Єгда же съгрѣши и прѣстѫпи заповѣди господьнѩ, изгнань бысть Адамь изь раю
1:2 [ἔλαβεν] Ἀδὰμ Εὔαν καὶ ἀνῆλθεν εἰς τὴν ἀνατολὴν καὶ ἔμεινεν ἐκεῖ ἔτη δέκα καὶ ὀκτὼ καὶ μῆνας δύο.	22:1 Et tulit Adam Evam et puerum et duxit eos ad orientem.	22(1):2 [*ms*] այնուհետև Արամ զնա եւ զմանուկն եւ սև զնոսա ի կողմ արեւելից, եւ եղև նա անդ ևտասն հանդերձ, եւ սաա լծան անէր ութսունևսան եւ ամիս երկու.	22(1):2 ხოლო ადამ წარმოუვანა ევა და ყრმაი იგი და მოუვანნა იგინი აღმოსავალით კერძო და დაადგრა მუნ. და იყვნეს აქესიხულენი წელნი მერვენი და თუენი იგი მეორე.	2.2а и поѥмь (Адамь) женѫ своѭ Кьѵгѫ и изьшьдь сѣде при Єдемѣ (ed. m: на мѣстѣ) прѣдь двьрьми раискыми .
	22:2 Et misit dominus deus per Michahel angelum semina diversa et dedit Adae et ostendit ei laborare et colere terram, ut habeant fructum, unde viverent ipsi et omnes generationes eorum.			
1:3 Καὶ ἐν γαστρὶ εἴληφεν Εὔα καὶ ἐγέννησε δύο υἱοὺς τὸν Διάφωτον τὸν καλούμενον Κάϊν καὶ τὸν Ἀμιλαβὲς τὸν καλούμενον Ἄβελ.	22:3 Postea enim concepit Eva et genuit filium, cui nomen Abel. et manebat Cain cum Abel in unum.	22(1):3 յդազաւ եւ ծնաւ որդի զկայենա որ անուանեաց եւ կոչեաց Հաբէլ դայեանկն], եւ բնակեցան ի միասին։	22(1):3 მიუდგა ევა და შვა სხუაი ძე, რომელსა უწოდა ქალმან ღმრთი- სამან აბელ და დაადგრა მუნ ურთი-ეთას.	
2:1 Καὶ μετὰ ταῦτα ἐγένοντο μετ' ἀλλήλων Ἀδὰμ καὶ Εὔα κοιμωμένων δὲ αὐτῶν, εἶπεν Εὔα τῷ κυρίῳ αὐτῆς Ἀδάμ·	23:1 Et dixit Eva ad Adam:	23(2):1 եւ ասէ եսա գնրամ.	23(2):1 მას ჟამსა ჰრქუა ევა ადამს:	

Pericope 7 *Cain and Abel* 26E

GREEK	LATIN	ARMENIAN	GEORGIAN	SLAVONIC
1:1 This is the story of Adam and Eve. After they had gone out of Paradise,				2.1 But after he committed the trespass and violated the command of the Lord, Adam was expelled from Paradise,
1:2 Adam [took] Eve and went to the east and abode there eighteen years and two months.	22:1 Adam took Eve and the boy and led them to the east.	22(1):2 Thenceforth Adam took Eve and the child and brought them to the eastern region, and he was there with her, and then eighteen years and two months were completed.	22(1):2 As for Adam, he took Eve and the child and he brought them into the eastern parts and he stayed there. And when the eighth year and the second month were completed	2.2a and (Adam) having taken his wife and left, he sat near Eden, (ed. on the spot) before the door of Paradise,
	22:2 The Lord God sent various seeds by Michael the angel, who gave them to Adam and showed them how to work and tend the ground, in order to have fruit, from which they and all their generations might live.			
1:3 And Eve conceived and bore two sons; Diophotos, who is called Cain and Amilabes who is called Abel.	22:3 Afterwards, Eve conceived and bore a son, whose name was Abel, and Cain and Abel remained together as one.	22(1):3 She became pregnant and bore a son, [Gap'at' whom the midwife named and called Abel;] and they dwelt together.	22(1):3 Eve became pregnant and bore another son whom the power of God called by the name Abel, and they remained there together.	
2:1 And after this, Adam and Eve were with one another and while they were sleeping, Eve said to Adam her lord:	23:1 Eve said to Adam:	23(2):1 Eve said to Adam,	23(2):1 At that time Eve told Adam,	

Pericope 7 Cain and Abel

GREEK	LATIN	ARMENIAN	GEORGIAN	SLAVONIC
2:2 Κύριέ μου, ἴδον ἐγὼ κατ' ὄναρ τῇ νυκτὶ ταύτῃ τὸ αἷμα τοῦ υἱοῦ μου Ἀμιλαβὲς τοῦ ἐπιλεγομένου Ἄβελ βαλλόμενον εἰς τὸ στόμα Κάϊν τοῦ ἀδελφοῦ αὐτοῦ καὶ ἔπιεν αὐτὸ ἀνελεημόνως. Παρεκάλει δὲ αὐτὸν συγχωρῆσαι αὐτῷ ὀλίγον ἐξ αὐτοῦ.	23:2 domine mi, dormiens vidi visum quasi sanguinem filii nostri Abel in manu Cain ore suo deglutientis eum. propterea dolorem habeo.	23(2):2 Տէր իմ, Արամ. ննջեցի եւ տեսանէի ի տեսլեան գիշերոյ, զի արիւն որդոյ իմոյ Արելի մտանէր բերան կայենի որդոյ մերոյ եղբաւր նորա եւ ումբէր զարիւն նորա անողորմ, եւ աղաչէր զնա Արել զի թողցէ սակաւիկ մի	23(2):2 "ფალო ჩემო, აღამ, დომლა შობა ჩემსა ვიხილე, ვითარძე სისხლი ძისა ჩემისა აბელისი შთავიდოდა პირსა კაენისა, ძმისა მისისასა, და შესუმიდა უწყალოდ. და ევედრებოდა აბელი, რაითამცა სისხლისა მისგან უტევა".	2.2b и видѣ Адамъ сьнь, како хощеть родити Каина и Авела брата ѥго, и видѣ како хощеть оубити Каинъ Авела, и въскрьбѣ Адамъ вельми.
2:3 Αὐτὸς δὲ οὐκ ἤκουσεν αὐτοῦ, ἀλλ' ὅλον κατέπιεν αὐτό. Καὶ οὐκ ἔμεινεν ἐπὶ τὴν κοιλίαν αὐτοῦ, ἀλλ' ἐξῆλθεν ἔξω τοῦ στόματος αὐτοῦ.		23(2):3 եւ ոչ թողոյր եւ ոչ անսայր նմա, այլ ումբէր զարիւն նորա բաւանդակ.	23(2):3 და მან არა ისმინა მისი, არამედ შესუა ყოველივე. და არა დაადგრა მუცელსა მისსა, არამედ გამოხდა გარე, დაჰბზია ყუელათა ასოთა მისთა და არა განეშორა გუამსა მისსა ყოლადვე".	2.3 тьгда прииде архаггель Михаиль къ Адаму и рече ѥму · Адаме, не скръби, ни изрьци ни имаи Каина въ срьдци своѥмь.
2:4 Εἶπε δὲ Ἀδάμ· Ἀναστάντες πορευθῶμεν καὶ ἴδωμεν τί ἐστι τὸ γεγονὸς αὐτοῖς, μήποτε ὁ ἐχθρὸς πολεμῇ τι πρὸς αὐτούς.	23:3 Et dixit Adam: Vae, ne forte interficiat Cain Abel! sed separemus eos ab invicem et faciamus eis singulas mansiones.	23(2):4a Ասէ Արամ զնա. Արդրեար սպանանէ կայենն զԱրել. այլ մեկնեսցուք զնոսա ի միմեանց. արասցուք նոցա խրամանչիւր տեղի եւ թողցուք զնոսա անդ. եւ մի տացուք ի մեզ տեղի չարին.	23(2):4a მიუგო აღამ ევას და ჰრქუა: "ნუუკუე მცა მოკლავი ევულე-ბი ძისა კაენ, განვაშორნეთ ურთი-ერთას და ვიყვნეთ მათ თანა, რაითა არა ვსცეთ ადგილი ჩვენ ცხვასა".	3.1 И тоу прѣбысть Адамъ при Едемѣ .н. лѣть, и тоу роди Каина и Авела, брата ѥго.

Pericope 7 *Cain and Abel*

GREEK	LATIN	ARMENIAN	GEORGIAN	SLAVONIC
2:2 "My lord, Adam, behold, I have seen in a dream this night the blood of my son Amilabes who is styled Abel being poured into the mouth of Cain his brother and he went on drinking it without mercy. But he begged him to leave a little of it. 2:3 Yet he hearkened not to him, but gulped it down completely; nor did it stay in his stomach, but came out of his mouth.	23:2 "My lord, while asleep I saw a vision like the blood of our son Abel on the hand of Cain who tasted it with his mouth. On account of this I am pained."	23(2):2 "My lord, Adam, I fell asleep and I saw in a night vision that the blood of my son Abel was entering the mouth of our son Cain, his brother, and he drank his blood without mercy. Abel beseeched him to leave a little, 23(2):3 and he did not leave (any), and did not hearken to him, but drank his blood completely."	23(2):2 "My lord Adam, in my sleep I saw that the blood of my son Abel was pouring into the mouth of Cain his brother and he drank it without mercy. And Abel beseeched him to leave him (a little) of his blood, 23(2):3 and he did not agree to hearken to him but he drank it completely and (it) did not remain in his stomach but it went forth and all his limbs were smeared with it and it could not at all be removed from his body."	2.2b and he saw a vision, how Cain and his brother Abel would be begotten, and he saw, how Cain would kill Abel, and Adam was very troubled. 2.3 Then the archangel Michael came to Adam and said to him, "O Adam, Adam, don't be troubled, don't speak about this and don't have Cain on your heart."
2:4 And Adam said, "Let us arise and go and see what has happened to them, (I fear) lest the adversary may be assailing them somewhere."	23:3 Adam said: "Woe, let not Cain kill Abel, but let us separate them from each other and make separate houses for them."	23(2):4a Adam said to Eve, "Surely Cain is killing Abel. Come, let us separate them from one another. Let us make individual places for them and leave them there, and let us not provide room in us for the evil one."	23(2):4a Adam replied to Eve and told her, "Lest Cain plan to kill him, let us separate them from one another, and let us be with them, so as to provide no room for anger."	3.1 And here, near Eden, Adam spent eighteen years, and here Cain and his brother Abel were born to him.

Pericope 7 *Cain and Abel*

GREEK	LATIN	ARMENIAN	GEORGIAN	SLAVONIC
	23:4 Et fecerunt Cain agricolam, Abel fecerunt pastorem, ut ita fuissent ab invicem separati.	23(2):4b եւ արարին նորա ոստ բանին այնմիկ, եւ աւէ զնոսա Արամ. Որդեակք իմ, արիք զնացէք իւրաքանչիւր տեղդ ձեր. Ցաբեան եւ զնացին նորա ոստ բանին այնորիկ:	23(2):4b და უკუეს ევრე, ვითარცა თქუა ადამ და ჰრქუა: "შვილნო ჩემნო, მოვედით და მიმოვებეთ თითოეულად ადგილსა თვისსა.	3.2 и по врѣмєни възрастєнию (възраста ю?) посьласта ихь къ скотомь в Курино мѣсто. 3.3 и ѥгда сьврьшишє сє .д҃і. лѣть, призьва Адамь жєнѫ своѫ Ѥвьгѫ и речє ѥи 'сьврьшишє сє лѣть .д҃і. и сьтвориль ѥсть Каинь крьвь на братѣ своѥмь Авєлѣ, якожє ѥсть ѹрєчєно, нємилостивьно
				3.4 изидємь, да видимь.
3:1 Πορευθέντες δὲ ἀμφότεροι εὗρον πεφονευμένον τὸν "Αβελ ἀπὸ χειρὸς Κάϊν τοῦ ἀδελφοῦ αὐτοῦ.	23:5 Et post haec interfecit Cain Abel. erat autem tunc Adam annorum CXXX. interfectus est autem Abel cum esset annorum CXXII.			3.5 Изьшьдьшє и обрѣтошє Авєла ѹбиѥна нємилостивьно рѫкоѫ Каиновоѫ.
3:2a Καὶ λέγει ὁ θεὸς Μιχαὴλ τῷ ἀρχαγγέλῳ· Εἰπὲ τῷ Ἀδὰμ ὅτι τὸ μυστήριον ὃ οἶδας μὴ ἀναγγείλῃς Κάϊν τῷ υἱῷ σου, ὅτι ὀργῆς υἱός ἐστιν. '		23(3):2a եւ ասա լեռ այսց բանից աւէ Աստուած զՄիքայէլ հրեշտակապետն. Գնա եւ ասա Արամայ թէ զխորհուրդդ որ գիտես, մի պատմեսցես քագլ Կայենի, զի որդի բարկութե(ան) է դա եւ սպանանէ զշարբէլ զեղբայր իւր.	23(3):2a მაშინ ჰრქუა ღმერთმან გაბრიელ ანგელოზსა:" არქუ ადამს ზრახვა საიდუმლოთო, რომელი უწყი, ნუ აუწყებ კაენს, რამეთუ საშობი რისხვისაი არს, რამეთუ მოკლვად არს მისგან ძმაი მისი,	3.6 и речє господь архаггєлоу Михаилоу· рьци Адамоу, нє изрьци ничьто сыноу своѥмоу Каиноу о дѣлѣ томьи ничьто нє вьскрьби, ни (нь?) вьсьхрани вь срьдьци своѥмь.

Pericope 7 *Cain and Abel*

GREEK	LATIN	ARMENIAN	GEORGIAN	SLAVONIC
	23:4 They made Cain to be a farmer, and Abel to be a shepherd that they might thus be separated from each other.	23(2):4b They acted according to this proposal. Adam said to them, "My sons, arise, go each of you to your place." They arose and went according to this proposal.	23(2):4b And they acted as Adam had said, and he told them, "My sons, come and let us disperse, each to his own place."	3.2 And when they were grown, they sent them to tend the flocks at a place called Cyrene. 3.3 And when fourteen years had passed, Adam called his wife Eve and said to her, "Fourteen years have passed and Cain has spilled his brother Abel's blood, as it was announced, in a merciless way. 3.4 Let us go out to see."
3:1 And they both went and found Abel murdered by the hand of Cain his brother.	23:5 But even after this, Cain killed Abel. Adam was then 130 years old. Abel was killed when he was 122 years old.			3.5 And when they went out they found Abel murdered in a merciless manner by the hand of Cain.
3:2a And God said to Michael the archangel: "Say to Adam: 'Reveal not the mystery that you know to Cain your son, for he is a son of wrath.		23(3):2a Then, after these proposals God said to the archangel Michael, "Go say to Adam, 'Do not relate the mystery that you know to Cain, for he is a son of wrath and he is killing Abel, his brother.	23(3):2a Then God told the angel Gabriel, "'[[Tell Adam]] Do not reveal to Cain the secret plan which you know, for he is a son of wrath, because his brother will be killed by him!'	3.6 And the Lord spoke to the archangel Michael, "Warn Adam, 'You should not say anything to your son Cain about this matter, and do not be troubled on account of it, instead keep it in your hearts.'"

Pericope 7 *Cain and Abel*

GREEK	LATIN	ARMENIAN	GEORGIAN	SLAVONIC
3:2b Ἀλλὰ μὴ λυποῦ· Δώσω σοι γὰρ ἀντ' αὐτοῦ ἕτερον υἱόν. Οὗτος δηλώσει πάντα ὅσα ποιήσῃς· Σὺ δὲ μὴ εἴπῃς αὐτῷ μηδέν.		23(3):2b բայց մի տրտմեցիր վասն նորա. տաց քեզ փոխանակ [նորա] զմէթ որ նման է առաջի պատուերին իմոյ և նա ցուցցէ զամենայն ինչ զոր արասցես. և ոչ եթէ ինչ ասասցես նման	23(3):2b არამედ ნუ შეჭუვნებისა ადამ მისთვის, რამეთუ აღუდგინო მის წილ სეთი, და ემსგავ-სოს იგი ხატსა ჩემსა, და გასწაოს შენ ყოველი, რომელი მოიხსენო, ხოლო ამას ნუვის აუწყებ თვინიერ ადამისა".	
3:3 Ταῦτα εἶπεν ὁ θεὸς τῷ ἀρχ-αγγέλῳ αὐτοῦ. Ἀδὰμ δὲ ἐφύλαξε τὸ ῥῆμα ἐν τῇ καρδίᾳ αὐτοῦ, μετ' αὐτοῦ καὶ ἡ Εὔα, ἔχον-τες τὴν λύπην περὶ Ἄβελ τοῦ υἱοῦ αὐτῶν.		23(3):3 զայս ասաց Աստուած գրեշտակին, և նա եկեաց խաաեցաւ Արամայ. և Արամ պահեաց զայս ի [սրտի] իւրում և տրտմեալ ինքն և եաւ:	23(3):3a ესე ჰრქუა უმერთმან ანგელოზსა მას და ანგელოზმაც მან ჰრქუა ადამს სიტყუაი ესე, ხოლო ადამ დაიმარხა სიტყუაი იგი გულსა შინა. და ჭმუნდეს ორნივე - ადამ და ცოლი მისი.	

Pericope 7 *Cain and Abel*

GREEK	LATIN	ARMENIAN	GEORGIAN	SLAVONIC
3:2b But do not be sad, for I will give you another son instead of him ; he shall show (to you) all that you shall do. Do not tell him anything.'"		23(3):2b However, do not be sad because of him; instead of him I shall give you Seth, who is like my first image, and he shall show all memories through me, and not only what you shall say to him.'"	23(3):2b However, let Adam not be sad, for I will raise up Seth for him instead of Abel, and he will resemble my image and [[he]] will teach you everything of which I have a memory. But do not reveal this to anyone but Adam!"	
3:3 Thus God spoke to his archangel. But Adam kept the word in his heart, and with him also was Eve, though they were sad concerning Abel their son.		23(3):3 God said this to the angel, and he came and spoke to Adam and Adam kept it in his own [heart]; and he and Eve were sad.	23(3):3a That is what God told the angel, and the angel spoke this word to Adam. Then Adam kept the word in his heart. And they both were sad, Adam and his spouse.	

Pericope 7 *Cain and Abel*

GREEK	LATIN	ARMENIAN	GEORGIAN	SLAVONIC
			23(3):3b და იყო ჟამი იგი, რამეთუ მოიკლა აბელი კაენისაგან, ძმისა მისისა, და პრქუა:" დასდვა უმერთმან აღსასრული ყოველთა კაცთაი, არა თუ სხუაი რაიმე იყო სიკუდილი იგი, არამედ კლვაი იგი, რომელ მოიკლა აბელ კაენისგან და მისცა უფრმან კაენისამან სიკუდილად, რამეთუ ნა- თესავი გულარძნილი იყო. 23(3):3c და იყვნეს ჟამნი, რომელსა აღსრულ იყვნეს კაენ და აბელი ველსა შინა მათსა, მოვიდეს ორნი ეშმაკნი, მსგავსნი აბელისი და კაენისი ხოლო ეშმაკი იგი ეშმაკსა მას ესხოდა, განრისხნა მას ზედა და მოიღო მახვილი ქვისაგან, რომელი იყო ქარწბია, და უკუეთა ყელი და მოკლა იგი	

Pericope 7 *Cain and Abel*

GREEK	LATIN	ARMENIAN	GEORGIAN	SLAVONIC
			23(3):3b And the time arrived when Abel was killed by Cain his brother and he (i.e., Adam) told her, "God has established an end for all human beings. Was death anything else but the killing by which Abel has been killed by Cain and Cain's jealousy delivered him to death because (Cain) was of a perverse race?" 23(3):3c And the time arrived when Cain and Abel had gone up towards their fields. Two demons resembling Cain and Abel came. Now, one demon reproached the other demon. He became angry with him and took a stone sword, which was of a transparent stone. He cut his throat and killed him.	

Pericope 7 *Cain and Abel*

GREEK	LATIN	ARMENIAN	GEORGIAN	SLAVONIC
			23(3):3d და ვითარცა იხილა კაენმან სისხლი იგი, მივიდა სწრაფით და აღიღო ქვა იგი ხელითა თვისითა, ხოლო ვითარცა იხილა აბელმან მიმავა-ლი მის ზედა, ევედრებოდა მას: "ნუ მომაკუდინებ, ძმაო კაენ". ხოლო მან არა ინება ვედრებაი მისი და დასთხია სისხლი აბელისი წინაშე მისა. და ტუვოდეს ადამ და ევა რაოდენ ჟამ მწუხარებითა დიდითა.	
4:1 Μετὰ δὲ ταῦτα ἔγνω Ἀδὰμ τὴν γυναῖκα αὐτοῦ καὶ ἐν γαστρὶ ἔσχεν καὶ ἐγέννησεν τὸν Σήθ.	24:1 Et post haec cognovit Adam uxorem suam et genuit filium et vocavit nomen eius Seth.	24(4):1 *bi jhu աշորիկ լզացաւ իւս եւ ծնաւ զՍէթ.*	23(4):1 და შემდგომად ამის შემდგა ადამი ცოლისა. მიუდგა ევა და შვა სეთი, მსგავსი ადამისი.	4-5.1 По томь роди сына Євьга и нарече име кмоу Сидь.
4:2 Καὶ λέγει Ἀδὰμ τῇ Εὔᾳ· Ἰδοὺ ἐγεννήσαμεν υἱὸν ἀντὶ Ἄβελ ὃν ἀπέκτεινεν Κάϊν. Δώσωμεν δόξαν καὶ θυσίαν τῷ θεῷ.	24:2 Et dixit Adam ad Evam: ecce genui filium pro Abel, quem occidit Cain.	24(4):2 *bi ասէ Ադամ ցեւա ի խասեմն իւրհանց ատ մինչանս. Աճաւ ծնաւ[ք] որդի փոխանակ Արելի զոր սպան Կայէն առաջի մեր.*	24(4):2 და ჰრქუა ადამ ევას: "აჰა ესერა ვშევ ძე აბელის წილ, რომელი მოაკუდინა კაენმან წინაშე ჩემსა".	4-5.2 и рече Євьга кь Адамоу: "азь родихь сына мѣсто Авела, югоже оуби Каинь. нь прииди, госп одинѥ мои, да въздаси (възьдамы?) хвалоу богоу и жрьтвоу принесемь кмоу.
	24:3 Et postquam genuit Adam Seth, vixit annos DCCC et genuit filios XXX et filias XXX, simul LXIII. et multiplicati sunt super terram in nationibus suis.			

Pericope 7 *Cain and Abel* 31E

GREEK	LATIN	ARMENIAN	GEORGIAN	SLAVONIC
			23(3):3d And when Cain saw the blood, he went quickly and took the stone in his hand(s). But when Abel saw him coming upon him, he begged him, "Do not make me die, O my brother Cain!" He, however, did not accept his prayer and he spilled Abel's blood in front of him. And Adam and Eve afflicted themselves all that time with great sadness.	
4:1 And after this, Adam knew Eve his wife, and she conceived and bore Seth.	24:1 After this Adam knew his wife and begot a son and called his name Seth.	24(4):1 After this, Eve became pregnant and bore Seth.	24(4):1 And after this, Adam entered his spouse and Eve became pregnant and bore Seth who resembled Adam.	4-5.1 Afterwards, Eve bore a son and called him Seth.
4:2 And Adam said to Eve: "Behold! we have begotten a son in place of Abel, whom Cain killed,	24:2 Adam said to Eve: "Behold, I have begotten a son in place of Abel, whom Cain killed."	24(4):2 Adam said to Eve when they were speaking with each other, "Behold, we have begotten a son in place of Abel, whom Cain killed before us."	24(4):2 Adam told Eve, "Behold, I have born a son in place of Abel, whom Cain killed before me."	4-5.2 And she said to Adam, "I have borne a son in the place of Abel, whom Cain killed; come my husband,
let us give glory and sacrifice to God."				that you may thank God, and that we may make an offering to Him."
see pericope 9	24:3 After Adam begot Seth, he lived for 800 years and begot 30 sons and 30 daughters -- 63 altogether -- and they were multiplied over the earth in its nations.	*see pericope 9*	*see pericope 9*	*see pericope 9*

25:1 Et dixit Adam ad Seth: audi, fili mi Seth, ut referam tibi, quae audivi et vidi. postquam eiecti sumus de paradiso ego et mater tua, 25:2 cum essemus in oratione, venit ad me Michahel archangelus nuntius dei. 25:3 Et vidi currum tamquam ventum et rotae illius erant igneae et raptus sum in paradisum iustitiae. et vidi dominum sedentem et aspectus eius erat ignis incendens intolerabilis. et multa milia angelorum erant a dextris et a sinistris currus illius. 26:1 Haec videns perturbatus sum et timor comprehendit me et adoravi coram deo super faciem terrae. 26:2 Et dixit mihi deus: ecce tu morieris, quia praeteristi mandatum dei, quia plus audisti vocem uxoris tuae quam tibi dedi in potestatem, ut haberes eam in voluntatem tuam. et audisti illam et verba mea praeteristi. 27:1 Et cum haec audivi verba dei, procidens in terram adoravi dominum et dixi: domine mi, omnipotens deus et misericors sancte et pie, ne deleatur nomen memoriae tuae maiestatis. sed converte animam meam, quia morior et spiritus meus exibit de ore meo. 27:2 Ne proicias me a facie tua quem de limo terrae plasmasti, nec postponas gratiae tuae quem nutristi. 27:3 Et ecce verbum tuum incedit mihi et dixit dominus ad me: quoniam figurantur dies tui factus es diligens scientiam, propter hoc non tolletur de semine tuo usque in seculum ad ministrandum mihi. 28:1 Et cum haec verba audivi, prostravi me in terram et adoravi dominum deum dicens: tu es aeternus deus et summus et omnes creaturae tibi dant honorem et laudem. 28:2 Tu es super omne lumen fulgens vera lux, vita vivens, incomprehensibilis magnitudinis virtus. tibi dant honorem et laudem spiritales virtutes. tu facis cum genere humano magnalia misericordiae tuae. 28:3 Postquam adoravi dominum, statim Michahel archangelus dei adprehendit manum meam et eiecit me de paradiso visitationis et iussionis dei. 28:4 Et tenens Michahel in manu sua virgam tetigit aquas quae erant circa paradisum et gelaverunt. 29:1 Et pertransivi et Michahel pertransivit mecum et reduxit me in locum, unde me rapuit. 29:2 Audi, fili mi Seth, et caetera mysteria sacramentaque futura quae mihi sunt revelata, qui per lignum scientiae comedens cognovi et intellexi, quae erunt in hoc seculo. [29.3 II,III,IV+temporali [III+futura]III quae facturus est Deus creaturae suae humano generi. 29:4 Apparebit Dominus in flamma ignis. ex ore maiestatis suae dabit omnibus mandata et praecepta (ex ore eius exiet gladius ex utraque parte acutus?) et sanctificabunt eum in domo habitationis maiestatis illius. et ostendet illis locum mirabilem maiestatis suae. 29:5 Et tunc aedificabunt domum domino deo suo in terra, qua pavit illos (quam praeparabit eis?), et ibi praeteribunt praecepta eius et accendetur sanctuarium eorum et terra eorum deseretur et ipsi dispergentur propter quod exacerbaverunt Deum. 29:6 Et iterum (die tertio?, septimo?) saluos faciet illos a dispersione illorum, et iterum aedificabunt domum Dei et exaltabitur novissime domus Dei maior quam prius. 29:7 Et iterum superabit iniquitas aequitatem. et post haec habitabit Deus cum hominibus in terris videndus. et tunc incipiet aequitas fulgere. et domus Dei in saeculum honorabitur et non poterunt adversa amplius nocere hominibus, qui sunt in Deo credentes. et suscitabit sibi Deus plebem fidelem, quam salvabit in secula seculorum. et impii punientur a deo rege suo qui noluerint amare legem illius. 29:8 Celum et terra noctes et dies et omnes creaturae obedient ei et non praeteribunt mandatum eius nec mutabunt opera sua. homines autem mutabuntur derelinquentes legem Domini. 29:9 Propter hoc repellet Dominus a se impios et iusti fulgebunt sicut sol in conspectu Dei. et in tempore illo purificabuntur homines per aquam a peccatis. 29:10 Condempnati autem erunt nolentes purificari per aquam. et felix erit homo, qui correxerit animam suam, quando erunt iudicia et magnalia dei inter homines et inquirentur facta eorum a Deo iusto iudice.]II,III,IV

Pericope 8 *Adam's Vision* 32E

25:1 Adam said to Seth: "Hear, my son Seth, let me recount for you what I have heard and seen. After I and your mother were cast out of the Garden, 25:2 when we were at prayer, the archangel Michael, the messenger of God, came to me. 25:3 I saw a chariot like the wind, and its wheels were afire, and I was caught up into the the Garden of the just. I saw the Lord seated, his face like fire burning intolerably. Many thousands of angels were at the right and the left of his chariot. 26:1 Seeing this, I was disturbed and fear seized me and I worshipped before God above the face of the earth. 26:2 Then God said to me: 'Behold, you shall die because you transgressed the commandment of God, because you harkened more to the voice of your wife whom I gave over to your control that you might have her in your will. You listened to her and transgressed my words.' 27:1 When I heard these words of God, falling down on the ground I worshipped the Lord and said: 'My Lord, Almighty and merciful God, holy and faithful, do not let the name of the memory of your majesty be destroyed, but turn my soul around, for I will die and my spirit will go forth from my mouth. 27:2 Do not cast me out from your sight, whom you formed from the dust of the earth, nor put me out from your grace whom you nourished. 27:3 Behold, your word has come over me.' Then the Lord said to me: 'Since your days are numbered, you have become attentive to knowledge. On account of this no one shall ever be taken from your offspring to minister unto me.' 28:1 When I heard these words, I prostrated myself on the ground and worshipped the Lord God saying: 'You are the eternal and most high God. All creatures give you honor and praise. 28:2 You are above all, the shining light, the true light, the living life, the Virtue of incomprehensible greatness. To you the spiritual virtues give honor and praise. With the human race you show the great deeds of your mercy.' 28:3 After I worshipped the Lord God, straightway Michael, the archangel of God, took my hand and threw me out of the the Garden of God's visitation and commanding. 28:4 Michael, holding in his hand a rod, touched the waters which surrounded the Garden and they froze. 29:1 Then I crossed over, and Michael crossed over with me and brought me again to the place from which he had taken me. 29:2 Hear also, my son Seth, the other mysteries and promised things to come which have been revealed to me. By eating of the tree of knowledge I have known and understood the things which are in this age, [29:3 II,III,IV+ temporary [III+future]III which God will do to his creation, the human race. 29:4 The Lord will appear in a flame of fire. From the mouth of his majesty he will give commandment and precepts to all (from his mouth will go forth a sword, sharp on both edges?) and they will sanctify him in the house of the dwelling of his majesty. He will show to them the marvelous place of his majesty. 29:5 Then they will build a house for the Lord their God in the land which he will prepare for them, and there they will transgress his precepts. Their sanctuary will be set afire, and their land shall be desolate, and they themselves will be dispersed because they provoked God. 29:6 But again, (on the third / seventh day ?) he will save them from their dispersion and they will build once more the house of God, and it will then be higher than it was before. 29:7 But once again, iniquity will conquer justice. After this, God will dwell, living with men on the earth. Then justice will begin to shine, and the house of the Lord will be honored forever. The opponents will no more be able to kill men who are believers in God. God will then receive unto himself a faithful people, whom he will save forever and ever. But the impious who did not wish to love his law will be punished by God their King. 29:8 Heaven and earth, night and day, and all creatures will obey him and will not transgress his commandment, nor will they alter his works. Men who forsake the law of the Lord, however, will be changed. 29:9 On account of this, the Lord will cast away from himself the impious, but the just will shine like the sun in the sight of God. At that time, men will be purified by water of their sins. 29:10 Those unwilling to be purified by water, however, will be condemned. Blessed will be the man who shall amend his soul when the judgments and great deeds of God will be among men. Their deeds will be investigated by God, the just judge."]II,III,IV

Pericope 9 *Illness of Adam*

GREEK	LATIN	ARMENIAN	GEORGIAN	SLAVONIC
5.1 Ἐποίησεν δὲ Ἀδὰμ υἱοὺς τριάκοντα καὶ θυγατέρας τριάκοντα. Ἔζησεν δὲ Ἀδὰμ ἔτη ἐνακόσια τριάκοντα.	30:1 Postquam factus est Adam annos DCCCCXXX,	30(5):1 եւ ապա յետ այնորիկ եղեն նորա ուստերք եւ դստերք երեսուն երեսուն, եւ անցին նորա: եւ էր Ադամ ի վերայ երկրի իսկ համբարր եւ երեսուն ամ,	30(5):1 და ამისსა შემდგომად მერმეცა ესხნეს ადამს ოცდაათ ძე და ოცდაათ ასული, რამეთუ ცხრა ათასნი წელნი ადამისნი ცხრაას ოცდაათ წელ. და მისგან განბნრავლდეს ქუეყანასა ზედა და დაემკნდეს მას ზედა. და ოდეს ადესრულა ცხრაას ოცდაათ ოცი წელი,	4-5.3 И роди Адамь сыновь .л. и дьщерии .л. и жить Адамь .д. сьть лѣть и .л.
5:2 Καὶ περιπεσὼν εἰς νόσον ἐβόησεν φωνῇ μεγάλῃ λέγων· Ἐλθέτωσαν πρὸς με οἱ υἱοί μου πάντες, ὅπως ὄψομαι αὐτοὺς πρὶν ἀποθανεῖν με.	30:2 sciens quoniam dies eius finiuntur dixit [II,III+ad Evam]II,III: congregentur ad me omnes filii mei, ut benedicam eos, antequam moriar, et loquar cum eis.	30(5):2 եւ ապա հիւանդացաւ Ադամ գահն մահու, եւ աղաղակեաց ի ձայն մեծ եւ ասէ. եկեցեն եւ ժողովեսցին առ իս ամենայն որդիք իմ, զի տեսից զնոսա յառաջ մինչ չեւ մեռայ իցեմ:	30(5):2 დასნეულდა ადამ, დადაად-ყო ხმითა დიდითა და თქუა: "შემეკრბით ჩემდა ყოველნი ნაშობნი ჩემნი და ვიხილნე ივნი ვიდრე სიკუდილადმდე ჩემდა".	4-5.4 и впаде вь болѣсть и възьпи гласомь велиемь и рече · сьберѣте се, чеда моя, кь мнѣ . 4-5.5 и убоя се Адамь вельми, понеже не знаше что ѥсть болѣсть.

Pericope 9 *Illness of Adam* 33E

GREEK	LATIN	ARMENIAN	GEORGIAN	SLAVONIC
5.1 And Adam begat 30 sons and 30 daughters and Adam lived 930 years;	30:1 After Adam reached the age of 930 years,	30(5):1 Then, after that, he had sons and daughters, 30 of each kind, and they grew up. Adam was upon the earth 930 years,	30(5):1 And again, after that, Adam had 30 sons and 30 daughters. For all the years of Adam were 930 years. And (those who were descended) from him multiplied over the earth and settled it. And when the 930 years were completed,	4-5.3 And Adam fathered thirty sons and thirty daughters, and he lived 930 years.
5:2 and he fell sick and cried with a loud voice and said, "Let all my sons come to me that I may see them before I die."	30:2 knowing that his days were ended, he said [II, III+to Eve]II,III: "Gather about me all my children that I might bless them before I die, and that I might speak with them."	30(5):2 and then Adam fell sick with a mortal affliction, and he cried out in a loud voice and said, "Let all my sons come and gather by me, so that I may see them first, before I die."	30(5):2 Adam fell ill and cried out in a loud voice and said, "Gather to me all my descendants and I will see them before my death."	4-5.4 And he fell ill and cried out in a loud voice and said, "My children, gather around me." 4-5.5 Adam, of course, was very anxious, since he didn't know what illness was.

Pericope 9 *Illness of Adam*

GREEK	LATIN	ARMENIAN	GEORGIAN	SLAVONIC
5:3 Καὶ συνήχθησαν πάντες· ἦν γὰρ οἰκισθεῖσα ἡ γῆ εἰς τρία μέρη. [καὶ ἦλθον πάντες ἐπὶ τὴν θύραν τοῦ οἴκου ἐν ᾧ εἰσήρχετο εὔξασθαι τῷ θεῷ.]	30:3 Et congregati sunt in tres partes ante conspectum eius coram oratorio, ubi adorabant dominum deum. [III+erat autem numerus XV milia virorum exceptis mulieribus et parvulis]III	30(5):3 եւ ժողովեցան առ նա ամենայն որդիք իւր որ էին ամենայն կողմ երկրին [եւ ժողովեցան առ նա ի դուռն տեղոյ որ մտանէր նա յաղաւթս կալ առ Տէր Աստուած:	30(5):3 და შემოკრბეს მისსა ყუველნი ნათესავნი მისნი, რომელნი დამკვიდრებულ იყვნეს, და დადგჳრა სამი ბანოფლო ჳელკანბისაო ნაშობთა მისთა. და შემოკრბეს ადამისა ყუველნი ნაშობნი მისნი, რამეთუ დამკჳდრებულ იყვნეს წინაშე კართა მისთა, ადგილსა მას, რომელი ქმნა ადამ, რომელსა შევიდოდა და ილოცვიდა ღმრთისა მიმართ.	4-5.6 и сьбраше се чеда юго и сташе на три страны.
5:4 Εἶπε δὲ αὐτῷ Σὴθ ὁ υἱὸς αὐτοῦ· Πάτερ Ἀδάμ, τί σοί ἐστι νόσος	30:4 Et interrogaverunt eum: [II, III+et cum congregasti essent omnes una voce dixerunt] II,III quid tibi est, pater, ut congregares nos? et quare iaces in lecto tuo?		30(5):4 და ჰრქუეს მეოთა მისთა:"რაი არს ესე, მამაო ადამ?"	6-7.1a И рече сынь юго Сидь · отьче, отьче Адаме, чьто юсть немощь твоя;
5:5 Καὶ λέγει· Τεκνία μου, πόνος πολύς συνέχει με. Καὶ λέγουσιν αὐτῷ· Τί ἐστι πόνος, τί ἐστι νόσος	30:5 Et respondens Adam dixit: filii mei, male mihi est doloribus. et dixerunt ad eum omnes filii eius: quid est pater male habere doloribus?		30(5):5 და მან ჰრქუა:"სნეულ ვარ, შვილნო ჩემნო". და ჰრქუეს მას:"რაი არს სნეული შენი, ანუ ვითარ დასნეულდი?"	6-7.1b и рече Адамь · ω чедо мою, болесть велика юсть вь мнѣ.
6:1 Καὶ ἀποκριθεὶς Σὴθ λέγει αὐτῷ· Μὴ ἐμνήσθης, πάτερ, τοῦ παραδείσου ἐξ ὧν ἤσθιες καὶ ἐλυπήθης [ἐπιθύμησας αὐτῶν.]	31:1 Tunc filius eius Seth dixit: domine forte desiderasti de fructu paradisi, ex quo edebas, et ideo iaces contristatus?	31(6):1 եւ ասէ որդի իւր Սէթ ցնա. Հայր իմ, միթէ դու ցանկայր դրախտին պտղովք կերակրէիր ի նմանէ եւ ի ցանկութենէ անտի տրտմեցար.	31(6):1 მიუგო სეთ, ძემან მისმან და ჰრქუა:"მამა ადამ, რაი არს შენ-და, ანუმცა მოგებენა ნაყოფი იგი სამოთხისა და გულმან გითქუა და სტკუე მისთჳს?"	6-7.2 И рѣше юмоу чеда юго · отьче, юда поминаюши блага раиская и того ради болиши тако;

Pericope 9 *Illness of Adam* 34E

GREEK	LATIN	ARMENIAN	GEORGIAN	SLAVONIC
5:3 And all assembled, for the earth was divided into three parts. [And they all came to the door of the house in which Adam would enter to pray to God]	30:3 They were gathered before his sight in three parts, in front of the oratory where he worshipped the Lord God. [III+They numbered 15,000 men, not counting women and children.]III	30(5):3 All his sons who were in every part of the world gathered by him. [They assembled by him inside the place which Eve had entered,] and he prayed to the Lord God.	30(5):3 And all his progeny gathered to him who had settled, and he divided the three parts of the earth among his descendants. And all Adam's descendants assembled by him, for they had taken a position before his doors, in the place which Adam had made, and into which he would enter and address his prayers to God.	4-5.6 And his children gathered around and stood on three sides.
5:4 And Seth his son said to him: "Father Adam, what is you pain?"	30:4 They asked him [II,III+and when they all had been gathered, they said with one voice]II,III: "What is wrong with you, father, that you have gathered us together? Why are you lying on your bed?"		30(5):4 And his sons told him, "What is this, Father Adam?"	6-7.1a And his son Seth said, "Father, Father Adam, what is your sickness?"
5:5 And he said, "My children, I am crushed by the burden of pain." "And they say to him, "What is pain, what is illness?"	30:5 Answering, Adam said: "My children, I am in great pain." All his children said to him: "What does (it) mean, father, to have great pain?"		30(5):5 [He told them, "I am sick, my sons." And they told him, "What is your illness] and how does a human being fall ill?"	6-7.1b Adam said, "My child, a great pain is in me."
6:1 And Seth answered and said to him: "Did you remember, father, the fruit of paradise of which you used to eat, and have you become sad [in yearning for it]?"	31:1 Then his son, Seth, said: "Lord, do you perhaps long for some of the fruit of paradise, which you used to eat, and therefore you lie there saddened?	31(6):1 His son Seth said to Adam, "My father, did you remember the fruit of the Garden, of which you used to eat, and have you become sad from that longing?	31(6):1 Seth, his son, replied to him and told him, "Father Adam, what is with you? Have (you) remembered, perchance, the fruit of the Garden, and you longed for it and have you become sad because of it?	6-7.2 And his children said to him, "Father, perhaps you are brooding about the delights of Paradise and for this reason it hurts you so."

Pericope 9 *Illness of Adam*

GREEK	LATIN	ARMENIAN	GEORGIAN	SLAVONIC
6:2 Ἐὰν οὕτως ἐστίν, ἀνάγγειλόν μοι καὶ ἐγὼ πορεύσομαι καὶ ἐνέγκω σοι καρπὸν ἀπὸ τοῦ παραδείσου. Ἐπιθήσω γὰρ κόπρον ἐπὶ τὴν κεφαλήν μου καὶ κλαύσομαι καὶ προσεύξομαι· καὶ εἰσακούσεταί μου κύριος καὶ ἀποστελεῖ τὸν ἄγγελον αὐτοῦ καὶ ἐνέγκω σοι ἵνα καταπαύσῃ ὁ πόνος ἀπὸ σοῦ.	31:2 Dic mihi et vadam ad proximas ianuas paradisi et mittam pulverem in caput meum et proiciam me in terram ante portas paradisi et plangam in lamentatione magna deprecans dominum. forsitan audiet me et mittet angelum suum ut adferat mihi de fructu quod desiderasti.	31[6]:2 Ասէ [այդպէս] իցէ ասա ինձ, զի գնացից մերձ ի դրախտն եւ արկից հող զգլխով իմով եւ լացից, զի թերեւս լուիցէ ինձ Աստուած ի սրտիղ անտի, զի բերցէ ինձ եւ քարասէ ի բէն ցաւոյ։	31(6):2 უკუეთუ ეგრეთ არს, მითხარ მე და მივიდე წინაშე სამოთხესა მას და გარეკვისხა მტუერი თავსა ჩემსა და ვტიროდე. და ისმინენ ჩემი ხოლო თუ ღმერთმან, და მოავლინოს ანგელოზი მისი და მომართუას მე ნა-ყოფი სამოთხისა, და მოჰკუეთოს შენ, რათა დასცხრე ტკივილისაგან შენისა".	6-7.3 и рече Сифь · отьче, азь идѫ сь материю своєю и принєсѫ оть рая, ѥда како ѹтолить ти сє. 6-7.4 Адамь рече · ω чедо, како да вьнидеши ты вь раи; 6-7.5 Сифь рече · отьче, изидѫ на пространо мѣсто противѫ раю и вьспла́чѫ сє изь срьдьца, ѥда како ѹслышить ны господь и припѹстить изь рая аггела и ѹтолить болѣсть твою.
6:3 Λέγει αὐτῷ ὁ Ἀδάμ· Οὐχί, υἱέ μου Σήθ, ἀλλὰ νόσον καὶ πόνους ἔχω.	31:3 Respondit Adam et dixit: non, fili mi, non desidero, sed infirmitatem et dolorem magnum habeo in corpore meo.	31(6):3 Ասէ ցնա Արամ. Ոչ է այդպէս [որդեակ իմ Սէթ] այլ հիւանդութիւն եւ ցաւ մարմնոյ իմոյ։	31(6):3 და ჰრქუა ადამ:" შვილო სეთ, არა ვჰნე არს, არამედ სნეულ ვარ და მელოს".	6-7.6 и рече Адамь · не тако, сынѹ мои, не тако, нь болѣсть чрѣвьнѫю имамь.
6:4 Λέγει αὐτῷ Σήθ· Καὶ πῶς σοι ἐγένοντο;	31:4 Respondit Seth: quid est dolor, domine pater, nescio; sed noli nobis abscondere, sed dic nobis [quia penitus ignoramus]III.	31(6):4 Ասէ ցնա Սէթ. Զո՞րպէս եղեւ քեզ այդ ցաւդ։	31(6):4 მიუგო სეთ:" მამაო, რაი არს სალმობაი, ანუ ვითარ გელმის?"	8-10.1 И рече Сифь · како ти ѥсть болѣсть, како ли ти прииде;

Pericope 9 *Illness of Adam* 35E

GREEK	LATIN	ARMENIAN	GEORGIAN	SLAVONIC
6:2 "If this be so, tell me, (and) I will go and bring you fruit from paradise. For I will set dung upon my head and will weep and pray that the Lord will hearken to me and send his angel (and bring me a plant from paradise), and I will bring it you that your pain may cease from you."	31:2 Tell me and I will go up to the entrance of paradise and cast dust on my head and throw myself on the ground before the gates of paradise, mourning in great lamentation, beseeching the Lord. Perhaps he will hear me and send his angel to bring me some of the fruit you desire."	31(6):2 If indeed [this] is the [case], tell me, so that I may go close to the Garden and cast dust upon my head and weep. For, perhaps God will give me of the fruit, that I might bring (it) to you, and this pain may be driven away from you."	31(6):2 If it is thus, tell me and I will go before the Garden and I will weep. And, if only God hears me, he will send his angel and he (the angel) will bring me the fruit of the Garden and I will bring it to you so that you may calm your distress."	6-7.3 And Seth said, "Father, I will go with my mother and bring something out of Paradise, by which perhaps your pain will be eased." 6-7.4 Adam, however, said, "My child, how will you be admitted into Paradise?" 6-7.5 Seth said, "Father, I will go to the great plaza before Paradise and cry out from my heart, perhaps the Lord will hear us and permit the angel (from Paradise) to come and your pain will be stilled."
6:3 Adam said to him: "Nay, my son Seth, but I have (much) sickness and pain! "Seth said to him: "And how has this come upon you?"	31:3 Adam answered and said: "No, my son, I do not desire it, even though I am suffering infirmity and great pain in my body."	31(6):3 Adam said to him, "It is not so, [my son, Seth]; rather do I have mortal sickness and pain."	31(6):3 And Adam told him, "My son Seth, it is not so, rather I am sick and I have pain."	6-7.6 And Adam said, "Not so, my son, not so, I have pain in my belly."
6:4 Seth said to him: "And how has this come upon you?"	31:4 Seth answered: "What is pain, my lord, father, for I do not know. Do not hide it from us, but tell us [III+ for inwardly we do not know.]III."	31(6):4 Seth said to him, "Through whom did this pain come to you?"	31(6):4 Seth replied to him, "Father, what is pain and how do you have pain?"	8–10.1 And Seth said, "In what way are you ill, how did it come over you?"

Pericope 10 *Adam's Story of the Fall*

GREEK	LATIN	ARMENIAN	GEORGIAN	SLAVONIC
7:1 Εἶπε δὲ αὐτῷ ὁ Ἀδάμ· "Ὅτε ἐποίησεν ἡμᾶς ὁ θεὸς ἐμέ τε καὶ τὴν μητέρα ὑμῶν, δι' ἧς καὶ ἀποθνῄσκω, ἔδωκεν ἡμῖν πᾶν φυτὸν ἐν τῷ παραδείσῳ, περὶ ἑνὸς δὲ ἐνετείλατο ἡμῖν μὴ ἐσθίειν ἐξ αὐτοῦ, δι' οὗ καὶ ἀποθνῄσκομεν.	32:1 Et respondit Adam et dixit: audite me, filii mei. quando fecit nos deus, me et matrem vestram, et posuit nos in paradisum et dedit nobis omnem arborem fructiferam ad edendum et interdixit nobis: de arbore scientiae boni et mali, quae est in medio paradisi, ne comedatis ex ea.	32(7):1 Ասէ ցնա Ադամ. Իբրեւ արար զմեզ Աստուած, զիս եւ զմայր քո, հրամայեաց մեզ ի ծառոյ ամենի ճաշակել.	32(7):1 ჰრქუა ადამ სეთის: "ოდეს შემქმნა მე და დედა შენი, და დამადგინა ჩუენ სამოთხესა მას ფუფუნებისასა ჭამად ბაყლოსა მისსა, ხოლო ერთი ხისგან უმშჭრის სამოთხესა, რომლისა გუ-ამცნო ღმერთმან ჩუენ, ვითარმედ ნუ სჭამთ.	8-10.2 и рече Адамь · егда сьтвори богь мене и матерь твою, и оть неѥ умираѥмь и вы вьси мрьтви будете, даде намь богь садъ раискыи, нь Ѥвьгы ради погубихомь
7:2 Ἤγγισε δὲ ἡ ὥρα τῶν ἀγγέλων τῶν διατηρούντων τὴν μητέρα ὑμῶν τοῦ ἀναβῆναι καὶ προσκυνῆσαι τὸν κύριον. Καὶ ἔδωκεν αὐτῇ ὁ ἐχθρὸς καὶ ἔφαγεν ἀπὸ τοῦ ξύλου, ἐγνωκὼς ὅτι οὐκ ἤμην ἔγγιστα αὐτῆς οὔτε οἱ ἅγιοι ἄγγελοι.		32(7):2 խաշիւաց զմեզ Սատանայ ի ժամուն իբրեւ վերացան հրշտակք[ն որ] պահապանք էին ծառոյն երկիրպագանել Աստուծոյ. յայնժամ կեր տուեալ Սատանայի ի քոյոյ մաւրն եկայք.	32(7):2 და აჰყუნეს დედასა თქუენსა გუელმან და აჴამ მას, რომლი- სათჳს აქ მოვკუდებით. ჟამ ოდეს იყო ვცუელთა მათ ანგელოზთა აღსლვა- ვისა თაყუანის- ცემად ღმერთისა, აჴყუნეს ოდე მტერმან და აჴამა მისგან	8-10.3 и . тогда приближи се часъ .s., виде Ѥвга диявола и поклони се, понеже сьтвори се аггельскымь образомь . и даде Ѥвзѣ оть древа, и преступи запо- вѣди госп- одьню, и сьнѣсть ѩже даде змия.
7:3 Ἔπειτα ἔδωκε κἀμοὶ φαγεῖν.		32(7):3a եւ ետ նաեւ ինձ՝ իբրեւ ոչ գիտէր.	32(7):3a და მან მაცყუნეს მე, შვილნო ჩემნო, რამეთუ არა უწყოდე.	
	32:2 Deus autem partem dedit paradisi mihi et matri vestrae: arborem orientalis partis et boreae quae est (et erubie que est?, et bone que est?, boree quod est?) contra aquilonem dedit mihi, et matri vestrae dedit partem austri et partem occidentalem.	32(7):3b Քանզի, որդեակ իմ Սէթ, բաժանեաց Աստուած զդրախտն ինձ եւ մաւր քո եւայի. որպէս զի արեւելուր մեր քոա, ինձ եւ զկողմ արեւելից եւ զ(հասրոֆ), եւ մաւր քո զկողմ արեւմտից եւ զ(հարաւոյ)):	32(7):3b და განვყოფ ჰყო ღმერთმან სამოთხე, მე და დედასა შენსა, ევას, რაოთაცა დავიცვათ იგი, ხოლო მე მომცა აღმოსავალთ კერძო და ჩრდილოთ, დედასა თქუენსა, ევას, მისცა სამხრით კერძო და დასავალთ.	

Pericope 10 *Adam's Story of the Fall*   36E

GREEK	LATIN	ARMENIAN	GEORGIAN	SLAVONIC
7:1 And Adam said to him: "When God made us, me and your mother, through whom also I die, he gave us power to eat of every tree which is in the Garden, but, concerning that one only, He charged us not to eat of it, and through this one we are to die.	32:1 Adam answered and said: "Hear me, my children. When God made us, me and your mother, and placed us in paradise and gave us all fruit-bearing trees for food, he forbade us, saying: 'Of the tree of the knowledge of good and evil, which is in the midst of paradise, you may not eat.'	32(7):1 Adam said to him, "When God made us, me and your mother, he gave us a command not to eat of that tree.	32(7):1 Adam told Seth, "Son, when God made us, your mother and me, he set us in the the Garden of delights [to eat its fruit.] But there was one plant in the middle of the Garden, (very) beautiful, concerning which God ordered us, 'Eat not of it.'	8-10.2 And Adam said, "When God created me and your mother, through whom we die and through whom you will all be mortal, he gave us the Garden in Paradise, which we lost on account of Eve.
7:2 And the hour drew near for the angels who were guarding your mother to go up and worship the Lord, And the enemy gave it to her and she ate from the tree. You know that I was not near her nor the holy angels.		32(7):2 Satan deceived us at the hour when [the] angels [who] were guardians of the tree ascended to worship God. Then, Satan caused Eve to eat that fruit;	32(7):2 And the serpent deceived your mother and caused her to eat of it, because of which, now, we are going to die. When it was the hour for the guardian angels [to ascend] to worship God, the enemy deceived her and she ate of it	8-10.3 At that time, when it was the sixth hour, Eve saw Satan and venerated him, because he came in the form of an angel, and he gave to Eve from the tree and she transgressed the commands of the Lord and ate of what the serpent had handed her."
7:3 Then she gave also to me to eat.		32(7):3a Eve gave [it] to me to eat when I did not know.	32(7):3a and she deceived me, my children, for I did not know.	
	32:2 God, however, gave part of the Garden to me, and part to your mother: to me he gave the tree of the eastern and northern part which is against the north, and to your mother he gave the southern and western part.	32(7):3b For, my son Seth, God divided the Garden between me and your mother Eve, that we might watch it. To me he gave the eastern portion and the [northern], and to your mother, the western and the [southern].	32(7):3b And God had divided the [Garden] between us---myself and your mother Eve-- so that we might guard it. As for me, he had given me the eastern and northern portion; to your mother Eve he had entrusted the southern and the western portion.	

Pericope 10 *Adam's Story of the Fall*

GREEK	LATIN	ARMENIAN	GEORGIAN	SLAVONIC
	33:1 Dedit nobis dominus deus angelos duos ad custodiendos nos.	33:1 *bi nikžup uhp hrkпunwuwň Հրեշտակք որ պահպանէին մեզ պարապանութեան զդրախտին մինչև ի ժամանակ լուսոյն.*	33:1 და უყვნეს ჩუენ თანა თითოეულად: ო˜ბ˜: ანგელოზნი ცვად ჩუენდა ვიდრე განთენებისა ჟამადმდე.	
	33:2 Venit hora ut ascenderunt angeli in conspectu dei adorare. statim invenit locum adversarius diabolus dum absentes essent angeli. et seduxit diabolus matrem vestram, ut manducaret de arbore inlicita et contradicta.	33:2 *բանզի Հասանզաց ար երկնեին [երկիր պագանեն Տեառն], ի ժամանակին իբրև նորա գնազին յերկինս յայնժամ խաբեազ Սատանայ զմայր ձեր, և նա пинե նմա ի մրդոյ անոր. գինաց Սատանայ եթէ ես ոչ էի и ոչ Հրեշտակք, յայնժամ նա пинե*	33:2 ხოლო ყოველსა დღესა აღხდიან ზედა. აღსლვასა დღე მასა აჰ-თუნა დედაი შენი გუელმან, და ხოლა მისგანი აკამა-ლა. და ოდეს არცა მე ვრთე, არცა ანგელოზნი.	8-10.4 И рєчє Сидь ・ кьто наоучи змию; 8-10.5 рєчє Адамь сыноу своюмоу・ сьтвори сє диꙗволь свѣтьль и аггєльскымь образомь приидє кь змии и рєчє юи ・ ты юси моудра много, ты даи оть дрѣва Квьзѣ да сьнѣсть и дасть Адамоу. 8-10.6 и тако сьтвори , и того ради болѣсти и сьмрьти прѣдахомь сє.
	33:3 et manducavit et dedit mihi.	33:3 *[խնոյ և նա իՆձ]*:	33:3 მეცა მაჟამა და არა გულისხმა-ვყავ.	
8:1 Καὶ ὠργίσθη ἡμῖν ὁ θεός· καὶ ἐλθὼν ἐν τῷ παραδείσῳ ὁ δεσπότης [ἔθηκε τὸν θρόνον αὐτοῦ καὶ] ἐκάλεσε φωνῇ φοβερᾷ λέγων· Ἀδάμ, ποῦ εἶ; καὶ ἵνα τί κρύβεσαι ἀπὸ προσώπου μου; Μὴ δυνήσηται κρυβῆναι οἰκία τῷ οἰκοδομήσαντι αὐτήν;	34:1 Et statim iratus est nobis dominus deus et dixit ad me dominus.	34(8):1 *Գիուցի այնուՀետև իբրև կերայ ի մրդոյ անոր եթէ բարկազաւ Սատանած ի վերայ մեր:*	34(8):1 ოდეს გჟამეთ, განრისხდა ღმერთი ჩუენდა	8-10.7 Тьгда приидє владыка и поставишє прѣстоль госпѡдьнь по срѣдѣ рая, и вьзва страшнымь гласомь ・ Адамє, Адамє, гдє юси; 8-10.8 азь рѣхь ・ нагь юсмь, госпѡди, и нє могоу изити .

Pericope 10 *Adam's Story of the Fall*

GREEK	LATIN	ARMENIAN	GEORGIAN	SLAVONIC
	33:1 The Lord God gave us two angels to watch over us.	33:1 We had twelve angels who went around with each of us, because of the guarding of the Garden, until the time of the light.	33:1 And there were twelve angels with each of us to guard us until the time of the dawn,	
	33:2 The hour came for the angels to ascend to the sight of God for worship. At once, the Devil, the enemy, found the place while the angels were absent. And the Devil deceived your mother so that she ate from the unlawful and forbidden tree."	33:2 Since, every day they would go forth [to worship the Lord], at the time when they went to the heavens, at that time Satan deceived your mother and caused her to eat of the fruit. Satan knew that I was not with her, nor the angels, at that time he caused her to eat.	33:2 but each day, they ascended (there). And at the moment of their ascent, the serpent deceived your mother and caused her to eat of the tree, for he had seen that I was not with her any more than the angels.	8-10.4 And Seth asked, "Who instructed the serpent?" 8-10.5 Adam said to his son, "The Devil changed himself into radiant form and came to the serpent in the form of an angel and said to it, 'You are very intelligent, give to Eve from the tree, she will taste it and also give it to Adam.' 8-10.6 And thus it happened and for this reason we have fallen prey to sickness and death.
	33:3 Then she ate it and gave it to me to eat.	33:3 [Afterwards, also, she gave (it) to me.]	33:3 She also made me eat of it and I did not understand.	
8:1 And God was angry with us, and the Lord came into the Garden [and set up his throne] and called me in a terrible voice and said: "Adam, where art you? And why do you hide from my face? Shall the house be able to hide itself from its builder?"	34:1 Immediately, the Lord God grew angry with us and said to me:	34(8):1 I knew then, when I ate the fruit, that God was angry with us.	34(8):1 When we had eaten, God became angry with us	8-10.7 Then the Master came, and in the center of Paradise his throne was set up, and he called out in a frightful voice, 'Adam, Adam, where are you?' 8-10.8 I said, 'I am naked, O Lord, and I cannot come out.'

Pericope 10 *Adam's Story of the Fall*

GREEK	LATIN	ARMENIAN	GEORGIAN	SLAVONIC
8:2 Καὶ λέγει· Ἐπειδὴ ἐγκατέλιπας τὴν διαθήκην μου, ὑπήνεγκα τῷ σώματί σου ἑβδομήκοντα πληγάς. Πρῶτον νόσος πληγῆς ὁ βιασμὸς τῶν ὀφθαλμῶν· δεύτερον πληγῆς ἀκοῆς καὶ οὕτως καθεξῆς πᾶσαι αἱ πληγαὶ παρακολουθοῦσαι τῷ σώματι.	34:2 eo quod dereliquisti mandatura meum et verbum meum quod confortavi tibi non custodisti, ecce inducam in corpus tuum LXX plagas; diversis doloribus ab initio capitis et oculorum et aurium usque ad ungulas pedum et per singula membra torquebimini. haec deputavit in flagellationem dolori uno cum arboribus (dolorum pro transgressione fructus arboris?). Haec autem omnia misit dominus ad me et omnes generationes nostras.	34(8):2 եւ ասէ Աստուած. Փոխանակ զի անցեր զուխտիւ իմով. ածից [ի] վերայ մարմնոյ քո հարուածսուն արիւն. ցաւ աչաց եւ ականջաց եւ ամենայն զառիւածող ընջգրրնգումս եւ համբերսցի զիս ի վերու Հասարութեանց որ պաշիս ի շարժարանս զի արձակեցէ զնոսա Աստուած ի վերին ժամանակս։	34(8):2 და გურქუა:" მეუ-რაცხ-ჰყავთ აღანაბი რომე და მეც მეუქრაცხ-გყენთ თქუენ. და მოვლი-ნა სამეუცდაათი სალმობა ჰურენ ზედა, თუალთა და ყურთა და ვიდრე ფერხთამდე, გუემად და სასწაულნო დაუხცებელი საუცხუანი. ესე მოყო მე უმერთმან წარსაწყმედელად აღსრულებისა".	8-10.9 и рече господь · никогда тако съкрыль се еси оть мене. кгда съкрываеши се оть мене, прѣстѹпиль еси заповѣди мок. 8-10.10 оумнож́ тѣло твок ранами и срьдьцѹ твокмѹ болести. 8-10.11 .а.-ая кза бѹдеть чрѣвоболь, .в.-ая кза очеболь и глѹхота . и по томь послѣдѹть вьсе кзы .о. и .в..

Pericope 10 *Adam's Story of the Fall* 38E

GREEK	LATIN	ARMENIAN	GEORGIAN	SLAVONIC
8:2 And he said to me: "Since you have abandoned my covenant, I have brought upon your body seventy-two strokes; first a stroke to the eyes, second a stroke to the hearing, and likewise in turn strokes shall follow upon (all parts of) the body."	34:2 'Because you have forsaken my mandate and have not kept my word which I entrusted to you, I will bring upon your body seventy afflictions. You will be racked with pains from the top of your head, eyes, and ears, to the toe-nails on your feet, and in every single member.' This he counted as punishment fitting in suffering [to the seriousness of our transgression] concerning the trees (of suffering for the transgression of the fruit of the tree?) The Lord sent all these ills upon me and all our generations."	34(8):2 God said, 'Because you transgressed my commandment, I shall bring seventy afflictions [upon] your body, pain of the eyes and ringing of the ears and all the joints.' It will be reckoned for me (?) among the afflictions of sickness which are preserved in the treasuries, so that God might send them in the last times."	34(8):2 and he told us, 'You have, therefore, scorned my commandment; I too will scorn you.' And he sent 70 evils upon us, to our eyes, and to our ears and as far as our feet, plagues and portents laid up in (his) treasuries. This God did to me to cause me to die a death."	8-10.9 And the Lord said, 'You have never hidden yourself from me." Since you hide from me, you have thus transgressed my commandment. 8-10.10 I will inflict your body abundantly with injuries and your heart with pains. 8-10.11 The first sickness will be a pain in the belly, the second sickness [will be] dimness of vision and deafness, and on top of this, there will follow seventy-two illnesses of all sorts besides.'"

Pericope 11 *Command to Retrieve Oil*

GREEK	LATIN	ARMENIAN	GEORGIAN	SLAVONIC
9:1 Ταῦτα δὲ λέγων ὁ Ἀδὰμ τοῖς υἱοῖς αὐτοῦ ἀνεστέναξε μέγα καὶ εἶπεν· Τί ποιήσω ὅτι ἐν μεγάλῃ λύπῃ εἰμί;	35:1 Haec dicens Adam ad omnes filios suos comprehensus est magnis doloribus et clamans magnis vocibus dicebat: quid faciam infelix, positus in talibus doloribus.	35(9):1 Զայս իբրև ասաց Ադամ յորդիսն իւր ՍԵԹ. ապաքաեցաւ և ասէ. Զի՞նչ առնեմ զի ի մեծ ցաւս եև յաշխատութիւնս եմ:	35(9):1 ესე რაი ეტყოდა ადამ ძესა თვისსა სეთის, ღაღადყო და თქუა: "რაი-მე ვყო?ოდის ერთასა შინა ვარ".	11-15.1 Тогда пакы въздьхноувь Адамь рече къ сыновомь своимь · великоу болѣзнь имамь, чеда моя.
9:2 Ἔκλαυσε δὲ ἡ Εὔα λέγουσα· Κύριέ μου Ἀδάμ, δός μοι τὸ ἥμισυ τῆς νόσου σου καὶ ὑπενέγκω αὐτό, ὅτι δι' ἐμὲ τοῦτό σοι γέγονεν, δι' ἐμὲ ἐν καμάτοις τυγχάνεις.	35:2 Et cum vidisset eum Eva flentem coepit et ipsa flere dicens: domine deus meus, in me transfer dolorem eius, quoniam ego peccavi. Et dixit Eva ad Adam: domine mi, da mihi partem dolorum tuorum, quoniam a me culpa haec tibi accessit.	35(9):2 Եւ զայս իբրև ասէ. Տէր իմ, Ադամ. արի ստիպիս ի ցաւող, զի ընկալայց և համբերեցից նմա. զի վասն իմ եղև ցաւքդ այդ որ եկեալ հասեալ են ի վերայ քո:	35(9):2 ტიროდით თქუა ევა: "უფალო ჩემო, ადამ, მომეც მე ზოგი სალმობათა შენთა და ერომაი ეგე შენი ვიტვირთო, რამეთუ ჩემ გამო არს სალმობაი შენი და მე ვეკადნეგე ერომანი ეგე".	11-15.2 тогда Евга сь плачемь рече емоу · господине, въстани, даи мьнѣ отъ болести твоее, да си оби подѣливѣ · отъ мене бо тако трьпиши болести.
9:3 Εἶπε δὲ Ἀδὰμ τῇ Εὔᾳ· Ἀνάστα καὶ πορεύου μετὰ τοῦ υἱοῦ ἡμῶν Σὴθ πλησίον τοῦ παραδείσου· καὶ ἐπίθετε γῆν ἐπὶ τὰς κεφαλὰς ὑμῶν καὶ κλαύσατε,	36:1 Et dixit Adam ad Evam: exsurge et vade cum filio meo Seth ad proximum paradisi [III=portas paradisi]III et mittite pul-verem in capita vestra et prosternite vos in terram et plangite in conspectu dei.	36(9):3 Ասէ ցևա Ադամ. Արի և ապաց որդոլ քո ՍԵԹաւ մերձ ի դրախտն և առ արկանէք հող զգլով ձերով և լացէք առաջի Աստուծոյ.	36(9):3 ჰრქუა ადამ ევას:" აღდეგ და მოვედ სეთის თანა, ძისა ჩემისა თანა სამოთხე, დასხით მოწო თავსა თქუენსა და ტიროდით წინაშე ღმრთისა,	11-15.3а рече Адамь къ Евзѣ · не възможно ѥсть подѣлити, нь въстани сь сыномь своимь Сидомь и иди противоу раю, и сь плачемь посыпающе прьсть на главѣ свои,

Pericope 11 *Command to Retrieve Oil*

GREEK	LATIN	ARMENIAN	GEORGIAN	SLAVONIC
9:1 As he said this to his sons, Adam groaned sore and said: "What shall I do? I am in great distress."	35:1 Saying this to all his children, Adam was seized with great pains, and crying out with a great voice, he said: "What shall I do, I who am unfortunate, being in so much pain?"	35(9):1 When Adam said this to his son Seth, he cried out and said, "What shall I do, for I am in great pains and toils."	35(9):1 When Adam said this to his son Seth, he cried out and said, "What shall I do? I am in great pain."	11-15.1 Then Adam sighed again and spoke to his sons, "I have a great pain, my children."
9:2 And Eve wept and said: "My lord Adam, rise up and give me half of your pain and I will endure it; for it is on my account that this has happened to you, on my account you have these troubles."	35:2 When Eve saw him, she began to cry and she herself crying said: "My Lord God, transfer his pain over to me, since it was I who sinned." Eve then said to Adam: "My lord, give me part of your pain, since by me this blame came upon you."	35(9):2 Eve wept and said, "My lord Adam. Arise, give me some of your pain, so that I might receive and bear it, for these pains which have come upon you, came about because of me."	35(9):2 Eve said, weeping, "My lord Adam, give me half of your sufferings and I will bear your present pain, for your suffering is due to me and it is I who caused these pains to come upon you."	11-15.2 Then Eve said to him amid tears, "Stand up, my husband, and give me a portion of your pain, we will both share it together; for on account of me you suffer such agony."
9:3 But Adam said to Eve, "Arise and go with my son Seth near to the Garden, and put earth upon your heads and weep	36:1 Adam then said to Eve: "Rise, go with my son, Seth, near the Garden [III=to the gates of the Garden]III and cast dust on your heads, and prostrate yourself on the ground, lamenting in the sight of God.	36(9):3 Adam said to her, "Arise, go with your son Seth, close to the Garden and there cast dust on your heads and weep before God.	36(9):3 And Adam told Eve, "Arise and go with Seth, my son, to the Garden; cast soil on your head and weep before God so that he might give us grace.	11-15.3a Adam, however, said to Eve, "It is impossible to share it, but rise up together with your son Seth and go to Paradise, and cry, while sprinkling dust on your heads,

Pericope 11 *Command to Retrieve Oil*

GREEK	LATIN	ARMENIAN	GEORGIAN	SLAVONIC
9:4 δεόμενοι τοῦ θεοῦ ὅπως σπλαγχνισθῇ ἐπ' ἐμοὶ καὶ ἀποστείλῃ τὸν ἄγγελον αὐτοῦ [εἰς τὸν παράδεισον,] καὶ δώσῃ μοι ἐκ τοῦ δένδρου ἐν ᾧ ῥέει τὸ ἔλαιον ἐξ αὐτοῦ καὶ ἐνέγκῃς μοι, καὶ ἀλείψομαι καὶ ἀναπαύσομαι ἀπὸ τῆς νόσου μου.	36:2 Forsitan miserebitur et transmittet angelum suum ad arborem misericordiae suae, de qua currit oleum vitae, et dabit vobis ex ipso modicum, ut me unguatis ex eo, ut quiescam ab his doloribus, ex quibus consumor.	36(9):4 *[Armenian text]*	36(9):4 რაითა წყალობაი ყოს ჩუენ ზედა და მოავლინოს ანგელოზი თვისი სამოთხედ, საღაცა არს ხე იგი ცხოვრებისაო, რომლისა გამოსდის ზეთი, რაითა კნინ გცეს ზეთი იგი. და მომართოთ მე იგი აქა და ვიცხო და განვისუენო სალმობათაგან ჩემთა.	11-15.3b ѥда како ѹслышить господь молитвѫ ваю и припѹстить ми отъ дрѣва маслиньна, да виждѫ ѥда како покоить ми сє болєсть.
9:5 [καὶ δηλώσω σοι τὸν τρόπον ἐν ᾧ ἠπατήθημεν τὸ πρότερον.]		36(9)5 *[Armenian text]*	36(9):5 მაშინ-ღა გაუჩყო შენ ყოველი იგი სახე, რომლითა განვიცადე-ნით".	

Pericope 11 **Command to Retrieve Oil** 40E

GREEK	LATIN	ARMENIAN	GEORGIAN	SLAVONIC
9:4 and pray God to have mercy upon me and send his angel to the Garden, and give me of the tree out of which the oil flows, and bring it me, and I shall anoint myself and shall have rest from my illness.	36:2 Perhaps he will take pity and send his angel over to the tree of his mercy from which flows the oil of life, and will give you a little of it with which to anoint me so that I may have rest from these pains with which I am consumed."	36(9):4 Perhaps God will pity me and send his angel to the Garden, and he will go to the place where the olive-tree stands, from which oil comes forth, and give you a little of it, so that you might bring it to me and I might anoint my bones and be separated from pain,	36(9):4 And (God) will send his angel to the Garden where the Tree of Life is, from which the oil flows out, so that he may give you a little of that oil. And you will bring it here to me and I will anoint myself and I will be healed of my sufferings.	11-15.3b perhaps God will hear your prayer and grant to me from the Tree of Oils, that I might learn if perhaps my pain may be eased."
9:5 And I will show you the way in which we were deceived at first."		36(9):5 and I might teach you this way...which we were tried formerly."	36(9):5 Then I will let you know the whole way in which we were tried.	

Pericope 12 *Encounter with Beast*

GREEK	LATIN	ARMENIAN	GEORGIAN	SLAVONIC
10:1 Ἐπορεύθη δὲ Σὴθ καὶ ἡ Εὔα εἰς τὰ μέρη τοῦ παραδείσου. [Καὶ πορευομένων αὐτῶν] εἶδεν ἡ Εὔα τὸν υἱὸν αὐτῆς καὶ θηρίον πολεμοῦντα αὐτόν.	37:1 Et abierunt Seth et mater eius contra portas paradisi; et dum ambularent, ecce subito venit serpens bestia et impetum faciens morsit Seth.	37(10):1 Գնացին այնուհետև Սէթ և նա ի կողմն ի դրախտին. մինչդեռ երթային, ահա նա [զդռոքին իր զի] զազան մի մարտնչէր ընդ Սէթ[այ] և խածանէր զնա. այլ սկսաւ նա և ասէ.	37(10):1 ესე და ესე, წარვიდეს სეთ და ევა, სადა-იგი იყო სამოთხე ადამისი. სლვასა მისსა იხილა ნაშობთა მისთაგანი რომელსა ებრძოდა მხეცი და ტირილად იყო ევა და თქუა:	11-15.4 И въставьши Ѥвьга съ сыномь своимь Сидомь прихождаше къ раю. 11-15.5 И видѣ Ѥвьга звѣра велия, именемь Котѹрь, гонеше изѣсти сына ѥѥ Сида.
10:2 Ἔκλαυσε δὲ ἡ Εὔα λέγουσα· Οἴμμοι οἴμμοι, ὅτι ἐὰν ἔλθω εἰς τὴν ἡμέραν τῆς ἀναστάσεως, πάντες οἱ ἁμαρτήσαντες καταράσονταί με λέγοντες ὅτι οὐκ ἐφύλαξεν ἡ Εὔα τὴν ἐντολὴν τοῦ θεοῦ.	37:2 Et cum vidisset Eva flevit dicens: heu mihi miserae, quoniam maledicta sum, quoniam non custodivi praecepta domini.	37(10)2 Եվ ետես եկեսն մայր դառնապատճին, անէծնայլ մեղաորք մեղադրին ինձ և ասասցեն թէ մայրն մեր ոչ լուաւ պատուիրանին Տեառն Աստուծոյ:	37(10):2 "ვა ჩემდა, რამეთუ ოდეს მოვროთ მე დღესა მას სასჯელო-სასა, ყოველნი შეცოდებანი ჩემნი მწვიდეს მე და არქუან: ვინცელად შენ არა დაიმარხე მცნებანი ღმრთისანი".	11-15.6а И въсплака сє Ѥвьга зѣло и рече· ѡ горє мнѣ, чєдо моѥ сладькоѥ, отъ селѣ до съврьшения и до .в.-го пришьствия клети мє хотеть вьси· менє бо ради вьса зла ѹмножише сє.

Pericope 12 *Encounter with Beast*

GREEK	LATIN	ARMENIAN	GEORGIAN	SLAVONIC
10.1 Then Seth and Eve went toward the direction of the Garden. [And while they were going,] Eve saw her son and wild beast assailing him.	37:1 Seth and his mother went away opposite the gates of the Garden. As they were walking, there suddenly appeared the serpent, the beast, who attacked and bit Seth.	37(10):1 Thereafter, Seth and Eve went in the direction of the Garden. As they were going, Eve saw that a wild beast was fighting with [her son] Seth and was biting him.	37(10):1 When they heard that, Seth and Eve went (to the place) where the Garden of Adam was. As she went she saw one of her descendants who was being attacked by a beast and (the beast) was biting the child.	11-15.4 And Eve arose along with her son Seth and set off for Paradise, 11-15.5 and Eve saw a huge animal, called Mongrel, which followed her son Seth, to devour him.
10:2 And Eve wept and said: "Woe is me; if I come to the day of the Resurrection, all those who have sinned will curse me saying: 'Eve has not kept the commandment of God.'"	37:2 When Eve saw this, she cried saying: "Alas, woe is me, for I am cursed because I did not keep the precepts of the Lord."	37(10):2 Eve began to weep and she said, "[When] the day of Judgment comes; all sins will be blamed upon me and (men) will say, 'Our mother did not hearken to the commandment of the Lord God!'"	37(10):2 Then Eve began to weep and said, "Woe is me, for when I arrive at the day of judgment, all my sins will burn me and (people) will tell me, 'In the first instance, it was you who did not observe God's orders.'"	11-15.6a Eve began to cry bitterly and said, "Woe is me, my sweet child, from now on until the end and until the second coming all will curse me, because it is on my account all sorts of evil have multiplied."

Pericope 12 *Encounter with Beast*

GREEK	LATIN	ARMENIAN	GEORGIAN	SLAVONIC
10:3 Καὶ εἶπε πρὸς τὸ θηρίον· Ὦ θηρίον πονηρόν, οὐ φοβήσει τὴν εἰκόνα τοῦ θεοῦ πολεμῆσαι αὐτήν; Πῶς ἠνοίγη τὸ στόμα σου; πῶς ἐνίσχυσαν οἱ ὀδόντες σου; πῶς οὐκ ἐμνήσθης τῆς ὑποταγῆς σου ὅτι πρότερον ὑπετάγης τῇ εἰκόνι τοῦ θεοῦ;	37:3 Et dixit Eva ad serpentem voce magna: bestia maledicta, quomodo non timuisti mittera te ad imaginem dei, sed ausus es pugnare cum ea? aut quomodo praevaluerunt dentes tui?	37(10):3 [Armenian text]	37(10):3 [Georgian text]	11-15.6b и възьпи къ сверю гласомь велиюмь и рече · 11-15.7 ѡ сверю, не боиши ли се иконы божияго образа, нь хощеши извести юго; како смеюши ѹста своя отврьсти на образь божии и обьявити зѫбы своѥ къ нѥмоу; како не помнѣши, сверю, како те хранѣхь роукою моюю;
11:1 Τότε τὸ θηρίον ἐβόησε λέγων· Ὦ Εὔα, οὐ πρὸς ἡμᾶς ἡ πλεονεξία σου οὔτε ὁ κλαυθμός, ἀλλὰ πρὸς σέ, ἐπειδὴ ἡ ἀρχὴ τῶν θηρίων ἐκ σοῦ ἐγένετο.	38:1 Respondit bestia voce humana: O Eva, numquid non ad vos est malitia nostra? nonne contra vos est furor noster?	38(11):1 [Armenian text]	38(11):1 [Georgian text]	11-15.8 тогда сверь рече къ ѥвьго, оть селѣ не имаши власти надь нами да повелѣваюши намь, понюже прѣжде оть тебе зачело се ѥсть .

Pericope 12 *Encounter with Beast* 42E

GREEK	LATIN	ARMENIAN	GEORGIAN	SLAVONIC
10:3 And she spoke to the beast: "You wicked beast, Do you not fear to fight with the image of God ? How was your mouth opened ? How were your teeth made strong? How did you not call to mind your subjection? For long ago you were made subject to the image of God."	37:3 Eve said to the serpent in a great voice: "O cursed beast, why are you not afraid to cast yourself at the image of God, but dare to fight against it? Why have your teeth prevailed?"	37(10):3 Eve called out against the wild beast and said, "O wild beast, how do you [not] fear the image of God, that you dared to fight with the image of God? How was your mouth open[ed] and your fangs bared, and your hair stood on end? How did you not remember the obedience which you formerly displayed, that your mouth was opened against the image of God?"	37(10):3 Eve called out and told the wicked beast, "O evil beast, have you no fear? [Did you dare] to fight with the image of God? How did you take it upon yourself to open your mouth and how have you (thought to) sink your teeth? Or how have you not recalled the first order of God and have opened your mouth against the image of God?"	11-15.6b And she screamed in a loud voice at the animal and said, 11-15.7 "O beast, aren't you afraid before the image of the divine countenance? Will you devour him? How do you dare to open your mouth against the image of God and to bare your teeth against him? Don't you remember, O beast, how I fed you with my own hand?"
11:1 Then the beast cried out and said: "It is not our concern, Eve, your greed and your wailing, but your own; for (it is) from you that the rule of the beasts has arisen.	38:1 The beast answered in a human voice: "O Eve, was our malice ever not against you? Isn't our anger against you?	38(11):1 Then the wild beast cried out and said to Eve, "In truth, our insolence is because of you, for the example came from you.	38(11):1 Then the beast replied to her and told Eve, "It is not from our greed that your discontent and your weeping come, but your discontent and your weeping come from your own greed, for at the beginning of creation, it was you who hearkened to the beast, the serpent.	11-15.8 Then the animal said to her, "O Eve, from now on you have no power over us to command us, for it has departed from you.

Pericope 12 *Encounter with Beast*

GREEK	LATIN	ARMENIAN	GEORGIAN	SLAVONIC
11:2 Πῶς ἠνοίγη τὸ στόμα σου φαγεῖν ἀπὸ τοῦ ξύλου περὶ οὗ ἐντείλατό σοι ὁ θεὸς μὴ φαγεῖν ἐξ αὐτοῦ; Διὰ τοῦτο καὶ ἡμῶν αἱ φύσεις μετηλλάγησαν.	38:2 Dic mihi, Eva, quomodo apertum est os tuum, ut manducares de fructu, quem praecepit tibi dominus deus ut non manducares:	38(11):2 [Armenian text]	38(11):2 [Georgian text]	11-15.9 како смѣяше ты отврѣсти ᲈста своя и сьнѣсти отъ древа, отъ нѥгоже ти не рече господь;
11:3 Νῦν οὖν οὐ δυνήσει ὑπενεγκεῖν, ἐὰν ἀπάρξωμαι ἐλέγχειν σε.	38:3 nunc autem non potes portare, si tibi incepero exprobrare?	38(11):3 [Armenian text]	38(11):3 [Georgian text]	11-15.10 за то и азъ хощᲈ ᲈбити тебе и извѣсти чеда твоя. 11-15.11 Тогда Евга не отвѣща ни что.
12:1 Λέγει ὁ Σὴθ πρὸς τὸ θηρίον. Κλεῖσαί σου τὸ στόμα καὶ σίγα καὶ ἀπόστηθι ἀπὸ τῆς εἰκόνος τοῦ θεοῦ ἕως τῆς ἡμέρας τῆς κρίσεως.	39:1 Tunc dixit Seth ad bestiam: increpet te dominus deus. stupe, obmutesce, claude os tuum, maledicte inimice veritatis confusio perditionis; recede de imagine dei usque in diem, quando dominus deus iusserit in comprobationem te adduci.	39(12):1 [Armenian text]	39(12):1 [Georgian text]	11-15.12 тогда Сидь рече къ звѣрю · да затвореть се ᲈста твоя до сᲈда, понѥже тако дръзнᲈше на образъ божии, и въ ложи своѥмь да прѣбываѥши въ вѣкы . и тако прѣбываѥть въ вѣкы.
12:2 Τότε λέγει τὸ θηρίον τῷ Σήθ· Ἰδοὺ ἀφίσταμαι ἀπὸ τῆς εἰκόνος τοῦ θεοῦ.	39:2 et dixit bestia ad Seth: ecce recedo, sicut dixisti, a facie imaginis dei.	39(12):2 [Armenian text]	39(12):2 [Georgian text]	
12:3 [Τότε ἔφυγε τὸ θηρίον καὶ ἀφῆκεν αὐτὸν πεπληγμένον] καὶ ἐπορεύθη εἰς τὴν σκηνὴν αὐτοῦ.	39:3 statim recessit plaga de dentibus a Seth.	39(12):3 [Armenian text]	39(12):3 [Georgian text]	

Pericope 12 *Encounter with Beast* 43E

GREEK	LATIN	ARMENIAN	GEORGIAN	SLAVONIC
11:2 How was your mouth opened to eat of the tree concerning which God commanded you not to eat of it? On this account, our nature also has been transformed. 11:3 Now therefore you cannot endure it, if I begin to reprove you."	38:2 Tell me, Eve. How could you open your mouth to eat the fruit which the Lord God commanded you not to eat. 38:3 Now, however, you are not able to bear it, if I should begin to reproach you?"	38(11):2 How was your mouth opened to dare to eat of the fruit concerning which God commanded you not to eat of it? 38(11):3 [Until he will change all of our natures, henceforth you are unable to resist that which I speak to you, or if I begin to rebuke you.]"	38(11):2 How did you dare to open your mouth and eat of the tree of which God had ordered you not to eat? You, [[on account]] of whom the aspect of everything has changed, 38(11):3 now, you will not be able to endure, if I start speaking and rebuking you."	11-15.9 How did you dare to open your mouth and eat from the tree, which the Lord did not allow you? 11-15.10 On account of this I will also kill you and devour your child." 11-15.11 At this Eve didn't answer.
12:1 Then Seth spoke to the beast, "Close your mouth and be silent and stand off from the image of God until the day of Judgment."	39:1 Then Seth said to the beast: "May the Lord God reproach you. Be mute, grow silent, close your mouth, cursed enemy of the truth, disorder of destruction. Fall back from the image of God until the day when the Lord God shall order you to be brought in for trial."	39(12):1 Then Seth said to the wild beast, "Close your mouth, O Satan. Get away from the image of God [until [[the day will come]] on which God will bring you to rebuke.]"	39(12):1 Seth replied to him and told the beast, "Let your mouth be closed and be silent, beast, and get away from us, the image of the divinity, until the day when God will have you standing (before him)."	11-15.12 Then Seth spoke to the beast, "Your mouth will be closed until the judgment, for you yourself were so bold against the image of God; you will stay in your lair right into eternity. And so it will remain even in eternity."
12:2 Then the beast said to Seth: "Behold, I stand off from the image of God."	39:2 The beast said to Seth: "Behold, I am going away, just as you have said, from the face of the image of God."	39(12):2 Then he said to Seth, "Behold, I am standing apart from you, the image of God."	39(12):2 Then also the beast told Seth, "Behold, then, I get away from you, image of God, dazzling (splendor) of God."	
12:3 [And the beast fled and left him wounded] and went to his hut.	39:3 At once the wound from its teeth disappeared from Seth.	39(12):3 The beast fled from him.	39(12):3 And when the beast had left them, the beast fled (far) from Seth and the wounded man went to the hut of Adam his father."	

Pericope 13 *Arrival at Paradise*

GREEK	LATIN	ARMENIAN	GEORGIAN	SLAVONIC
13:1 Ἐπορεύθη δὲ Σὴθ μετὰ Εὔας πλησίον τοῦ παραδείσου. Καὶ ἔκλαυσαν δεόμενοι τοῦ θεοῦ ὅπως ἀποστείλη τὸν ἄγγελον αὐτοῦ καὶ δώσει αὐτοῖς τὸ ἔλαιον τοῦ ἐλέου.	40:1 Seth autem et mater eius ambulaverunt in partes paradisi propter oleum misericordiae, ut ungerent Adam infirmum. et pervenientes ad portas paradisi tulerunt pulverem de terra et posuerunt super caput suum. et prostraverunt se in terram super faciem suam et coeperunt plangere cum gemitu magno deprecantes dominum deum, ut misereretur Adae in doloribus suis et mitteret angelum suum dare eis oleum de arbore misericordiae suae.	40(13):1 *[Armenian text]*	40(13):1 *[Georgian text]*	16-17.1 И прииде Сидь кь раю сь матєрию своєю, плачюще се и рыдающе и вьпиюще кь богѹ, посыпающе прьстию главѣ свои.
13:2a Καὶ ἀπέστειλε ὁ θεὸς Μιχαὴλ τὸν ἀρχάγγελον καὶ εἶπεν αὐτῷ·	41:1 [NIC+ *Orantibus autem eis horas multas et deprecantibus ecce angelus Michahel apparens eis dixit:* ego missus sum ad te a domino, ego sum constitutus a domino super corpus humanum. tibi dico,	41(13):2a *[Armenian text]*	40(13):2a *[Georgian text]*	16-17.2a и пирп ѹсти господь архаггєла Михаила, и рєчє Сидѹ
13:2b Σὴθ ἄνθρωπε τοῦ θεοῦ, μὴ κάμῃς εὐχόμενος ἐπὶ τῇ ἱκεσίᾳ ταύτῃ περὶ τοῦ ξύλου ἐν ᾧ ῥέει τὸ ἔλαιον ἀλεῖψαι τὸν πατέρα σου Ἀδάμ·	41:2 [Seth homo dei, noli lacrimare orando et deprecando propter oleum ligni misericordiae, ut perunguas patrem tuum Adam pro doloribus corporis sui.	41(13):2b *[Armenian text]*	40(13):2b *[Georgian text]*	

Pericope 13 *Arrival at Paradise*

GREEK	LATIN	ARMENIAN	GEORGIAN	SLAVONIC
13:1 And Seth went with Eve near the Garden,	40:1 Seth and his mother then walked to the region of the Garden for the oil of mercy to anoint the sick Adam.	40(13):1 Seth, [with] Eve, went close to the Garden,	40(13):1 As for Seth, he went with Eve to the Garden.	16-17.1 And Seth came with his mother to Paradise,
and they wept there praying to God to send his angel and give them the oil of mercy.	Arriving at the gate of the Garden, they picked up dust from the ground and cast it on their heads, and prostrated themselves on the ground and began to lament with a great moan, beseeching the Lord God that He might have mercy on Adam in his pains, and send his angel to give them some oil from the tree of his mercy	and they wept with loud lament and asked God to send an angel to help them.	And they were weeping close to the wall of the Garden, and there they supplicated God to send them his angel.	they cried and sobbed and entreated God, sprinkling their heads with dust.
13:2a And God sent the archangel Michael and he said to Seth:	41:1 *[NIC+After they had prayed and pleaded for many hours, behold, the angel Michael appeared to them and said: "I was sent to you by the Lord. I was given power over the human body.*	41(13):2a God sent to them the angel Michael, who is prince of souls, and [he spoke these words to them],	41(13):2a [And God sent to them the archangel Michael,] who is in charge of the souls, and he told Seth,	16-17.2a And God sent his archangel Michael and he spoke to Seth,
13:2b "Seth, man of God, weary not yourself with prayers and entreaties concerning the tree which flowed with oil to anoint your father Adam.	41:2 *[I tell you, Seth, man of God, do not weep, praying and pleading for the oil of the tree of mercy to anoint your father Adam on account of the pains of his body.*	41(13):2b "Seth, [man of God]: Do not labour to supplicate for the oil which issues forth from the tree—that oil of joy—to anoint your father Adam.	41(13):2b "Man of God, do not labor to supplicate thus concerning the olive tree, in order to anoint your father Adam.	

Pericope 14 *Michael's Reply*

GREEK	LATIN	ARMENIAN	GEORGIAN	SLAVONIC
13:3 Οὐ γενήσεταί σοι νῦν [ἀλλ' ἐπ' ἐσχάτων τῶν ἡμερῶν. τότε ἀναστήσεται πᾶσα σὰρξ ἀπὸ Ἀδὰμ ἕως τῆς ἡμέρας ἐκείνης τῆς μεγάλης ὅσοι ἔσονται λαὸς ἅγιος. 13:4 [Τότε αὐτοῖς δοθήσεται πᾶσα εὐφροσύνη τοῦ παραδείσου καὶ ἔσται ὁ θεὸς ἐν μέσῳ αὐτῶν. 13:5 [Καὶ οὐκ ἔσονται ἔτι ἐξαμαρτάνοντες ἐνώπιον αὐτοῦ ὅτι ἀρθήσεται ἀπ' αὐτῶν ἡ καρδία ἡ πονηρὰ καὶ δοθήσεται αὐτοῖς καρδία συνετιζομένη τὸ ἀγαθὸν καὶ λατρεύειν θεῷ μόνῳ.]	42:1 [Quia nullo modo poteris ex eo accipere, nisi in novissimis diebus, quando completi fuerint quinque milia et quingenti anni. 42:2 [Tunc veniet super terram amantissimus rex dei resuscitare corpus Adae et cum eo resuscitare corpora mortuorum. 42:3 [Et ipse filius dei veniens baptizabitur in flumine Jordanis et dum egressus fuerit de aqua Jordanis, tunc de oleo misericordiae suae perunguet omnes credentes in se. 42:4 [Et erit oleum misericordiae in generationem et generationem eis, qui renascendi sunt ex aqua et spiritu sancto in vitam aeternam. 42:5 [Tunc descendens in terris amantissimus filius dei Christus introducet patrem tuum Adam in paradisum ad arborem misericordiae.] NIC	42(13):3a Այդ այժմ ոչ ումի լինել. բայց այս ի ժամանակին իբրեւ լնուն եւ կատարին ամբ կատարածին. 42(13):3b յայնժամ եկեսցէ սիրելին Քրիստոս, յարուցանել զմարմինն Ադամայ, վասն յանցանաց նորա որ եղեն. 42(13):3c եկեսցէ ի Յորդանան եւ մկրտեսցի [ի] նմանէ եւ յորժամ ելցէ նա ի ջրոյ անտի, յայնժամ եկեսցէ Մ՛իրայէլ եւ խղումն գծմնեքեան ամէնք զնոր Ադամ նովաւ. 42(13):4 եւ այս լէտ այնորիկ դունին այրխաւկան լինիցի ամենայն զազանաց երկրի որ յարիցեն ի յարութեան, եւ լինիցին արժանաւորբ մտանել ի դրախտն անդր. եւ եւ ամէնց զնուաա խղով այնուհէ.	42(13):3a აწვე არა უფალ არს, არამედ მერმეთა ჟამთა, ოდეს აღესრუ- ლოს ხუთათასი წელი. 42(13):3b ხოლო მეხუთათასსა და ნახევარსა წელსა მოვიდეს ქუე- ყანად საყუარელი იგი ძე ღმრთისაი, ქრისტე, აღდგინებად გუამისა მის ადამისა დაცემისა მისგან გარდასლვითა მცნებათაითა. 42(13):3c მოვიდეს და ნათელ-იღოს იორდანესა მდინარესა. და ოდეს მიერ წყლით გამოვიდეს ზეთითურთ, და სცხოს იგი მას 43(13):4 და ყოველთა ნათესავთა მისთა, რათა აღდგენ ქამსა მას აღდგომისასა. თქუა უფალმან: და შევიყუანნე მჱნ სამოთხედ და ვსცხო მათ საცხებელი ესე.	

Pericope 14 *Michael's Reply* 45E

GREEK	LATIN	ARMENIAN	GEORGIAN	SLAVONIC
13:3 For it shall not be yours now, [*but at the end of the times. Then shall all flesh be raised up from Adam till that great day,—all that shall be of the holy people.*	42:1 [*For in no wise can you receive any until the last days, after 5500 years have passed.*	42(13):3a This cannot be now: but then, at that time when the years of the end are filled and completed,	42(13):3a This is not to be right now but in the future times, when five thousand years have been completed. Then, at the 5500 year	
13:4 [*Then shall the delights of the Garden be given to them and God shall be in their midst* 13:5 [*And they shall no longer sin before his face, for the evil heart shall be taken from them and there shall be given them a heart understanding the good and to serve God only.*]	42:2 [*Then the most loving king of God will come upon the earth to resurrect the body of Adam and, with him, the bodies of the dead.*	42(13):3b then the beloved Christ will come to resurrect Adam's body, because of his sins which took place.	42(13):3b the beloved Son of God, Christ, will come upon the earth to re[[surrect]] Adam's body from his fall, because of the transgression of the commands.	
	42:3 [*The very Son of God, when he comes, will be baptized in the river Jordan, and when he comes forth from the water of the Jordan, he will then anoint all who believe in him with the oil of his mercy.*	42(13):3c He will come to the Jordan and be baptized [by] him, and when he will come forth from the water, then Michael will come and anoint the new Adam with the oil of joy.	42(13):3c He will come and he will be baptized in the river Jordan. And as soon as he will have come forth from the water, with the (anointing) of oil, he will anoint him, him	
	42:4 This oil of mercy will be from generation to generation on those who are reborn of water and the Holy Spirit into eternal life.	42(13):4 Then, after that, it shall happen in the same fashion to all the wild beasts of the earth, who will arise in resurrection and be worthy of entering the Garden. I shall anoint them with that oil.	43(13):4 and all his descendants, so that they will rise at the time of the resurrection. The Lord said, 'I will admit them into the Garden and I will anoint them with that unction.'	
	42:5 [*Then, the most loving Son of God will descend into the earth and lead your father, Adam, back into the Garden to the tree of mercy.*] NIC			

Pericope 15 *Return to Adam*

GREEK	LATIN	ARMENIAN	GEORGIAN	SLAVONIC
13:6 Σὺ δὲ πάλιν πορεύου πρὸς τὸν πατέρα σου, ἐπειδὴ ἐπληρώθη τὸ μέτρον τῆς ζωῆς αὐτοῦ εἴσω τριῶν ἡμερῶν· ἐξερχομένης δὲ τῆς ψυχῆς αὐτοῦ, μέλλεις θεάσασθαι τὴν ἄνοδον αὐτῆς φοβεράν.	43:1 Tu autem, Seth, vade ad patrem tuum Adam, quoniam completum est tempus vitae illius. adhuc sex dies tunc exibit anima eius de corpore et, cum exierit, videbis magna mirabilia in caelo et in terra et in luminaribus caeli.	43(13):6 Բայց դու գնա առ Ադամ հայրն քո, քանզի լցան ժամանակք կորա. մինչեւ վեցից աւուրս [ումեք] տակաւանել զարմանալիս բազումս յերկինս եւ յերկրի եւ ի [լուսաւորս] ամենայն որ յերկինս է.	43(13):6 ხოლო აწ მოვედ მამისა შენისა ადამისა, რამეთუ აღსრულე-ბულ არიან დღენი ცხოვრებისა მისთანი, სამ დღე გამოვიდეს სული გვამისაგან მისისა და იხილნეს საკვირველებანი მრავალნი ცათა შინა.	16-17.2b чловѣче божии, възврати сє кь отьцоу своємоу, понєжє приближиль сє ѥсть ѥмоу дьнь смрьти, и нє имать врачьбы .
14:1a Εἰπὼν δὲ ταῦτα ὁ ἄγγελος ἀπῆλθεν ἀπ' αὐτῶν.	43:2 Haec dicens Michahel statim recessit a Seth. 43:3 et reversi sunt Eva et Seth. ac tulerunt secum [III+ ramusculum et odor]III odoramenta hoc est nardum et crocum et calaminthen et cinamomum. [III+***legenda de ligno crucis***]III	43(14):1a Զայս իբրեւ խաւսեցաւ հրեշտակն, թափտիտ եղեւ ընդ ձառով դրախտին.	43(14):1a ესე რაი თქუა ანგელოზმან მან, და დაეფარა ნერგსა მას ქუეშე სამოთხისა.	16-17.3 и дадє ѥмоу .г. проуты (от древа, оть нѥгожє изгнань бысть) . пєвги, кєдрь и купарисъ. 16-17.4 И възємь Сидь проуты и принєсє кь отьцоу своємоу.
14:1b Ἦλθε δὲ Σὴθ καὶ ἡ Εὔα εἰς τὴν σκηνὴν ὅπου ἔκειτο ὁ Ἀδάμ.	44:1 Et cum pervenissent Seth et mater eius ad Adam dixerunt ei [III+omnia, quae gesta fuerant in via, et dixit]III, quia bestia serpens morsit Seth.	44(14):1b եկին այսուհետեւ Սէթ եւ մայր ի տատրակարն առ Ադամ կայր հանդուցեալ. պատմեաց Ադամ ամակ ձառոյն կերակրոյն յանցմանն.	43(14):1b ხოლო სეთი და ევა წარვიდეს ქალავანსა მას ადამისა. და ტიროდა ადამ ჭყლლებასა მას მჴეცისასა	16-17.5 и видѣ Ядамь и позна и въздьхноувь зѣло и сьвить сєбѣ вѣньць и възложи на главоу свою 16-17.6 и призъва чєда своя и вьноучєта ихь .

Pericope 15 *Return to Adam* 46E

GREEK	LATIN	ARMENIAN	GEORGIAN	SLAVONIC
13:6 But do go back to your father since the term of his life is filled in three days, and when his soul goes forth you will see its awesome ascent."	43:1 But you, Seth. go to your father, Adam, for the time of his life is complete. Six days hence, his soul will go forth from his body, and, when it does, you will see great wonders in heaven and on earth, and in the lights of heaven."	43(13):6 But you, go to Adam your father, for his times will be full in three days and you [have] to see many wonders in heavens and upon earth and in all [luminaries] which are in the heavens."	43(13):6 But now, go to your father Adam, because the days of his times are completed. (In) three days his soul will go out of his body and numerous wonders will be seen in the heavens."	16-17.2b "Man of God, go back to your father, for his day of death is drawing near, and there is no cure for him."
14:1a After the angel said these things it left them.	43:2 Saying this, Michael at once withdrew from Seth.	43(14):1a When the angel had spoken this, he disappeared behind a tree of the Garden.	43(14):1a When the angel had told that to him, (immediately) he was hidden underneath the plant of the Garden.	16-17.3 And he gave him three branches (from the tree, on account of which he was expelled): from the spruce, from the cedar, and from the cyprus.
				16-17.4 And Seth took the branches and brought them to his father.
	43:3 Seth and Eve went home, carrying with them [III+a small branch and incense]III spices — nard, crocus, calaminth, and cinnamon. [III +*** Legend of the Wood of the Cross***]III			
14:1b And Seth and Eve came to the hut where Adam was lying.	44:1 When Seth and his mother reached Adam, they said to him [III+ all that had been done on the way, and said]III that the beast, the serpent, had bitten Seth.	44(14):1b Thenceforth, Seth and Eve came to the hut where Adam lay sick. Adam remembered about the transgression of the eating of the tree,	44(14):1b Now, Seth and Eve departed for Adam's hut. And Adam wept because of the wound of the beast	16-17.5 And Adam saw and recognized them, and with a heavy sigh he coiled a wreath, and set it on his head,
				16-17.6 and [Adam] called his sons and grandchildren to him.

Pericope 16 *Adam's Rebuke of Eve*

GREEK	LATIN	ARMENIAN	GEORGIAN	SLAVONIC
14:2 Λέγει δὲ Ἀδὰμ τῇ Εὔᾳ· Ὦ Εὔα, τί κατειργάσω ἐν ἡμῖν; Ἐπήνεγκας ἐφ' ἡμᾶς ὀργὴν μεγάλην, ἥτις ἐστὶ θάνατος κατακυριεύων παντὸς τοῦ γένους ἡμῶν.	44:2 Et dixit Adam ad Evam: quid fecisti? induxisti nobis plagam magnam, delictum et peccatum in omnem generationem nostram. et hoc quod fecisti post mortem meam refert filios tuos,	44(14):2 ևւ ասէ ցևա. Ո՜վ, զի՞նչ արարեր. կամ որպիսի զայ ածեր ի վերայ մեր և ի վերայ զաւակի մերոյ.	44(14):2 და ჰრქუა ევას:" რაი იყო ჰყენ, რამეთუ მოიწია ჰყენ ზედა გუემაი, და ყოვლისა ნათესავისა ჰყენისა.	
14:3 Λέγει Ἀδὰμ τῇ Εὔᾳ· Κάλεσον πάντα τὰ τέκνα ἡμῶν καὶ τὰ τέκνα τῶν τέκνων ἡμῶν καὶ ἀνάγγειλον αὐτοῖς τὸν τρόπον τῆς παραβάσεως ἡμῶν.		44(14):3a արդ այսուհետև որպէս զիա՞րդ եղև լսանական պատմեսցես որդոց որդ.	44(14):3a რამეთუ რაი არიან შეცოდებანი შენნი, აწუყვე შვილთა შენთა,	
		զի լռայ ասասիկ ի պակասել գաևորո[հանս] խնոյ.		
	44:3 quoniam qui exsurgent a nobis laborantes non sufficient sed deficient et maledicent nos dicentes:	44(14):3b զի դուցէ հերևւ մևրանիցրիմթ. եկեցցեն աշխատութիմբ ի վերայ երկրի, և աշխատուցին անեծացի աղգ որ եղեալ են ի մէ[ն]ջ, և կորուսցեն զմեզ և ասասցեն եթէ	44(14):3b რამეთუ ჰყენ მოვკუდეთ, მე და შენ, და განუტინნენ ჯირნი ქუეყანასა ზედა. ყოველნი ნათესავნი, რომელნი არიან გამოსრულნი ჰყენ- გან, გუწყევდენ ჰყენ და თქუან, ვითარმედ:	
	44:4 quoniam omnia mala intulerunt nobis parentes nostri, qui ab initio fuerunt. 44:5 haec audiens Eva coepit lacrimare et ingemescere. [III+***legenda de ligno crucis***]III.	44(14):4 Հայր մեր և մայր մեր ածին զ[չարիս զայս] ի վերայ մեր.	44(14):4 "მამა- დედათა ჰყენთა მოიღეს ჯირი ესე ჰყენ ზედა".	

Pericope 16 *Adam's Rebuke of Eve* 47E

GREEK	LATIN	ARMENIAN	GEORGIAN	SLAVONIC
14:2 And Adam said to Eve: "O Eve, What have you done to us? You have brought great wrath upon us which is death which will rule over our entire race."	44:2 Adam said to Eve: "What have you done? You have brought on us a great affliction, fault and sin unto all our generations. What you have done will be passed on to your children after my death,	44(14):2 and he said to Eve, "Oh, what did you do? What sort of pain did you bring upon us and upon our seed?	44(14):2 and he told Eve, "What has been done with us? For an evil has come upon us and upon all our descendants.	
14:3 And Adam said to Eve: "Call all our children and the children of our children and tell them the manner of our transgression."		44(14):3a Now, then, tell your children how the sin took place; for, behold, I am weakened unto the exhaustion of my strength.	44(14):3a Indeed, tell your children what your sins are:	
	44:3 for those who arise from us will not have all they need from their labors, but will be lacking. They will curse us, saying:	44(14):3b For, perhaps, when we die, toils will come upon the earth and all the generations who will issue from u[s] will labor. And they will curse us and say,	44(14):3b for we will die, you and I, and misfortunes will spread over the earth. All the descendants who have come forth from us will curse us saying,	
	44:4 "Our parents, who were from the beginning, brought all these evils on us.'"	44(14):4 'Our father and our mother brought [these evils] upon us.'"	44(14):4 'It was our father and mother who brought this misfortune upon us.'"	
	44:5 Hearing this, Eve began to weep and moan. [***III + Legend of the Wood of the Cross***]			

Pericope 17 EVE'S TALE: *Portions of Adam and Eve*

GREEK	LATIN	ARMENIAN	GEORGIAN	SLAVONIC
15:1 Τότε λέγει ἡ Εὔα πρὸς αὐτούς· Ἀκούσατε, πάντα τὰ τέκνα μου καὶ τὰ τέκνα τῶν τέκνων μου, κἀγὼ ἀναγγελῶ ὑμῖν πῶς ἠπάτησεν ἡμᾶς ὁ ἐχθρός.	[44](15):1 Ժամանակի լայ ականս նա, եւ ասէ. Եկայք լուարուք իմձ եւ պատմեցից ձեզ զառակս զայս, որպէս զիարդ եղեն յանցանք մեր:	[44](15):1 მაშინ ტიროდა იგი-ყო ევა და თქუა: "ისმინეთ ჩემი, შვილნო ჩემნო, და გითხრა თქუენ, ვითარ შეგვცთუნვნეთ:.	18-20.1 Събравшимъ се чедомъ кго, и бысть въсѣхъ числомь двѣ хилиадѣ людеи, и въпросише глаголюще · о мати наша, ты вьса знакши отьца нашего Адама съкровеньна и объявлкньна, повѣждъ намъ, мати наша, чьто се дивьнок видимь; 18-20.2 тогда Кквга рече · прѣпоручаю вамь, чеда моя, яко прѣльсти насъ врагъ, да не прѣльстить и васъ прѣзь законъ нашъ.
15:2 Ἐγένετο ἐν τῷ φυλάσσειν ἡμᾶς τὸν παράδεισον, [ἐφυλάττομεν] ἕκαστος ἡμῶν τὸ λαχόν τι αὐτῷ μέρος ἀπὸ τοῦ θεοῦ· ἐγὼ δὲ ἐφύλαττον ἐν τῷ κλήρῳ μου νότον καὶ δύσιν.	[44](15):2 ի ժամանակին յորժամ պահէր հայր ձեր զվիճակ բաժանի իւրոյ զոր տուեալ էր նմա յԱստուծոյ, եւ ես պահէր իմում վիճակին ի կողմանէ հարաւոյ [եւ արեւմտից]	[44](15):2 და ოდეს ვამი თქუენი სცვიდა თვისსა სამოთხისა ნაწილსა ლმოსავალით და ჩრდილოთ, ხოლო მე ვსცევდი თვისსა ნაწილსა დასავა-ლით და სამხრით.	18-20.3 Адамъ блюдѣше раи отъ въсточьнык страны и сѣверьною страну, азъ же събљюдахъ западьною и пладьноую страну .
15:3 Ἐπορεύθη δὲ ὁ διάβολος εἰς τὸν κλῆρον τοῦ Ἀδάμ, ὅπου ἦν τὰ θηρία,	[44](15):3 գնաց Սատանայ ի վիճակ հաւր ձերոյ, ուր էին գազանքն, կոչեաց զամնն եւ ասէ գնա. Արի եկ դու առ իս.	[44](15):3 და მოვიდა ეშმაკი ნაწილსა ადამისასა. და ოყვნეს მუნ მხეცნი.	
15:4 ἐπειδὴ τὰ θηρία ἐμέρισεν ὁ θεός, τὰ ἀρσενικὰ πάντα δέδωκε τῷ πατρὶ ὑμῶν καὶ τὰ θηλυκὰ πάντα δέδωκεν ἐμοί. [καὶ ἕκαστος ἡμῶν τὸ ἑαυτοῦ ἐτήρει.]	[44](15):4 քանզի գգազանս բաժանեաց Աստուած եւ իւր մեզ գարուսն իւր հաւր ձերոյ եւ գէգուսն իւր ինձ, եւ սնուցանէաք մէք լուռ իւրաքանչիւր որում հասեալ էր	[44](15):4 რამეთუ მხეცთაცა განგვყუბნა უფალმა: მამალი ყოველი მისცა ადამ და დედალი ყოველი მომცა მე. და თვითოეულად ვზრდიდით მათ.	18-20.4 Адамь сьблюдаше звѣри мужьскыи поль, азъ же събљюдахъ звѣри женьскыи поль .

Pericope 17 EVE'S TALE: *Portions of Adam and Eve* 48E

GREEK	LATIN	ARMENIAN	GEORGIAN	SLAVONIC
15:1 Then said Eve to them: "Hear all my children and children's children and I will relate to you how the enemy deceived us.		[44](15):1 Then Eve began to weep and said, "Come near me and I will tell you this way, how our sin took place.	[44](15):1 Then Eve began to cry and she said, "Now hearken to me, my children, and I will tell you how we were tricked.	18-20.1 When all his children had assembled themselves--and they were altogether nearly two thousand people--they bid Eve, saying, "Our Mother, you know every secret and open thing of our father Adam, tell us, our mother, what does this incredible manifestation which we see mean?" 18-20.2 Then Eve said, "I will share with you, my children, in what manner our enemy deceived us, so that he will not be able to incite you as well against our law.
15:2 It befell that we were guarding the Garden, each of us [was guarding] the portion allotted to us from God. Now I guarded in my lot, the west and the south.		[44](15):2 At the time when your father was guarding the lot of his portion which had been given to him by God and I was guarding in my lot, at the southern [and western side],	[44](15):2 It happened, (then), that your father was guarding his portion of the Garden, the east and the north, while I was guarding my own portion, the west and the south.	18-20.3 Adam watched the eastern and northern sides of Paradise, I guarded the western and southern side.'
15:3 But the Devil went to Adam's lot, where the male creatures were.		[44](15):3 Satan went to your father's lot, where the wild beasts were. He summoned the serpent and said to him, 'Arise, come to me!'	[44](15):3 And the Devil came to Adam's portion. And there were beasts there,	
15:4 For God divided the creatures; all the males he gave to your father and all the females he gave to me. [Each of us guarded his own portion.]		[44](15):4 For God had divided the wild beasts and given them to us—the male ones he gave to your father and the female ones he gave to me. We used to nourish them according to whichever of us it had been allotted.	[44](15):4 for the Lord had also divided the beasts between us. All (that were) male He had given to Adam, and all (that were) female, He had given to me. And we each fed our own ones.	18-20.4 Adam guarded the male animals, I tended the female animals.

Pericope 18 EVE'S TALE: *Satan and the Serpent* (Gen 3:1a)

GREEK	LATIN	ARMENIAN	GEORGIAN	SLAVONIC
16:1 Καὶ ἐλάλησε τῷ ὄφει ὁ διάβολος λέγων· 'Ανάστα, ἐλθὲ πρός με [καὶ εἴπω σοι ῥῆμα ἐν ᾧ ὠφειληθῇς.] Καὶ ἀναστὰς ἦλθε πρὸς αὐτόν.		[44](16):1 *bi aut Statnalaj gaidū. Arļi ek dņi at ļu bi aabū ṗeq ṗaū ifi ḳiś, ņ ra∫ lfiūļi ṗeq.*	[44](16):1 ოდეს მოვიდა ეშმაკი ნაწლოსა მას მადის თჳუენისასა, მოუწოდა ეშმაკმან გუელსა მას და ჰრქუა:" ადეგ და მოვედ ჩემდა და გაუწყო შენ სარგებელი სიტყვისაი".	18-20.5 и тако вьниде дия воль вь страноу оноу, отъ коудоу бѣше Адамъ, и призьва змию къ себѣ и рече ки ты ѥси любовьна оу бога, та ра(зв ѣ) всѣхь вещеи тебѣ хощеть вѣровати.
16:2 Καὶ λέγει αὐτῷ ὁ διάβολος· 'Ακούω ὅτι φρονιμώτερος εἶ ὑπὲρ πάντα τὰ θηρία. ['Εγὼ δὲ ἦλθον κατανοῆσαί σε· εὗρον δέ σε μείζονα πάντων τῶν θηρίων] καὶ ὁμιλῶ σοι· [ὅπως προσκυνεῖς τὸν ἐλαχιστότερον]		[44](16):2a *Θայսմ̄ա̄ ekū at fu aidū, bi aut glīū Statnalaj. Lībū qi pūmasuum bū qni ṗaū qalbūsajū qaqasīū, bi bu ekfi ūbuwbej qṗeq [bi qaṁ qṗeq jambīnajū qaqasīū]. qi čiṗ īmaū ḫaūšaqnoj od. uṗajfu bi Asaū taṗi ebaqnr ambīnajū qaqasaq. nojūbu bi qni:* [44](16):2b *bi aṗaū jojmaū qūasfū qaqasū bṗkṗ ṗaqasbj Asaū lasa bi aut gasdū. Gnē ū qņ bṗkṗ ṗaqasbū Asaū ambīnajū asauat. karaq qni bu beqbaj ṗaū qūas. qīaū od bṗkṗ ṗaqasbū ataqṗūq įinunj, aj aṗaupi ē iṗoṗū bṗkṗ ṗaqasbj atasaṗū.*	[44](16):2a მაშინ მოვიდა გუელი იგი და ჰრქუა ეშმაკმან გუელსა მას, ვითარმედ:" უბრძნეს ხარ შენ ყოველთა პირუტყუთა და მოსრულ ვარ განცდად მეცნიერებისა შენისა, რამეთუ ადამან მისცის სახელებთა ყოველთა პირუტყუთა, ევრეცა შენ ზედა, [44](16):2b ოდესიგი მოვიდიან ყოველბო პირუტყუნი თაყუანის-ცემად ადამისა დღითი-დღე და ღლითი-დღედ, ყოველსა დღესა მიხვიდე შენცა თაყუანის-ცემად. პირველად მისსა შენ დაბადებული ხარ, ღიდი ესე, და კნინსა მას თაყუანის-სცემ!	

Pericope 18 EVE'S TALE: *Satan and the Serpent* (Gen 3:1a)

GREEK	LATIN	ARMENIAN	GEORGIAN	SLAVONIC
16:1 And the Devil spoke to the serpent saying, "Rise up, come to me [and I will tell you a word whereby you may have profit]." And he arose and came to him.		[44](16):1 Satan said to the serpent, 'Arise, come to me and I will tell you something which is of profit to you.'	[44](16):1 When the Devil came to your father's portion the Devil summoned the serpent and told him,"Arise and come to me, and I will teach you a useful word."	18-20.5 And so the enemy entered in from that side on which Adam was, and he called the serpent to himself and said to it, 'You are loved by God, therefore she (Eve) will give credence to you before any other creature.'
16:2 And the Devil said to him: "I hear that you are wiser than all the beasts, [I have come to observe you. I have found you greater than all the animals] and I have come to converse with you. [Nevertheless you worship the lesser.]		[44](16):2a Then the serpent came to him and Satan said to it, 'I hear that you are wiser than all the wild animals and I have come to see you. [I found] that there is none like [you] in your cunning [among all the animals]. Even as Adam gave nourishment to all the wild beasts, so also you did."	[44](16):2a Then, the serpent came and the Devil told the serpent, "I ([hear)] that you are wiser than all the animals and I have come to test your knowledge, for Adam gives food to all the animals, thus also to you.	
		[44](16):2b And then, when the wild beasts went to worship Adam, Satan went with them and said to the serpent, 'Why do you worship Adam every morning? You came into being before him: why is it that you, who are the former one, worship the later? Rather should the younger worship the older.	[44](16):2b When then all the animals come to bow down before Adam from day to day and from morning to morning, every day, you also come to bow down. You were created before him, as old (as you) are, and you bow down before this younger one!	

Pericope 18 EVE'S TALE: *Satan and the Serpent* (Gen 3:1a)

GREEK	LATIN	ARMENIAN	GEORGIAN	SLAVONIC
16:3 Διὰ τί ἐσθίεις ἐκ τῶν ζιζανίων τοῦ Ἀδὰμ [καὶ τῆς γυναικὸς αὐτοῦ καὶ οὐχὶ]ἐκ τοῦ παραδείσου; Ἀνάστα καὶ ποιήσωμεν αὐτὸν ἐκβληθῆναι ἐκ τοῦ παραδείσου ὡς καὶ ἡμεῖς ἐξεβλήθημεν δι' αὐτοῦ.		[44](16):3 ընդէ՞ր երկիր պաշանես. կամ կերակրիս դու յնասիայ, եւ ոչ կերակրիս դու ի պտղոյ դրախտին։ Աղէ. արի, եկ դու ատ ի, եւ յուր դիր քեզ ասեմ քեզ. Հանցուք զնա ի դրախտէս, որպէս զմեզ. զի զարձաք մեք մտցուք ի դրախտ անդր։	[44](16):3 და რაისა სჭამ ნარჩევსა ადამისსა და ცოლისა მისისასა, და არა ნაყოფთა კეთილთა სამოთხისათა? აღდეგ მოვედ და ისმინე ჩემი რაითა გამოვჰხადოთ ადამ გარეშე ზღუდესა სამოთხისასა, ვითარცა ჩუენ გარე ვართ. და, ვინ უწყის, ვითარ ჩუენ ნუუკუე შევიდეთ სამოთხესა".	
16:4a Λέγει αὐτῷ ὁ ὄφις· Φοβοῦμαι μήποτε ὀργισθῇ μοι ὁ θεός.		[44](16):4a եւ ասէ ասէն. Պիղէս եւ կամ գին՞ որ մարթասցուք հանել զնա ի դրախտէն։	[44](16):4a და ჰრქუა გუელმან: "ვითარ გამოვჰხადოთ?"	
16:4b Λέγει αὐτῷ ὁ διάβολος· Μὴ φοβοῦ· γενοῦ μοι σκεῦος κἀγὼ λαλήσω διὰ στόματός σου ῥήματα πρὸς τὸ ἐξαπατῆσαι αὐτούς.		[44](16):4b Ասէ Սատանայ ցասն. Լեր դու ինձ ի կերպս քո քաս, եւ ես խասեցայց ընդ բերան քո քան. որպէս մարթասցուք մեք ատել։	[44](16):4b მიჰუგო ეშმაკმან და ჰრქუა გუელსა მას: "საკუთრველ მექმენ და მე ვეტყუელ დედაკაცსა მას პირითა შენითა სიტყუათა, რომლითა შევა-ტყუთ".	18-20.6 и наꙋчи ю вьсе и посьла ю кь мьнѣ .

Pericope 18 **EVE'S TALE:** *Satan and the Serpent* (Gen 3:1a)

GREEK	LATIN	ARMENIAN	GEORGIAN	SLAVONIC
16:3 Why do you eat of the tares of Adam [and his wife and not] of the Garden? Rise up and we will cause him to be cast out of the Garden, even as we were cast out through him."		[44](16):3 Why do you worship (Adam) or (why) are you fed by Adam and are not fed by the fruit of the Garden? Come on, rise up, come to me and hear what I say to you. Let us expel Adam from the Garden like us so that we may re-enter the Garden.'	[44](16):3 And why do you eat (food) inferior [to Adam's and his spouse's and not the good fruit of the Garden? But come and hearken to me so that we may have Adam expelled from the wall of the Garden just as we are outside. Perhaps we can reenter somehow to the Garden."	
16:4a The serpent said to him, "I fear lest the Lord be wroth with me."		[44](16):4a The serpent said, 'In what way or how can we expel him from the Garden?'	[44](16):4a And the serpent told him, "How can we have them excluded?"	
16:4b The Devil said to him: "Fear not, only be my vessel and I will speak through your mouth words to deceive them."		[44]16:4b Satan said to the serpent, 'Be you, in your form, a lyre for me and I will pronounce speech through your mouth, so that we may be able to help."	[44]16:4b The Devil replied and told the serpent, "Be a sheath for me and I will speak to the woman through your mouth a word by which we will trick them."	18-20.6 And he instructed it in everything and sent it to me.

Pericope 19 EVE'S TALE: *Serpent's Approach* (Gen 3:1b-3)

GREEK	LATIN	ARMENIAN	GEORGIAN	SLAVONIC
17:1 Καὶ εὐθέως ἐκρεμάσθη ἐκ τῶν τειχέων τοῦ παραδείσου. Καὶ ὅτε ἀνῆλθον οἱ ἄγγελοι τοῦ θεοῦ προσκυνῆσαι, τότε ὁ Σατανᾶς ἐγένετο ἐν εἴδει ἀγγέλου καὶ ὕμνει τὸν θεὸν καθάπερ οἱ ἄγγελοι.		[44](17):1 *bկpս ալունչեստու երկրեանն ատ իս, եւ կախեցին զոտս իւրեանց զորմով դրախտին: Իրրեւ վերացան հրեշտակքն յերկրպագութիւն Տեառն, եւ յայնժամ եղեւ Սատանայ ի կերպս հրեշտակի եւ ալրնէէր զննտուած գալրնութիւնս հրեշտակաց. խոնարհեցաւ եւ ատ որմուն, եւ մին դնէր ալրնութեանց նորալ.*	[44](17):1 და მოვიდეს ორივე ერთად, დაამჴკიდეს თავი მათი ზღუდესა სამოთხისასა, მას ჟამსა, ოდეს აღვიდეს ანგელოზნი თაყუანის-ცემად ღმრთისა, მაშინ გარდაიქცა ეშმაკი იგი ხატად ანგელოზისად, გალობდა გალობთა ანგელოზთაითა და მე ვიჯვირობდი ზღუდელ მიმართ სამოთხისა-ად სმენად გალობისად.	18-20.7 змия мьнѣщи, яко аггель ѥсть, и прииде кь мьнѣ.
17:2 Καὶ παρέκυψεν ἐκ τοῦ τείχους καὶ εἶδον αὐτὸν ὅμοιον ἀγγέλου.		[44](17):2a *Հայեցալ եւ տեսի զնա ի նմանութին հրեշտակի. դարձեալ իրրեւ Հայեցալ եւ ոչ տեսի զնա:*	[44](17):2a განვიცადე და ვიხილე იგი მსგავსად ანგელოზისა. და მეყ-სეულად ყინომ იქმნა,	18-20.8a и диявол сьтвори сѥ аггельскымь образомь и прииде свѣтль велико, поющє пѣснь аггельскую, яко и аггель.
		[44](17):2b *Գնաց ալունչեստու եւ կոչեաց գամձն, եւ աստ զնա. Արի եկ դու ատ իս զի մինչց ի քեզ եւ խատացցալց ընդ բերան քո, որչափ եւ ալարտ իցէ իմձ խասնեցի:*	[44](17):2b რამეთუ წარვიდა იგი მოყუანებად გუელისა მის და ჰრქუა მას:" აღდეგ და მოვედ და ვიყო მე შენ თანა და ვიტყოდი მე პირთა შენითა, რაი ჯერ-არს სიტყუად შენდა".	

Pericope 19 **EVE'S TALE:***Serpent's Approach* (Gen 3:1b-3) 51E

GREEK	LATIN	ARMENIAN	GEORGIAN	SLAVONIC
17:1 And instantly he hung himself from the wall of the Garden, and when the angels ascended to worship God, then Satan appeared in the form of an angel and sang hymns like the angels.		[44](17):1 Then the two of them came to me and hung their feet around the wall of the Garden. When the angels ascended to the worship of the Lord, at that time Satan took on the form of an angel and began to praise God with angelic praises. I knelt down by the wall and attended to his praises.	[44](17):1 And the two of them came together and they allowed their heads to hang on the wall of the Garden at the time when the angels had ascended to prostrate before God. Then the Devil changed himself into the image of an angel; he sang the praises of the angels. And I was gazing in the direction of the wall to hear the praises.	18-20.7 The serpent believed that it was an angel, and came to me.
17:2a And he bent over the wall and I saw him, like an angel.		[44](17):2a I looked and saw him in the likeness of an angel; when I looked again, I did not see him.	[44](17):2a I stared, and I saw him like an angel and at once he became invisible	18-20.8a And the Devil had changed to the form of an angel and came here with radiance, singing an angel's song, just like an angel,
		[44](17):2b Then he went and summoned the serpent and said to him, 'Arise, come to me so that I may enter into you and speak through your mouth as much as I will need to say.'	[44](17):2b for he had gone forth to bring the serpent. And he told him, 'Arise and come and I will be with you and I will speak through your mouth that which is proper for you to say.']	

Pericope 19 EVE'S TALE: *Serpent's Approach* (Gen 3:1b-3)

GREEK	LATIN	ARMENIAN	GEORGIAN	SLAVONIC
		[44](17):2c ծայլժամ եղև նմա սիրտ ևւ բանի, ևւ եկն դարձեալ ի պարիսպ դրախտին, աղաղակեաց ևւ ասէ. Ով կին, դու որ ի դրախտիդ փափկութեան կուրացեալ ես. արի եկ դու առ իս ևւ ասացից քեզ բանս ինչ:	[44](17):2c სასჱ ექმნა მას გუელი იგი ზრუდისა სამოთხისად. და შთა- ცუა გუელსა მას ეშმაკი, შთამოჰკიდა თავი თვისი ზღუდესა მას სამოთხი-სასა, ღაღად-ყო და თქუა: "ჰაი შენდა დედაკაცო, რომელი-ეგე ხარ სამო-თხესა ფუფუნებისასა. რომელი-იგი ბრმა ხარ, მოვედ ჩემდა და გარქუ რაიმე სიტყუაი საიდუმლოი".	
Καὶ λέγει μοι· Σὺ εἶ ἡ Εὕα; Καὶ εἶπον αὐτῷ· Ἐγώ εἰμι. Καὶ λέγει μοι· Τί ποιεῖς ἐν τῷ παραδείσῳ;		[44](17):2d ես իբրև գնացի առ նա, ասէ ցիս. Դու ե՞ս Եվա. եւ ասացի. Այո, ես եմ: Պատասխանի ետ եւ ասէ. Զի՞նչ գործես ի [դրախտի] այդր.	[44](17):2d და ვითარ მივედ, მრქუა მე: "ევა!" და ვარქუ: "აჰა ესერა ვარ". მომიგო და მრქუა მე: "რასა ზამ შენ სამოთხესა შინა?"	
17:3 Καὶ εἶπον αὐτῷ· Ὁ θεὸς ἔθετο ἡμᾶς ὥστε φυλάσσειν καὶ ἐσθίειν ἐξ αὐτοῦ.		[44](17):3 Ասեմ ցնա. Աստուած եդ զմեզ ի դրախտի պահապանութեան:	[44](17):3 მიუგე და ვარქუ: "ღმერთმან დამადგინა ცვად სამოთხისა და ჭამად".	
17:4 Ἀπεκρίθη ὁ διάβολος διὰ στόματος τοῦ ὄφεως· Καλῶς ποιεῖτε, ἀλλ' οὐκ ἐσθίετε ἀπὸ παντὸς φυτοῦ.		[44](17):4 Պատասխանի ետ Սատանայ եւ ասէ ցիս ընդ բերան աւձին. Բարի է գործդ. բայց աղէ ուտէք դուք [զամենայն] ծառոցդ որ ի դրախտի աստէն:	[44](17):4 მომიგო ეშმაკმან მან და მრქუა მე ჰოროთა გუელისათა: კეთილად სჭამთ თქუენ ნაყოფსა ყოვლისაგან ხისა, რომელ არს სამოთხე- სა მას შინა?"	18-20.8b и рече кь мьнѣ: вьса ли раиская сьнѣдоуете;

Pericope 19 EVE'S TALE:*Serpent's Approach* (Gen 3:1b-3)   52E

GREEK	LATIN	ARMENIAN	GEORGIAN	SLAVONIC
		[44](17):2c At that time the serpent became a lyre for him, and he came again to the wall of the Garden. He cried out and said, 'Oh, woman, you who are blind in this Garden of delight, arise come to me and I will say some words to you.'	[44](17):2c He took on the form of the serpent (to go) close to the wall of the Garden and the Devil slipped inside the serpent and he allowed his head to hang on the wall of the Garden. He cried out and said, 'Shame on you, woman, you who are in the the Garden of delight (and) who are blind! Come to me and I will tell you a certain secret word.'	
And he said to me: "Are you Eve? "And I said to him, "I am." And he said to me, "What do you do in the Garden?"		[44](17):2d When I went to him, he said to me, 'Are you Eve?' I said, 'Yes, I am.' He replied and said, 'What do you do in [the Garden]?'	[44](17):2d And when I had come, he said to me, 'Eve!' and I said to him, 'Here I am.' He replied to me and told me, 'What do you do in the Garden?"	
17:3 And I said to him, "God set us to guard and to eat of it."		[44](17):3 I said to him, 'God set us to guard the Garden',	[44](17):3 I replied to him and told him, 'God has set me to guard the Garden and eat (of it).'	
17:4 The Devil answered through the mouth of the serpent: "You do well but you do not eat of every plant."		[44](17):4 Satan replied and said to me through the mouth of the serpent, 'This work is good, but come, do you eat of [all] the trees which are in the Garden?'	[44](17):4 The Devil replied to me and told me through the mouth of the serpent, 'Well (done!) Do you eat the fruit of every tree which is in the Garden?'	18-20.8b and said to me: 'Do you eat from everything in Paradise?'

Pericope 19 EVE'S TALE: *Serpent's Approach* (Gen 3:1b-3)

GREEK	LATIN	ARMENIAN	GEORGIAN	SLAVONIC
17:5 Κἀγὼ εἶπον· Ναί, ἀπὸ πάντων ἐσθίομεν, παρὲξ ἑνὸς μόνου ὅ ἐστι μέσον τοῦ παραδείσου περὶ οὗ ἐνετείλατο ἡμῖν ὁ θεὸς μὴ ἐσθίεν ἐξ αὐτοῦ, ἐπεὶ θανάτῳ ἀποθανεῖσθε.		[44](17):5 Ասեմ Այո, յամենայնէ կերակրիմք, բայց միայն ի միոջէն ծառոյ որ է հուկ ի մէջ դրախտին, վասն որոյ պատուիրեաց Աստուած մեզ թէ մի կերակրիք ի նմանէ. ապա եթէ ուտիցէք մահու մեռանիջիք.	[44](17):5 მოუგე და ვარქუ:" მე, ვჭამთ ყოველისავე ნაყოფსა, გარნა ერ- თისა მის ხისა, რომელ არს შუა სამოთხესა ამას, რამეთუ ღმერთმან გუამცნო ჩუენ, ვითარმედ ნუ სჭამთ მისგანსა, რაითა არა სიკუდილითა მოკუდეთ".	18-20.9 азь мнѣщи, яко аггель ѥсть, понѥже прииде отъ Адамовы страны, и глаголахъ кь нѥмоу · ѥдино дрѣво речє намъ господь не ясти, ѥже ѥсть по срѣдѣ рая.

Pericope 19 EVE'S TALE: *Serpent's Approach* (Gen 3:1b-3)

GREEK	LATIN	ARMENIAN	GEORGIAN	SLAVONIC
17:5 And I said: "Yea, we eat of all, save one only, which is in the middle of the Garden, concerning which, God charged us not to eat of it, for, you shall die the death."		[44](17):5 I said to him, 'Yes, we eat of all of them except only of that one tree which is in the very middle of the Garden, concerning which God commanded us, "Do not eat of it, for if you eat you will surely die."'	[44](17):5 I replied to him and told him, 'Yes, [we] eat all the fruit except for only one tree which is here in the middle of the Garden, for God ordered us, 'Do not eat of it, so that you will not die a death.'	18-20.9 And at that time I took him for an angel, because he had come from Adam's side, so I said to him, 'From one tree the Lord commanded us not to eat, the one which stands in the middle of Paradise.'

Pericope 20 EVE'S TALE: *Temptation of Eve* (Gen 3:4-6b)

GREEK	LATIN	ARMENIAN	GEORGIAN	SLAVONIC
18:1 Τότε λέγει μοι ὁ ὄφις· Ζῇ ὁ θεὸς ὅτι λυποῦμαι περὶ ὑμῶν· [ὅτι ὡς κτήνη ἐστέ.] οὐ γὰρ θέλω ὑμᾶς ἀγνοεῖν. Δεῦρο οὖν καὶ φάγε νόησον τὴν τιμὴν τοῦ ξύλου.		[44](18):1 Ցայնժամ ասէ առն. Կենդան է Տէր, զի մեծ հոգամ վասն [ձեր] զի իբրեւ անասուն էք, վասն զի խորհուրդ Աստուծոյ ի ձէնջ, այլ ոչ կամիմ ես եթէ տգէտք լինիցիք. արդ ցնա դու եւ կեր ի ծառոյ անտի. եւ տեսանեմ զինչ լինելոց է քեզ պատուի։	[44](18):1 მაშინ მრქუა გუელმან მან: "ჰკჳვე მე ოჳკუებთვის, რამეთუ ხართ თქუენ ვითარცა პირუტყუნი. შურდა თქუენი ღმერთისა და არა ვათუ-ლნა თქუენ, ხოლო მე არა მნებავს უმეცრებაი თქუენი, არამედ მოვედ და ჭამე და იხილო დიდებულებაი იგი, რომელ ყოფად არს შენ თანა".	18-20.10 Дияволь рече · много жалю васъ, понеже не разоумѣюта ничьто, нь си глаголю вамь · то дрѣво ѥсть блажає вьсѣхь дрѣвь.
18:2 Ἐγὼ δὲ εἶπον αὐτῷ· Φοβοῦμαι μήποτε ὀργισθῇ μοι ὁ θεὸς καθὼς εἶπεν ἡμῖν.		[44](18):2 Եւ ասեմ ցնա. Երկնչիմ գուցէ մեռանիմ որպէս ասաց ցմեզ Աստուած։	[44](18):2 ხოლო მე ვარქუ: "მეშინის მე, ნუუკუე მოვკუდე, ვითარცა თქუა უფლთმან".	
18:3 Καὶ λέγει μοι· Μὴ φοβοῦ· ἄμα γὰρ φάγῃς, ἀνοιχθήσονται σου οἱ ὀφθαλμοὶ καὶ ἔσεσθε ὡς θεοὶ γινώσκοντες τί ἀγαθὸν καὶ τί πονηρόν.		[44](18):3 Պատասխանի ետ առն Հանդերձ Սատանայիւ եւ ասէ ցիս. Կենդանի է Տէր, զի ոչ մեռանիք, այլ որժամ կերակիք բանին աչք ձեր եւ լինիցիք որպէս զԱստուած ճանաչել զբարի եւ զչար։	[44](18):3 მომიგო გუელმან მან და მრქუა: "რაოდენ სიკუდილო, ანუ ვითარ მოკუდეთ? სიკუდილო ცხორებაი არს". მიუგვე და ვარქუ: "არა უწყი მე". მომიგო და მრქუა: "ცხოველ არს უფალი, რაითა არა მოჰკუდეთ, არამედ რომელსა ჟამსა სჭამოთ, განებუენენ თუალნი თქუენნი და იცნეთ მეცნიერ, ვითარცა უფალი, კეთილისა და ბოროტისა".	18-20.11 аще сьнѣсте оть дрѣва того, то яко бози бѫдете и свѣтли бѫдете яко и аггели.

Pericope 20 EVE'S TALE: *Temptation of Eve* (Gen 3:4-6b)

GREEK	LATIN	ARMENIAN	GEORGIAN	SLAVONIC
18:1 Then the serpent said to me, "As God lives! I am grieved on your account [that you are like animals,] for I would not have you ignorant. Come hither and eat and perceive the honor of that tree."		[44](18):1 Then the serpent said, 'As the Lord lives, I am greatly concerned about [you] for you are like beasts, since God has withheld (it) from you, but I do not wish you to be ignorant. Come on, come and eat of the tree, and you see what honour will be yours.'	[44](18):1 Then the serpent told me, 'I am distressed for you, for you are like the animals. God was jealous of you and he has not permitted you, but as for me, I do not desire your ignorance. Rather come, eat and you will see the glory which is to be with you.'	18-20.10 The Devil said, 'I am very sorry for you, because you don't understand, but I will tell you this: that tree is better than all the others.
18:2 But I said to him, "I fear lest God be angry with me as he told us."		[44](18):2 I said to him, 'I fear lest I die as God said to us.'	[44](18):2 However, I told him, 'I am afraid of dying, perhaps, as God said.'	
18:3 And he said to me: "Fear not, for as soon as you eat of it your eyes will be opened and you too shall be as gods knowing what is good and what is evil.		[44](18):3 The serpent, together with Satan, replied and said to me, 'As the Lord lives, you (will) not die, but when you eat, your eyes (will be) opened and you will become like God, knowing good and evil.	[44](18):3 The serpent replied to me and told me, 'What is death and how does one die? Death is life!' I replied to him and told him, 'I do not know.' He replied to me and told me, 'God is living, just thus you (pl.) will not die, but at the moment when you (pl.) eat, your eyes will be opened and you will be instructed, like God, about good and evil.	18-20.11 If you taste from that tree, you would become like gods and radiant like the angels.'

GREEK	LATIN	ARMENIAN	GEORGIAN	SLAVONIC
18:4 Τοῦτο δὲ γινώσκων ὁ θεὸς ὅτι ἔσεσθε ὅμοιοι αὐτοῦ ἐφθόνησεν ὑμῖν καὶ εἶπεν· Οὐ φάγεσθαι ἐξ αὐτοῦ.		[44](18):4 *·այց գիտ[աց] Աստուած եթէ նմանողք լինիք նմա. նենգեաց ձեզ, զի ասաց եթէ մի կերակրիք ի նմանէ.*	[44](18):4 უწყოდა ღმერთმან, რამეთუ მსგავს მისა იქნებოდით და შურ- და ღმერთსა თქუენი, მისთვის გრქუა თქუენ ღმერთმან, ვითარმედ: ნუ სჭამთ მისგანსა.	
18:5 Σὺ δὲ πρόσχες τῷ φυτῷ καὶ ὄψει δόξαν μεγάλην. ['Εγὼ δὲ προσέσχον τῷ φυτῷ καὶ εἶδον δόξαν μεγάλην περὶ αὐτοῦ. Εἶπον δὲ αὐτῷ ὅτι ὡραῖον τοῖς ὀφθαλμοῖς κατανοῆσαι.]		[44](18):5 *եւ ասէ. Հայեաց դու ի ծառն եւ տես զինչ փառք են շուրջ զծառովն։ Ասեմ ցնա. [եւ իբրեւ հայեցայ ի ծառն եւ տեսի զի մեծ փառք էին շուրջ զնովաւ].*	44(18):5 მივედ ხესა მას და იხილე გარეიმოს მისსა დიდებულებაი მისი". ხოლო ვითარცა მივედ და ვიხილე გარემო მისა დიდებულებაი მისი. და ვთქუ:	
18:6 'Εφοβήθην δὲ λαβεῖν ἀπὸ τοῦ καρποῦ. Καὶ λέγει μοι· Δεῦρο καὶ δώσω σοι· ἀκολούθει μοι.		[44](18):6 *Բարի է ծառն եւ հաճոյ թուեցաւ յաչս իմ, բայց զնալ եւ առնուլ ի մրգոյ անտի ոչ կարեմ. երկնչիմ. [ասէ ե]թէ ոչ երկնչիս դու բեր ինձ ի մրգոյ անտի եւ կերայց, զի ծանեայց եթէ իցեն բանք քո ճշմարիտ թէ ոչ. կոչեաց այնուհետեւ աւձն զիս եւ ասէ. Եկ բաց զդուռն ինձ եւ մտից եւ տաց քեզ ի մրգոյ անտի։*	[44](18):6 კეთილ არს ხე ესე და საცნაურ არს თუალთა ჩემთა ნაყოფი მისი, ხოლო მე მიყოფად ხელისა და მოღებად მეშინის, ხოლო შენ თუ არა გეშინის, მომართუ მე და ვჭამო და ვცნა, უკუეთუ ჭეშმარიტ არიან სიტ-ყუანი შენნი ესე. ანუ არა". მომიგო გუელმან მან და მრქუა:" მოვედ და განმიღე მე კარი და გეც შენ მისგანი".	

Pericope 20 **EVE'S TALE:***Temptation of Eve* (Gen 3:4-6b)   55E

GREEK	LATIN	ARMENIAN	GEORGIAN	SLAVONIC
18:4 But God knew that you would be like Him, so he envied you and said, 'You shall not eat of it.'		[44](18):4 But God kn[ew] that you (will) become like him; he deceived you, that he said, "Do not eat of it."'	[44](18):4 God knew that you would become like him and God was jealous of you. Because of that God told you, "Do not eat of it!"	
18:5 But, do give heed to the plant and you will see its great glory." [I gave heed to the plant and saw its great glory. I said to him that it was pleasing to the eyes to look at.]		[44](18):5 And he said, 'Look at the tree and see what glory is around the tree.' When I looked at the tree, I saw (that) great glory was around it. I said to him,	[44](18):5 [Look at] the tree and see the glory around it.' As for me, when I had gone and I had seen its glory around it then I said,	
18:6 Yet I feared to take of the fruit.		[44](18):6 'The tree is good and it looks pleasing to me, but I cannot go and take of the fruit: I am afraid. [Come here! I]f you are not afraid, bring me of the fruit and I will eat, so that I may know whether your words are true or not.'	[44](18):6 'This tree is good and its fruit is worthy of notice in my eyes. However, I am afraid to stretch out my hand and take (it). But you, if you are not afraid, bring it to me and I will eat (of it) and I will know whether your (present) words are true or not.'	
And he said to me: "Come hither, and I will give it you. Follow me."		Then the serpent called to me and said, 'Come, open the gate for me and I will enter and I will give you of the fruit.'	The serpent replied to and told me, 'Come, open the gate and I will give you of it.'	

Pericope 21 EVE'S TALE: *Eve's Oath*

GREEK	LATIN	ARMENIAN	GEORGIAN	SLAVONIC
19:1a Ἤνοιξα δὲ καὶ εἰσῆλθεν ἔσω εἰς τὸν παράδεισον καὶ διώδευσεν ἐμπροσθέν μου. Καὶ περιπατήσας ὀλίγον ἐστράφη καὶ λέγει μοι·		[44](19):1a Իրիւ եկն եմուտ գնաց սակաւիկ մի ի մէջ դրախտին եւ դարձի առ.	[44](19):1a და ვითარ მივედ და განვლე კარი, და ვითარცა შემოვიდა სამოთხე, წარვიდა და დადგა მცირედ.	
		[44](19):1b ասէ եւ. Զի՞ առեր դարձի.	[44](19):1b მიუგე და ვარქუ მას:" რაისა სდგა?" ხოლო მან, შვილნო ჩემნო, იწყო ზაკუად ჩემდა მომართ.	
19:1c Μεταμεληθεὶς οὐ δώσω σοι φαγεῖν. [ταῦτα εἶπε θέλων εἰς τέλος δελεάσαι με. Καὶ λέγει μοι]		[44](19):1c ասէ ցիս. Գուցէ իբրեւ քեզ տամ ուտել, ռանին աչք քո եւ լինիցիս իբրեւ զԱստուած, նենգեցաւ Ադամայ եւ ոչ տաս ուտել նմա ի մրգոյ ասաի եւ լինի նա իբրեւ զաստուած առաջի քո.	[44](19):1c მომიგო და მრქუა:" ადისთვის ვდეგ მე, რამეთუ შევინანე, ნუუკუე შენ გეც, და სჭამო და განგებრენ თუალნი შენნი და იყო შენ ვითარცა ღმერთი და სცნა კეთილი და ბოროტი და განჰვალნე და გუჟრდეს ადამისთვის და არა აჭამო მას და იყოს იგი ვითარცა პირუტყვი შენ წინა- შე, ვითარცა თქუენ იყვენით წინაშე ღმრთისა, რამეთუ შურდა ღმერთისა თქუენი.	

Pericope 21 EVE'S TALE: *Eve's Oath* 56E

GREEK	LATIN	ARMENIAN	GEORGIAN	SLAVONIC
19:1a And I opened (it for him) and he entered the Garden and went before me. He walked a little way, then turned and said to me:		[44](19):1a When he entered, he proceeded a little way into the Garden and stopped.	[44](19):1a And when I had gone to open the gate for him and he had entered the Garden, he went forth, and then he stopped a little.	
		[44](19):1b I said, 'Why did you stop?'	[44](19):1b I replied to him and said, 'Why have you stopped?'	
19:1c "I have changed my mind and I will not give you (something) to eat [These things he said wishing to trap me in the end. And he said to me:]		[44](19):1c He said to me, 'Perhaps, when I shall give you to eat and your eyes are opened and you become like God, you will deceive Adam and will not give him to eat of the fruit and he will become like a beast before you.	[44](19):1c But he, my children, began to use trickery with me. He replied to me and told me, 'If I have stopped it is because I changed my mind for fear that, perhaps if I should give you of it and you eat it, and your eyes will be opened and you will become like God, and you will know good and evil, and you will become prideful and become jealous of Adam and you will not make him eat of it, and he will be like an animal before you, as you were before God, because God was jealous of you.	

Pericope 21 EVE'S TALE: *Eve's Oath*

GREEK	LATIN	ARMENIAN	GEORGIAN	SLAVONIC
19:1d ἐὰν μὴ ὀμόσῃς μοι ὅτι δίδης καὶ τῷ ἀνδρί σου.		[44](19):1d այլ եթէ կամիս դու երդուիր ինձ Հշմարիտ եթէ տացես նմա դուտել եւ ոչ ծածկեսցես առն քո Ադամայ:	[44](19):1d უკეთუ გინებს მეფუცე მე ჭეშმარიტად, ვითარმედ მე თუ გაჭამო შენ, არა გმურდეს ადამისთვის, ქმრისა შენისა, არამედ აჭამო და სცე მასცა".	
19:2 Ἐγὼ δὲ εἶπον αὐτῷ ὅτι οὐ γινώσκω ποίῳ ὅρκῳ ὀμόσω σοι, πλὴν ὃ οἶδα, λέγω σοι· μὰ τὸν θρόνον τοῦ δεσπότου καὶ τὰ χερουβὶμ καὶ τὸ ξύλον τῆς ζωῆς ὅτι δώσω καὶ τῷ ἀνδρί μου.		[44](19):2 Աասեմ ցնա. Զերդումն ես ինչ ոչ գիտեմ թէ որով երդնում [քեզ], բայց դոր գիտեմ ասեմ քեզ. տեսաւք դրախտի եւ քերովբէիւք եւ սերովբէիւք, եւ որ սատր Հայր ի լերկինս եւ իջանել ի դրախտս. թէ կերայց եւ ձանեսայց զամենայն ինչ [ոչ խորհեցից], այլ տաց տունել առն իմում Ադամայ:	[44](19):2 მიუგე და ვარქუ მას:" ფიცა არა ვიცი, ვითარ გეფუცო შენ?" და მარქუა მე:" თქუ, ვფუცავ ჩერგუთა მათ სამოთხისათა და ქებინთა ზედა, ჩომელთა ზედა ზის მამაი, და გარდამოხდის სამოთხესა მას უკეთუ ვჭა-მო და ვცნა ყოველი, არა მურდეს, არამედ ვსცე ადამსცა".	
19:3 Ὅτε δὲ ἔλαβεν ἀπ' ἐμοῦ τὸν ὅρκον, τότε ἦλθε [καὶ ἐπέβη ἐπ' αὐτὸν] καὶ ἔθετο ἐπὶ τὸν καρπὸν ὃν ἔδωκε μοι φαγεῖν τὸν ἰὸν τῆς κακίας αὐτοῦ, τοῦτ' ἐστι τῆς ἐπιθυμίας, ἐπιθυμία γάρ ἐστι κεφαλὴ πάσης ἁμαρτίας. Καὶ κλίνας τὸν κλάδον ἐπὶ τὴν γῆν ἔλαβον ἀπὸ τοῦ καρποῦ καὶ ἔφαγον.		[44](19):3 Իբրեւ երդմամբ ընկալաւ զիս, ապա առաւշրիդրեաց ինձ եւ տարաւ զիս ի ձառ անտուր, եւ եդ ինքն ի ձառ, եւ եդ ևա գնաս[ր]ըտութիւնն ի պտողդ նորա, այսինքն ցանկութիւն մեղաց, պտունկութիւր, շնութիւն, ազահմութիւր. եւ խոնարՀեցոյց դոստա ձառողն, մինչեւ երկիր, եւ առի կայձման ի մրդոյ անտի եւ կերայ:	[44](19):3 და ოდეს მოიღო ჩემ ზედა ფიცი, შემქრა მე, მცა ხისა მისგანი და ვჭამე.	18-20.12a и азь чюхь такова слова и югда сьндохь оть древа того,

Pericope 21 EVE'S TALE: *Eve's Oath*

GREEK	LATIN	ARMENIAN	GEORGIAN	SLAVONIC
19:1d unless you swear to me that you will give also to your husband."		[44](19):1d But you, if you wish, swear to me truly that you will give him to eat, and will not deceive your husband Adam.'	[44](19):1d If you want it, swear to me truly that, if I make you eat it, you will not be jealous of Adam, your husband, but will make him eat of it and give of it also to him.'	
19:2 But I said, "I do not know what sort of oath I should swear to you? Yet what I know, I say to you: By the throne of the Master, and by the Cherubim and the Tree of Life, I will give also to my husband to eat."		[44](19):2 I said to him, 'I do not know any oath by which I can swear [to you], but I will say to you that which I do know: By the plants of the Garden and by the Cherubs and the Seraphs and (by) the Father who sits in the heavens to descend to the Garden, if I eat and learn everything, [I shall not withhold], but I will give to my husband Adam to eat.'	[44](19):2 I replied to him and told him, 'I do not know any oath, how could I swear to you?' And he told me, 'Say: I swear by the plants of the Garden and by the Cherubs upon which the Father sits and (upon which) he descends to the Garden, that if I eat and know all, I will not be jealous but will give of it also to Adam."	
19:3 And when he had received the oath from me, he came [and entered] and placed upon the fruit which he gave me the poison of his wickedness -- which is (the sense of) desire, for it is the beginning of every sin -- and he bent the branch to the earth and I took of the fruit and I ate.		[44](19):3 When he had caught me through an oath, he then led me and brought me to the tree and he went forth to the tree. He set the deception in its fruit, that is desire of sins, harlotries, adulteries, greeds. He lowered the branches of the tree to the earth. Then I took some of the fruit and I ate.	[44](19):3 And when he had made me take the oath, he bound me (to it), gave me of the tree and I ate it.	18-20.12a And I listened to these words and as I tasted from the tree,

Pericope 22 EVE'S TALE: *Eve's Recognition of Sin* (Gen 3:7a)

GREEK	LATIN	ARMENIAN	GEORGIAN	SLAVONIC
20:1 Καὶ ἐν αὐτῇ τῇ ὥρᾳ ἠνεῴχθησαν οἱ ὀφθαλμοί μου καὶ ἔγνων ὅτι γυμνὴ ἤμην τῆς δικαιοσύνης ἧς ἤμην ἐνδεδυμένη. Καὶ ἔκλαυσα λέγουσα·		[44](20):1 Եւ ի ժամուն այնմիկ զբացան իմ աչքր իմոյք էթէ մերկացայ ես ի փառացն զոր զգեցեալ էր. այսուհետև սկսայ լալ եւ ասեմ.		18-20.12b тогда отврьзоста се очи мои и видѣхь яко и нага ѥсмь, и въсплакахь се ѕѣло, чьто сьтворихь. дияволь же невидимь бысть.
20:2 Τί τοῦτο ἐποίησας ὅτι ἀπηλλοτριώθην ἐκ τῆς δόξης μου [ἧς ἤμην ἐνδεδυμένη;]		[44](20):2 Զի՞նչ արարեր ինձ [այլ ոչ ես ճանէր ես վասն մարտին զոր եղեալ էր ինձ] Օշնամի. ժամանեալ զիմացի այսուհետեւ եթէ այս առաջնորդեցէ ինձ յանդունդս դժոխոց.		
20:3 ῎Εκλαιον δὲ καὶ περὶ τοῦ ὅρκου. Ἐκεῖνος δὲ κατῆλθεν ἀπὸ τοῦ φυτοῦ καὶ ἄφαντος ἐγένετο.		[44](20):3 Զայս իբրեւ արար Սատանայ էջ ի ծառոյ անտի, եւ եղեւ թաքստեա ի դրախտին.		18-20.12c диаволь же невидимь бысть.
20:4 ᾿Εγὼ δὲ ἐζήτουν ἐν τῷ μέρει μου φύλλα ὅπως καλύψω τὴν αἰσχύνην μου καὶ οὐχ εὗρον· ἄπαντα γὰρ τὰ φυτὰ τοῦ ἐμοῦ μέρους κατερρύη τὰ φύλλα, παρὲξ τοῦ σύκου μόνου.		[44](20):4 եւ ես խնդրէի ի դրախտին յամեն, լմում կողմանէ տերեւս ծառոց ծածկել զմերկութիւն իմ, եւ ոչ գտանէր, քանզի ի ժամուն այնմիկ տերեւաթափ լեալ էր ամենայն ծառք դրախտին, բայց միայն ի թզենւոյ անտի.	[44](20):4 რო... შიშუელობაი ჩემი და არა ვჰპოვე ყოველთა მათ ხეთა თანა, რამეთუ ჩომელსა ჯამსა ვჰპოვე ყოველთა მათ ხეთა სამოთხისათა, ნაფოტისა ჩემისათა, ფურცელი დაცჳვეოდა.	21-22.1 Азь же сьбирахь листвиѥ смоковьно да покрыю срамоту мою, 21-22.2 понеже яко бѣше раздѣлѥнь раи, половина Адамоу а половина мьнѣ, коѥ дрѣвиѥ бѣше вь мою страноу, вьсе листвиѥ поврьже,
20:5 Λαβοῦσα δὲ φύλλα ἀπ' αὐτοῦ ἐποίησα ἐμαυτῇ περιζώματα· [καὶ ἔστι παρὰ τὸ φυτὸν ἐξ οὗ ἔφαγον.]		[44](20):5a առի եւ ծածկեցի զմերկութիւն իմ. եւ կացի առ ծառոյն յորմէ կերայ.	[44](20):5a მოვედ მისგან და ვქმენ საფარველად ჩემდა და დავღა ხესა მას თანა, რომელისაგან ვჭამე. შელოდნი ჩემო.	21-22.3 смоковьница не поврьже. 21-22.4a и възехь оть листвия и прѣпоясахь се и вьнидохь подь дрѣво,

Pericope 22 EVE'S TALE: *Eve's Recognition of Sin* (Gen 3:7a) 58E

GREEK	LATIN	ARMENIAN	GEORGIAN	SLAVONIC
20:1 And in that very hour my eyes were opened, and I knew that I was naked of the righteousness with which I had been clothed, and I wept and said to him: 20:2 "Why have you done this that I have been deprived of the glory [with which I was clothed]?"		[44](20):1 At that hour I learned with my eyes that I was naked of the glory I with which I had been clothed. Thenceforth, I began to weep and said, [44](20):2 'What did you do to me?' [But I was no longer mortified about the war which (the) enemy had made against me;] then I learned, thenceforth, that he will lead me to the depths of hell.		18-20.12b immediately my eyes were opened and I saw that I was naked, and I cried bitterly about what I had done.
20:3 But I wept also about the oath, which I had sworn. But he descended from the tree and vanished.		[44](20):3 When Satan did this, he descended from the tree and hid in the Garden.		18-20.12c The Devil, however, became invisible.
20:4 And I began to seek, in my nakedness, in my part for leaves to hide my shame, but I found none, for, as soon as I had eaten, the leaves showered down from all the trees in my part, except the fig-tree alone.		[44](20):4 In my parts of the Garden I sought leaves of a tree to cover [my nakedness], and I could not find any on all the trees. For, at that hour all the trees of the Garden became leafless, except for the fig-tree alone.	[44](20):4 [... (I was searching for leaves to cover)...] my nakedness and found none on all the trees, for at the moment at which I had eaten, the leaves from all the trees of the Garden, in my portion, fell down.	21-22.1 I, however, gathered fig leaves to cover my shame. 21-22.2 Because of how Paradise was apportioned, the one half to Adam, and the other to me, all the trees in my half had let fall all their leaves.
20:5 I took leaves from it and made for myself a girdle [and it was from the same plant of which I had eaten].		[44](20):5a I took (its leaves) and covered my nakedness, and I stood by the tree of which I had eaten.	[44](20):5a I took some and made a covering for myself and stood by the tree of which I had eaten, my children.	21-22.3 The fig tree, however, did not do this. 21-22.4a And I took from its leaves and wrapped myself and went under the tree, from which I had tasted,

Pericope 22 EVE'S TALE:*Eve's Recognition of Sin* (Gen 3:7a)

GREEK	LATIN	ARMENIAN	GEORGIAN	SLAVONIC
		[44](20):5b երկեաս որդեակ իմ Մեթ վասն երդմանն զոր երդուայ եթէ տաց ուտել առն իմում Ադամայ։	[44](20):5b შემეშინა ფიცისა მისგან, რომლისგან ვფუცე სამოთხისა რომლისა(!) და ვთქჳ, ვითარმედ ადამსცა ვაჭამო.	

Pericope 22 EVE'S TALE: *Eve's Recognition of Sin* (Gen 3:7a)

GREEK	LATIN	ARMENIAN	GEORGIAN	SLAVONIC
		[44](20):5b I was afraid, my son Seth, because of the oath I swore that I would give my husband Adam to eat.	[44](20):5b I was afraid because of the oath which I had sworn by the Garden and in which I had said, 'I will make Adam eat of it as well.'	

Pericope 23 EVE'S TALE: *Temptation of Adam* (Gen 3:6b-3:7)

GREEK	LATIN	ARMENIAN	GEORGIAN	SLAVONIC
21:1 Καὶ ἐβόησα αὐτῇ τῇ ὥρᾳ λέγουσα· Ἀδάμ, Ἀδάμ, ποῦ εἶ; Ἀνάστα, ἐλθὲ πρὸς με καὶ δείξω σοι μέγα μυστήριον.		[44](21):1 Աղաղակեցի ի ձայն մեծ Ադամայ. Արի եկ առ իս եւ ես ցուցից քեզ զառակս զայս:		21-22.4b отъ нѥгоже сънѣдохъ и възьвахъ гласомь великъмь къ Адамү, глаголю · Адамє, Адамє, гдє ѥси; 21-22.5 въстани и прииди къ мьнѣ, да ти исповѣмь чюдо.
21:2a Ὅτε δὲ ἦλθεν ὁ πατὴρ ὑμῶν		[44](21):2 Յայնժամ Ադամ մեծ փառաւք իւրով եկն առ իս.	[44](21):2a მაშინ მოვიდა მამაი თქუენი ადამ,	
			[44](21):2b ვგრე ვსობა, ვითარმედ მხეცი შემზჴდა სამოთხესა და მარქუა მე:" რასა ჰჴამ, ანუ რაი არს შენ თანა ფურცელი ეგე ლეღვისაი?"	21-22.6a И приидє Адамъ къ мьнѣ,
21:2b εἶπον αὐτῷ λόγους παρανομίας οἵτινες κατήγαγον ἡμᾶς ἀπὸ μεγάλης δόξης.			[44](21):2c მოუგე და ვარქუ:" არა ვნებავს თხრობაი ჩემი, რამეთუ გნე- ბავს ჩემი?ვიყვენით ვიდრე დღეინდელად დღედე. ვითარცა პირუტყუნი.	
21:3 Ἅμα γὰρ ἦλθεν, ἤνοιξα τὸ στόμα μου καὶ ὁ διάβολος ἐλάλει καὶ ἠρξάμην νουθετεῖν αὐτὸν λέγουσα· Δεῦρο κύριέ μου Ἀδὰμ ἐπάκουσόν μου καὶ φάγε ἀπὸ τοῦ καρποῦ τοῦ δένδρου οὗ εἶπεν ἡμῖν ὁ θεὸς τοῦ μὴ φαγεῖν ἀπ' αὐτοῦ καὶ ἔσει ὡς θεός.			[44](21):3 ვითარცა განვიცადე, რომელისა-იგი ვურქუა ჩუენ ყდალმან, ვითარმედ ნუ შჴამთ მისგანსა, და ვიხილე დიდებაი მისი, მოვილე და ვჴამ მისგანი და ვცან კეთილი და ბოროტი. აწ ჴამე შენცა და იყო ვითარ- ცა ღმერთი"	21-22.6b и азъ отврьзохъ оуста моя, и дияволь глаголаше въ мьнѣ о дрѣвѣ и разоумѣ, ѥда како сънѣсть и тьи."

Pericope 23 EVE'S TALE: *Temptation of Adam* (Gen 3:6b-7)   60E

GREEK	LATIN	ARMENIAN	GEORGIAN	SLAVONIC
21:1 And I cried out in that very hour, "Adam, Adam, where are you? Rise up, come to me and I will show you a great mystery."		[44](21):1 I cried out to Adam in a loud voice, 'Arise, come to me and I will show you this way.'		21-22.4b and called in a loud voice to Adam, saying, 'Adam, Adam, where are you? 21-22.5 Stand up and come here so that I can share something incredible with you.'
21:2a But when your father came,		[44](21):2 Then Adam came to me with his great glory,	[44](21):2a Then your father Adam came.	
			[44](21):2b He had thought thus: that a beast had entered the Garden and he said to me, 'What are you shouting for and why do you have this fig-leaf on yourself?'	21-22.6a And Adam came to me
21:2b I spoke to him words of transgression which have brought us down from our great glory.			[44](21):2c I replied to him and I told him, 'Don't you wish me to tell you something or do you wish me to? Until today we were like animals.	
21:3 For, when he came, I opened my mouth and the Devil was speaking, and I began to exhort him and said, "Come hither, my lord Adam, hearken to me and eat of the fruit of the tree of which God told us not to eat of it, and you shall be as a God."			[44](21):3 When I understood [that of which] the Lord had said to us, 'Do not eat of this' and when I saw its splendor, I took of it and ate of it and I learned good and evil. Now, eat also of it and you will you become like God.'	21-22.6b and I opened my mouth and the Devil spoke through me about the tree and about knowledge, so that he would also want to taste of it.

Pericope 23 EVE'S TALE: *Temptation of Adam* (Gen 3:6b-3:7)

GREEK	LATIN	ARMENIAN	GEORGIAN	SLAVONIC
21:4a Καὶ ἀποκριθεὶς ὁ πατὴρ ὑμῶν εἶπεν· Φοβοῦμαι μήποτε ὀργισθῇ μοι ὁ θεός.			[44](21):4a ამდიგო და მრქუა მე ადამ:"მეშინის, ნუუკუე განბორისხნეს მე უფალი და მრქუას მე: მცხებაი ჩემო, რომელი გამცენ შენ, არა დაიმარხე".	
21:4b Ἐγὼ δὲ εἶπον· Μὴ φοβοῦ· ἅμα γὰρ φάγῃς ἔσει γινώσκων καλὸν καὶ πονηρόν.			[44](21):4b ხოლო მე ვარქუ მას:" ჩემ ზედა იყოს ბრალი ესე, უკეთუ გაიოხოს შენ, ესრეთ თქუ:" დედაკაცი ესე, რომელი შენ მომეც, მისი ბრალი არისო. გემო იხილე დიდებისა ამის".	
21:5 Καὶ τότε ταχέως πείσασα αὐτόν, ἔφαγεν. Καὶ ἠνεῴχθησαν αὐτοῦ οἱ ὀφθαλμοὶ καὶ ἔγνω τὴν γύμνωσιν αὐτοῦ.		[44](21):5 եւ ևատու պատել նմա ի մրգոյ ածոյի. եւ արարի զնա իբրեւ զիս. եւ եւս այնուհետեւ առ ւնբրեւ ծխինոյն. եւ ծածկաց զմերկութիւն իւր:	[44](21):5 მაშინ ვეცა მისგან, ჭამა და იქმნა ვითარცა მე. და მოღო მანცა ღელვისა ფურცელი და დაითარა შიშუღლებაი მისი.	21-22.7a И сьнѣде Адамь и отврьзостѣ се очи ɪємоу и видѣ наготоу мою и своѭ.
21:6 Καὶ λέγει μοι· Ὦ γύναι πονηρά, τί κατειργάσω ἐν ἡμῖν; Ἀπηλλοτρίωσάς με ἐκ τῆς δόξης τοῦ θεοῦ.				21-22.7b и рече ми · ѡ жєно, чьто сьтвори мьнѣ; 21-22.8 почьто оудалихомь сє оть милости божиɪє;

Pericope 23 **EVE'S TALE:** *Temptation of Adam* (Gen 3:6b-7) 61E

GREEK	LATIN	ARMENIAN	GEORGIAN	SLAVONIC
21:4a And your father answered and said, "I fear lest God be angry with me.			[44][21]:4a Adam replied to me and told me, 'I fear lest God be angry with me and tell me, "You did not keep my commandment which I gave to you!"'	
21:4b And I said to him, "Fear not, for as soon as you have eaten you shall know good and evil."			[44](21):4b But I told the father, 'This blame shall be on me. If He asks you, say thus: "This woman whom you have given me said she is to blame for that; [[she told me]]: See the flavor of this glory!"'	
21:5 And speedily I persuaded him, and he ate and his eyes were opened and he too knew his nakedness.		[44](21):5 and I gave him to eat of the fruit, and I made him like me. Subsequently, he, too, came (and) took a fig leaf and covered his nakedness.	[44](21):5 Then I gave [him of it and he ate of it and became like me, and he also took a leaf of the fig tree and covered his nakedness with it.]	21-22.7a And Adam tasted, and his eyes were opened, and he saw his and my nakedness,
21:6 And to me he said, "O wicked woman! what have you done to us? You have deprived me of the glory of God."				21-22.7b and he said to me, 'O wife, what have you done to me? 21-22.8 Why have we departed from the grace of God?'

Pericope 24 EVE'S TALE: *Entry of God* (Gen 3:8-13)

GREEK	LATIN	ARMENIAN	GEORGIAN	SLAVONIC
22:1 Καὶ αὐτῇ τῇ ὥρᾳ ἠκούσαμεν τοῦ ἀρχαγγέλου Μιχαὴλ σαλπίζοντος [ἐν τῇ σάλπιγγι αὐτοῦ] καὶ καλοῦντος τοὺς ἀγγέλους καὶ λέγοντος·		[44](22):1 Եւ այնորհիկ լուաք զի Գաբրիէլ հրեշտակն փող հարկանէր եւ կոչեաց զհրեշտակսն ամենայն եւ ասէր ցնոսա.	[44](22):1 შემდგომად ამისა გუესმა ანგელოზისაგან, ვითარმედ დასცა საყჳრსა. უფლოდ ანგელოზთა და ჰრქუა:	23-24.1 Тогда ѹслышахомь вь нєбєсныхь гласъ арха҃гг҃єла Михаила, призываѫ агг҃елы всє и глагол҄ѫ имь ·
22:2 Τάδε λέγει κύριος· Ἔλθατε μετ' ἐμοῦ εἰς τὸν παράδεισον καὶ ἀκούσατε τοῦ κρίματος ἐν ᾧ κρινῶ τὸν Ἀδάμ. Καὶ ὡς ἠκούσαμεν τοῦ ἀρχαγγέλου σαλπίζοντος, εἴπομεν· Ἰδοὺ ὁ θεὸς εἰς τὸν παράδεισον ἔρχεται κρῖναι ἡμᾶς. Ἐφοβήθημεν δὲ καὶ ἐκρύβημεν.		[44](22):2 Զայս ասէ Տէր. եկայք առ իս զի ձայր հանդերձ իջէք(ց) եւ ի դրախտն, եւ լուարուք դուք դատաստանի իմում զոր ինձ դատեմ եւ զԱդամ: Եւ իբրեւ լուաք մեք զայս փողոյ հրեշտակին գիտացաք եթէ Ասուած գալոց է ի դրախտս դատել զմեզ.	[44](22):2 "ესრეთ იტყჳს უფალი, მოვედით სამოთხეს, ისმინეთ სასჯელი, რომელსა ვჰსჯო". მრქუა ადამ: "ვცოდით, ვითარმედ ღმერთი სამოთხისა მოვალს დასჯად ჩუენდა". შევჰშინდეს და დავიმალენით.	23-24.2 тако глагол҄єть господь · сънидємь вь раи да ѹслышитє сѫдъ, гдѣ ѥстъ съгрѣшиль Адамь и како да сѫждѹ ѥмѹ.
22:3 Καὶ ἦλθεν ὁ θεὸς εἰς τὸν παράδεισον ἐπιβεβηκὼς ἐπὶ ἅρματος χερουβίμ, καὶ οἱ ἄγγελοι ὑμνοῦντες αὐτόν. ἐν ᾧ δὲ ἦλθεν ὁ θεὸς [εἰς τὸν παράδεισον,] ἐξήνθησαν τὰ φυτὰ τοῦ κλήρου τοῦ Ἀδὰμ καὶ τὰ ἐμὰ πάντα ἐστερεῖτο.		[44](22):3 եւեկալ ի կառս քերոբէից. եւ հրեշտակք աւրհնէին զնա. երկաք այսեհետու եւ ի Ճաշակի եղաք. եկն Ասուած ի դրախտն եւ ծաղկեցան ամենայն տունկք դրախտին.	[44](22):3 და მოვიდა ღმერთი სამოთხედ მკდომარე ქერობინთა ზედა და წინაშე მისსა გალობდეს ანგელოზნი. მოვლდ-ვიდა სამოთხეს, აღმოსცენდეს ყო ფურცელი ვამოთი ყოველმან ხემან	23-24.3 и сьнидє госп одь на рамѹ хєровимьскѹѭ и множьство аггєль, поѭщєє нємльчьнѫѭ пѣснь, славѧщє бога нєпрѣстанно.
22:4 Καὶ ὁ θρόνος τοῦ θεοῦ ἐστηρίζετο ὅπου ἦν τὸ ξύλον τῆς ζωῆς.		[44](22):4 եւ արկ գահոյք իւր մերձ առ ծառն կենաց:	[44](22):4 და დადგეს საყდარნი ხესა მას თანა ცხორებისასა.	23-24.4 и ста по срѣдѣ рая прѣстоль госп одьнь. 23-24.5 адамово дрєвиѥ цвьтѫшє цвѣтиѥмь вєлиѥмь, моѩ страны дрєвиѥ ѹвєло бѣ и отьпало.

Pericope 24 EVE'S TALE: *Entry of God* (Gen 3:8-13)

GREEK	LATIN	ARMENIAN	GEORGIAN	SLAVONIC
22:1 And in that same hour, we heard the archangel Michael blowing [with his trumpet] and calling to the angels and saying:		[44](22):1 After that, we heard the angel Gabriel blowing a trumpet and summoning all the angels and saying to them,	[44](22):1 After which we heard from an angel that (God) blew the trumpet. He (had) summoned the angels and told them,	23-24.1 Then we heard the voice of the archangel Michael in the heavenly realm, who called together all the angels and said to them:
22:2 "Thus says the Lord, Come with me to the Garden and hear the judgment with which I shall judge Adam." And when we heard the archangel sound the trumpet we said, "Behold God is coming into the Garden to judge us." We feared and we hid.		[44](22):2 'Thus says the Lord, "Come to me so that I [may] descend to the Garden with you, and listen to my judgement with which I will judge Adam."' When we heard the sound of the angel's trumpet, we knew that God was about to come to the Garden to judge us.	[44](22):2 'Thus says the Lord, "Come to the Garden and hear the sentence by which we are going to judge (them).'" Adam [[told me]], 'We have sinned, for God is going to come to judge us.' We were afraid and we hid.	23-24.2 'Thus says the Lord, "We will go down to Paradise to hold a hearing where Adam has sinned, and I will pronounce the verdict on him."'
22:3 And God came into the Garden, mounted on the chariot of his Cherubim with the angels proceeding before him and singing hymns of praises. As God entered [the Garden,] the plants of Adam's portion flowered but all mine were bereft of flowers.		[44](22):3 He set forth upon the Cherub chariot and the angels were praising him; consequently, we were afraid and hid. God reached the Garden and all of the plants of the Garden flowered.	[44](22):3 And God came to the Garden sitting upon the Cherubim and the angels were singing hymns before him. When he had arrived at the Garden, at once all (the) tree(s) cast off their (its) foliage,	23-24.3 And the Lord came down on the shoulders of the Cherubim and a host of angels with him, singing the eternal song, glorifying God without end.
22:4 And the throne of God was fixed where the Tree of Life was.		[44](22):4 He set up his throne clos[e] to the Tree of Life.	[44](22):4 and thrones were set up near the Tree of Life.	23-24.4 And the throne of God was set up in the center of Paradise. 23-24.5 The trees of Adam burst forth in great blossoms, the trees of my half became withered and all their leaves were fallen.

Pericope 24 EVE'S TALE: *Entry of God* (Gen 3:8-13)

GREEK	LATIN	ARMENIAN	GEORGIAN	SLAVONIC
23:1 Καὶ ἐκάλεσεν ὁ θεὸς τὸν Ἀδὰμ λέγων· Ἀδάμ, ποῦ ἐκρύβης; νομίζεις ὅτι οὐχ εὑρίσκω σε; Μὴ κρυβήσεται οἶκος τῷ οἰκοδομήσαντι αὐτόν;		[44](23):1 Կոչեաց Աստուած զԱդամ եւ ասէ. Ադամ, Ադամ, ո՞ւր ես. համարիս թէ թաքուցեալ ես եւ ասես թէ ոչ գտանէ զիս. մի՞թէ թաքչել կարէ շինուածն ի շինողէ անտի, զի թաքուցեալ ես առ ծառովդ ճիշթեւոյ:	[44](23):1 და უფლოდ უფლოდ ღმერთმან ადამს და ჰრქუა: "ადამ, ადამ, სადა ხარ, მე დამემალები? ანუ ჰგონა დამალვის საქმე მაშენებელსა თვისსა, ანუ ჰრაისა დამალულ ხარ ხესა თანა სამოთხისასა?"	23-24.6 и възва господь Адама · Адаме, Адаме ·
23:2 Τότε ἀποκριθεὶς ὁ πατὴρ ὑμῶν εἶπεν· Οὐχί κύριε, οὐ κρυβόμεθά σε ὡς νομίζοντες ὅτι οὐχ εὑρισκόμεθα ὑπὸ σοῦ· ἀλλὰ φοβοῦμαι ὅτι γυμνός εἰμι καὶ ᾐδέσθην τὸ κράτος σου, δέσποτα.		[44](23):2 Պատասխանի ետ Ադամ եւ ասէ. Ոչ Տէր, ոչ թէ թաքուցեալ համարիցեմք թէ ոչ գտանիցեմք զիս, այլ երկեայ, զի մերկ եմ, եւ ամաչեմ.	[44](23):2 მაშინ მოუგო მამამან თქუენმან და ჰრქუა: უფალსა: "დამალ-ღა ვარ მე, ჰამეთუ მეშინის, შემუელ ვარ და მრცხუენის".	23-24.7 Адамъ рече · господи гласъ твои услышахъ и обоѧхъ сѧ зѣло, понеже нагъ ѥсмь ·
23:3 Λέγει αὐτῷ ὁ θεός· Τίς σοι ὑπέδειξεν ὅτι γυμνὸς εἶ εἰ μὴ ὅτι ἐγκατέλιπας τὴν ἐντολήν μου [ἣν παρέδωκά σοι] τοῦ φυλάξαι αὐτήν;		[44](23):3 Ասէ ցնա Աստուած. Ո՞ բացոյց քեզ մերկ լինել, եթէ ոչ թողեալ էր քո զպատուիրանն իմ զոր ետուի քեզ պահել զնա:	[44](23):3 მოუგო ღმერთმან და ჰრქუა: "ვინ გითხრა შენ, ვითარმედ შიშუელ ხარ? ნუუკუე შეჰრაცხ-ჰყავ მცნება ჩემი, რომელი გამცენ შენ?"	23-24.8 и рече господь къ нѥмоу · кто ти повѣда, ꙗко нагъ ѥси, аще не бы сьнѣлъ отъ дрѣва, ѥгоже ти рѣхъ не ꙗсти; 23-24.9 и поꙗшѧ насъ аггели и свѣрѣпо гонѣхоу ны.
23:4 Τότε Ἀδὰμ ἐμνήσθη τοῦ λόγου οὗ ἐλάλησα αὐτῷ [ὅτε ἤθελον ἀπατῆσαι αὐτὸν] ὅτι ἀκίνδυνόν σε ποιήσω παρὰ τοῦ θεοῦ.		[44](23):4 Յայնժամ լիշեաց Ադամ զբանն զոր ասաց նմա զորդի եւ պատճէ. ասէ Ադամ. Կինս զոր ետուր, սա խաբեաց զիս եւ կերայ:	[44](23):4 მაშინ მოეხსენა ადამ სიტყუაი იგი ჩემი, რომელი ვთქუ, ვითარმედ: ნუ ზრუნავ, არამედ ჰამ ზედაცა ოყოს ესე · და თქუა ადამ: "უფალო, დედაკაცი ესე, რომელ მომეც მე, მან მაცოჳნა".	

Pericope 24 EVE'S TALE: *Entry of God* (Gen 3:8-13) 63E

GREEK	LATIN	ARMENIAN	GEORGIAN	SLAVONIC
23:1 And God called Adam saying, "Adam, where are you hiding? Do you think that I won't find you? Can the house be hidden from the presence of its builder?"		[44](23):1 God summoned Adam and said, 'Adam where are you?' Do you think that you have hidden and do you say, "He does not know me?" Can the building hide from the Builder, that you hide near that olive-tree?'	[44](23):1 And God summoned Adam [and told him,] 'Adam, Adam, where are you? [Are you hiding from me? Or how will a house hide from its builder? Or why have you hidden near the tree of the Garden?'	23-24.6 And the Lord called Adam, 'O Adam, Adam.'
23:2 Then your father answered; "It is not because we think we can't be found by you, Lord, that we hide, but I was afraid, because I am naked, and I was ashamed before your might, (my) Master."		[44](23):2 Adam replied and said, 'No, Lord, it is not that having hidden, I think that you will not find me, but I was afraid, for I am naked and I am ashamed.'	[44](23):2 Then your father replied and told the Lord, 'I have hidden because I am afraid: I am naked and I am ashamed.']	23-24.7 Adam said, 'Lord, I heard your voice and was terribly afraid, since I am naked.'
23:3 God said to him, "Who showed you that you are naked, unless you has forsaken my commandment, [which I gave to you] to keep."		[44](23):3 God said to him, 'Who showed you to be naked, if you have not abandoned my commandment which I gave you to observe?'	[44](23):3 God replied to him and told him, 'Who told you that you are naked? Have you scorned the commandment which I gave you?'	23-24.8 And the Lord said to him, 'Who told you that you are naked, unless you have tasted from the tree, of which I told you not to taste?' 23-24.9 And the angel took us and brusquely drove us away.

Pericope 24 EVE'S TALE: *Entry of God* (Gen 3:8-13)

GREEK	LATIN	ARMENIAN	GEORGIAN	SLAVONIC
Καὶ στραφεὶς πρός με εἶπεν· Τί τοῦτο ἐποίησας; 23:5 Κἀγὼ εἶπον ὅτι ὁ ὄφις ἠπάτησέ με.		եւ դարձաւ առ իս եւ ասէ. Ընէ՞ր արարեր զայդ։ [44](23):5 Թշեցի իս զբան սաիրն եւ ասեմ. Աւձն խաբեաց զիս։	მაშინ მომექცა მე და მარქუა:" რაი ჰყავ?" [44](23):5 მე მოვახსენე სიტყუაი იგი გუელისა მის და ვთქუ, ვითარმედ: "გუელმან მაცთუნა მე".	

Pericope 24 EVE'S TALE: *Entry of God* (Gen 3:8-13)

GREEK	LATIN	ARMENIAN	GEORGIAN	SLAVONIC
23:4 Then Adam remembered the word which I spoke to him [when I wished to deceive him] "I will make you secure before God;"		[44](23):4 Then Adam remembered the injunction which He had spoken to him, to do and observe. Adam said, 'This woman, whom you gave, deceived me and I ate.'	[44](23):4 Then Adam remembered my word(s) which I had said, 'Do not be concerned for (the blame) for it will lie upon me.' And Adam said, 'Lord, it is this woman whom you gave to me who deceived me.'	
and he turned and said to me: "Why have you done this?" 23:5 And I said, "The serpent deceived me."		He turned to me and said, 'Why did you do that?' [44](23):5 I recalled the serpent's speech and said, 'The serpent deceived me.'	Then He turned towards me and told me, 'What have you done?' [44](23):5 And I remembered the serpent's word and I said, 'It is the serpent who deceived me!'	

65 Pericope 25 EVE'S TALE: *Judgment of Adam and Eve* (Gen 3:14-19)

GREEK	LATIN	ARMENIAN	GEORGIAN	SLAVONIC
24:1 Καὶ λέγει ὁ θεὸς τῷ Ἀδάμ· Ἐπειδὴ παρήκουσας τὴν ἐντολήν μου καὶ ἤκουσας τῆς γυναικός σου, ἐπικατάρατος ἡ γῆ ἕνεκα σοῦ.		[44](24):1 եւ ասէ այնուհետեւ Աստուած Ադամա՛. Փոխանակ զի լուար ձայնի կնոջ քո եւ անցեր զպատուիրանաւ իմով, նախատեալ լինիցին դու ի վերայ երկրի.	[44](24):1 მიუგო ღმერთმან ადამს და ჰრქუა:"რაისა ისმინე ცოლისა შენისაი და შეურაცხ-ჰყავ მცნებაი ჩემი? წყეულ იყავნ ქუეყანაი საქმეთა შინა შენთა,	
24:2 Ἐργάσει αὐτὴν καὶ οὐ δώσει τὴν ἰσχὺν αὐτῆς· ἀκάνθας καὶ τριβόλους ἀνατελεῖ σοι καὶ ἐν ἱδρῶτητι τοῦ προσώπου σου φάγει τὸν ἄρτον σου.		44.24.2 վաստակեալ երիցես ի նմա [եւ նա մի՛ տացէ քեզ զզօրութիւն իւր]. փուշ եւ տատասկ[ն] բուսցի քեզ. քրտամբ երեսաց քոց կերիցես զհաց քո.	[44](24):2 იქმოდე ქვა და არა გამოგცეს ნაყოფი, ეკალსა და კუროსთავ-სა აღმოგიცენებდეს შენ, ოფლითა პირისა შენისაითა სჭამდე პურსა.	
24:3 Ἔσει δὲ ἐν καμάτοις πολυτρόποις, [καμῇ καὶ μὴ ἀναπαύσῃ] θλιβεὶς ἀπὸ πικρίας, καὶ μὴ γεύσει γλυκύτητος, θλιβεὶς ἀπὸ καύματος καὶ στενωθεὶς ἀπὸ ψύξεως. [Καὶ κοπιάσεις πολλὰ καὶ μὴ πλουτήσεις καὶ παχυνθήσει καὶ εἰς τέλος μὴ ὑπάρξεις.]		[44](24):3 եւ մի՛ լիցի քեզ հանգիստ. բաղցիցես եւ յագեսցիս եւ ներքսցիս ի դառնութեւն. եւ ապա ճաշակ[եսցես] ի քաղցրութեւն. ճգնեսցիս ի տապոյ եւ ներքսցիս ի ցրտոյ. աղքատասցիս եւ մեծասցիս, [գիրասցիս եւ տկարասցիս]	[44](24):3 იყავ შენესითა მრავალითა, შრომითა შუერ და არა განისუე- ნო, გჳობდე და არა განსძღე, იჭირვოდე სიმწარისაგან და არა განსძღე, გემო არა იხილო სიტკბოებისაგან, გჭირდეს სიცხისაგან და გევნებოდეს ყინელისაგან, დაგლახაკნეთ და არა გამდიდრნეთ, ჭამდეთ და არა განსყე- ნეთ, განსტფეთ ცეცხლითა და არა განნწყრდეთ, ილტო... წყლითა და განყუ- ნენ	

Pericope 25 EVE'S TALE: *Judgment of Adam and Eve* (Gen 3:14-19) 65E

GREEK	LATIN	ARMENIAN	GEORGIAN	SLAVONIC
24:1 God said to Adam: "Since you transgressed my commandment and hearkened to your wife, cursed is the earth on your account. 24:2 You shall work it and it shall not give its strength: thorns and thistles shall spring up for you and in the sweat of your face you shall eat your bread. 24:3 You shall be in manifold toils [and you shall not rest]; you shall be crushed by bitterness, but of sweetness you shall not taste. You shall be crushed from heat and constrained by cold. [You shall struggle greatly and not become rich and you shall grow fat, but in the end you will not be.]			[44](24):1 Subsequently God said to Adam, 'Because you obeyed your wife's voice and transgressed my commandment, you will be condemned upon the earth. [44](24):2 You will toil upon it, [and it will not give you its strength]; thorns and thistl[es] will sprout forth for you. By the sweat of your brow you shall eat your bread [44](24):3 and you shall have no rest; you [shall hunger] and you shall be sated and you shall be afflicted by bitterness then you shall eat of sweetness; you shall be tormented by heat and afflicted by cold; you shall be pauperized and become great; [you shall grow fat and you will be weakened	[44](24):1 God replied to Adam and told him, '[[Because]] you hearkened to your wife and scorned my commandment, let the earth be cursed in your deeds. [44](24):2 May you work it and it will give you no fruit; it will sprout only thorns and thistles for you. By the sweat of your brow you shall eat bread. [44](24):3 May you be with many sighs, toil in labors and have [[no]] rest. You shall hunger and you shall [[not]] be sated. You shall be affected by bitterness and you shall [[not]] taste sweetness; you shall be tormented by heat and will undergo cold; you (pl.) shall be pauperized and you shall [[not]] be enriched; you shall eat and shall [[not]] grow fat; you shall warm yourselves with fire, and you shall not be heated. You will fle[[e (to soak yourselves]] with water and it will draw back.	

Pericope 25 EVE'S TALE: *Judgment of Adam and Eve* (Gen 3:14-19)

GREEK	LATIN	ARMENIAN	GEORGIAN	SLAVONIC
24:4 Καὶ ὦν ἐκυρίευες θηρίων ἐπαναστήσονταί σοι ἐν ἀκαταστασίᾳ, ὅτι τὴν ἐντολήν μου οὐκ ἐφύλαξας.		[44](24):4 եւ որոյ] տիրէիր գազանաց յարիցեն ի վերայ քո անզգամութեամբ, վասն զի անցեր դու պատուիրանաւ իմով եւ ոչ պահեցեր։	[44](24):4 და მხეცთა, რომელთა ზედა შენ უფლებდი, იგინი შენ ზედა აღდგენ. დაუმტკიცებელ იყო, რამეთუ მცნებანი ჩემნი არ დაიმარხენ".	
25:1 Στραφεὶς δὲ πρός με ὁ κύριος λέγει· Ἐπειδὴ ἐπήκουσας τοῦ ὄφεως καὶ παρήκουσας τὴν ἐντολήν μου, ἔσει ἐν καμάτοις καὶ ἐν πόνοις ἀφορήτοις.		[44](25):1 Դարձաւ Աստուած եւ ասէ ցիս. փոխանակ զի լուար դու սատնի [եւ անցեր պատուիրանաւ իմով] լիցիր դու ի վաստակս եւ ի ցաւս.	[44](25):1 მომექცა მე და მრქუა: "რაისა ისმინე შენ გუელისა და დაუ- ტევენ მცნებანი ჩემნი, რომელნი გამცენ შენ? იყავ შრომათა შინა და სალმობათა,	
25:2 Τέξει τέκνα ἐν πολλοῖς τρόποις καὶ ἐν μιᾷ ὥρᾳ ἔλθεις τοῦ τεκεῖν καὶ ἀπολέσεις τὴν ζωήν σου ἐκ τῆς ἀνάγκης σου τῆς μεγάλης καὶ τῶν ὀδυνῶν.		[44](25):2 ծնցիս որդիս բազումս, եւ ի ժամանակի ծննդեան վարեանեսցի[ս ի] կեանս քոյ, եւ ի մեծ վշտաց քոյ եւ ի ցաւոց	[44](25):2 შევ ნაყოფი მრავალი. და ოდეს შვა, წარსწირო ცხორებაი შენი ურვათა და სალმობათა,	
25:3 Ἐξομολογήσει δὲ καὶ εἴπεις· Κύριε, κύριε, σῶσόν με καὶ οὐ μὴ ἐπιστρέψω εἰς τὴν ἁμαρτίαν τῆς σαρκός, [ἀλλὰ καὶ πάλιν ἐπιστρέψεις.]		[44](25):3 խոստովանեսցիս բերանով քոյով եւ ասասցես. ե՛թէ ապրեցայց ի վշտացս յայսցանէ, ոչ եւս արարից զմեղս յայսմ հետ. եւ իբրեւ եկեսցեն ի վշտացն, դարձ արասցիր դու ատամանէն յերկիր այսր.	[44](25):3 ფუკელოდ განერე ჭირთა მათ, არცარა მოიქცე ქმნისად, და განაფიცხე გული შენი ბრძოლისა მისგან დიდისა, რომელ დადვა გულსა მან შენ თანა,	
25:4 Διὰ τοῦτο ἐκ τῶν λόγων σου κρινῶ σε, διὰ τὴν ἔχθραν ἣν ἔθετο ὁ ἐχθρός ἐν σοί. Στραφήσει δὲ πάλιν πρὸς τὸν ἄνδρα σου, καὶ αὐτός σου κυριεύσει.		[44](25):4 զի ի բերանոյ քումմէ դատապարտեսցիր, վասն զի խոստովանեսցար ի տագնապեալ ցաւս ե՛թէ ոչ դարձայց լերկիր այսր. եւ ապա դարձաւ ի [սոսա. ցաւոք] ծնցիս որդիս եւ զձեռդ դարձիր առ այր քո, եւ նա տիրեսցէ քեզ։	[44](25):4 მოიქცე მეყსეულად მშვე. ჭყვილითა შევ ნაშობი შენი და მოქყალებით მოიქცე ქმნისა შენისა და იგი შენ ზედა უფლებდეს".	

Pericope 25 EVE'S TALE: *Judgment of Adam and Eve* (Gen 3:14-19) 66E

GREEK	LATIN	ARMENIAN	GEORGIAN	SLAVONIC
24:4 The beasts, over whom you ruled, shall rise up in rebellion against you, for you have not kept my commandment."		[44](24):4 and] the beasts [which] you ruled will rise up against you malignantly, because you transgressed my commandment and did not observe (it).'	[44](24):4 And the beasts over whom you (sing.) used to rule shall rise up against you. You shall be weakened because you have not kept my commandments.'	
25:1 And the Lord turned to me and said: "Since you has hearkened to the serpent, and transgressed my commandment, you shall suffer torments and intolerable pains;		[44](25):1 God turned and said to me, 'Because you obeyed the serpent [and transgressed my commandment,] you shall suffer torments and pains.	[44](25):1 God turned to me and told me, 'Why did you hearken to the serpent and abandon my commandments which I commanded you? (May you) be in toils and pains;	
25:2 you shall bear children in much trembling and in one hour you shall come to the birth, and lose your life, from your sore trouble and anguish.		[44](25):2 You shall bear many children and at the time of birth [you shall] bring your life [to] an end and, from your great agonies and pains	[44](25):2 ((may you) give birth to many fruits and when you give birth to them you will despair of your life because of the torments and pains.	
25:3 But you shall confess and say: "Lord, Lord, save me, and I will turn no more to the sin of the flesh." [But even another time you shall so turn.]		[44](25):3 you shall promise with your mouth and say, "If I survive these agonies, I shall never go back to my husband." And when you emerge from the agonies, you shall return immediately to the earth.	[44][25]:3 (You shall promise yourself) that if you are ever delivered from the agonies, you will never go back to [[your husband]] and you will harden your heart in view of the great combat which the serpent instituted with you.	

67 Pericope 25 EVE'S TALE: *Judgment of Adam and Eve* (Gen 3:14-19)

GREEK	LATIN	ARMENIAN	GEORGIAN	SLAVONIC
26:1 Μετὰ δὲ τὸ εἰπεῖν μοι ταῦτα, εἴπεν τῷ ὄφει ἐν ὀργῇ μεγάλῃ λέγων· Ἐπειδὴ ἐποίησας τοῦτο καὶ ἐγένου σκεῦος ἀχάριστον ἕως ἂν πλανήσῃς τοὺς παρειμένους τῇ καρδίᾳ ἐπικατάρατος σὺ ἐκ πάντων τῶν κτηνῶν.		[44](26):1 եւ [լ]եւ ասելոյն իմձ զայս ամենայն, բարկացաւ Տէր ի վերայ աւձին բարկութեամբ մեծաւ եւ ասէ. Փիսանակ զի արարեր դու զայդ եւ եղեր քսար [մոլորեցուցանել լքեալ սրտիւք], անիծեալ լիջիր դու ամենայն անասնոց.	[44](26):1 ოდეს მრქუა მე ესე ყოველი, განრისხნა გუელსა ზედა რისხვითა და მრქუა მას:" წარწყმდი შენცა და წყულ იყავ ყოველთა შორის პირუტყუთა,	
26:2 Στερηθήσει τῆς τροφῆς σου ἧς ἤσθιες καὶ χοῦν φάγει πάσας τὰς ἡμέρας τῆς ζωῆς σου. Ἐπὶ τῷ στήθει καὶ τῇ κοιλίᾳ πορεύσει ὑστερηθεὶς καὶ χειρῶν καὶ ποδῶν σου·		[44](26):2 արգելցիր դու ի կերակրոց քոց [զոր կերակրէիր]. Տող կերակուր լիցի քեզ եւ ի վերայ լանջաց եւ որովայնի քում գնասցես. արգելցին ոտք քո եւ ձեռք քո	[44](26):2 მოაკლდი საზრდელისაგან შენისა, რომელსა სჭამდი, და მიწა იყავნ საჭმელად შენდა ყოველთა დღეთა ცხორებისა შენისათა, მკერდითა და მუცლითა შენითა ხვიდოდე შენ. მოაკლდეს შენგან ხელნი და ფერხნი შენი	
26:3 Οὐκ ἀφεθήσεταί σοι ὠτίον οὔτε πτέρυξ οὔτε ἓν μέλος τούτων ὧν σὺ ἐδελέασας ἐν τῇ κακίᾳ σου καὶ ἐποίησας αὐτοὺς ἐκβληθῆναι ἐκ τοῦ παραδείσου.		[44](26):3 եւ մի լուիցին ականջք[?] քո. [եւ մի ինչ լանդամող քոց. նմանութիւն խաչին գործիս իմ բերիցէ լերկիր. վասն այսորիկ զոր դու խաբեցեր. լքեալ եւ խցեալ լիցիր դու վասն չարութեան սրտի քո.	[44](26):3 და ნუ იყვნენ ყურნი და ფრჴხილნი შენი და ნუ იყოფინ ნუცა ერთი ასო შენი, დაგასაჯენ შენ პატიოსანმან ჯუარმან, რომელი ადლოს ძემან ჩემმან ქუეყანასა ზედა, საცთურისა მისთვის, რომელი აცთუნე ადამი. არამედ შენ იყავ კუალადვე მგლიანცა და განსხეულ (!) უკეთურებითა გულისა შენისათა.	

Pericope 25 EVE'S TALE: *Judgment of Adam and Eve* (Gen 3:14-19) 67E

GREEK	LATIN	ARMENIAN	GEORGIAN	SLAVONIC
25:4 And on this account, from your own words I will judge you, by reason of the enmity which the enemy has planted in you. And you shall return again to your husband and he will rule over you."		[44](25):4 For you shall be condemned by your own mouth, since you promised when the pain was acute, "I will never go back to this earth" and then you returned to [the same. In pain] you shall bear children and in pity you shall return to your husband and he will rule over you.'	[44](25):4 (But may you) return at once to the same point, may you bear your offspring in hurt and return in pity (lit: begging for alms) to your husband, and he will rule over you.'	
26:1 After he said these things to me, he spoke to the serpent in great wrath saying: "Since you has done this, and become a thankless vessel until you has deceived the innocent hearts, be cursed (more than) all beasts.		[44](26):1 After he had said all this to me, the Lord became very angry at the serpent and said, 'Because you did this and became a lyre [to lead astray those who were weak of heart], be cursed more than all the animals.	[44](26):1 [When he had said all this to me, he became very angry with the serpent,] and God told the serpent, 'You, too, perish and be cursed among all the animals.	
26:2 You shall be deprived of the food which you ate and you shall eat dust all the days of your life; on your breast and your belly you shall walk and be robbed of hands and feet.		[44](26):2 Be withheld from your foods [which you used to eat]. Dust will be your food and you shall go upon your breast and your stomach; your feet and hands will be withheld	[44](26):2 (May you) be withheld from your food which you used to eat and (may) the soil be to you as food all the days of your life; you shall go on your breast and on your stomach; your hands and your feet will be taken from you.	

68 Pericope 25 EVE'S TALE: *Judgment of Adam and Eve* (Gen 3:14-19)

GREEK	LATIN	ARMENIAN	GEORGIAN	SLAVONIC
26:4 Καὶ θήσω ἔχθραν ἀνὰ μέσον σοῦ καὶ ἀνὰ μέσον τοῦ σπέρματος αὐτῶν· αὐτός σοῦ τηρήσει κεφαλὴν καὶ σὺ ἐκείνου πτέρναν ἕως τῆς ἡμέρας τῆς κρίσεως.		[44](26):4 թշնամութիւն եդից ի մէջ քո եւ զաւակին Ադամայ. դու նորա գարշապարին սպասես եւ նա քում գլխոյդ. մինչեւ յաւրն յորում տանջեսցիք:	[44](26):4 და დავდვა მტერობაი შორის შენსა და შორის ნათესავისა მისგან დედაკაცისა, იგი დმზირდეს თავსა შენსა და შენ დმზირდე ბრჯალ- სა მისსა ვიდრე ღედმდე სასჯელისა".	

Pericope 25 EVE'S TALE: *Judgment of Adam and Eve* (Gen 3:14-19) 68E

GREEK	LATIN	ARMENIAN	GEORGIAN	SLAVONIC
26:3 May you have neither ears nor wings, not even one of the limbs with which you ensnared them in your malice and so caused them to be cast out of the Garden;		[44](26):3 and your ear[s] will not hear, and [none of your limbs.] A likeness of the cross will bring my son to the earth, because of him whom you deceived. Be disabled and broken because of the evil of your heart.	[44](26):3 And (may you) have neither ears nor nails and may not even one limb remain for you. Let the precious cross which my Son will take upon the earth condemn you because of the deceit by which you deceived [Adam]. But may you again [be exhausted and broken] because of the evil of your heart.	
26:4 and I will put enmity between you and their seed: he shall lie in wait for your head and you [shall lie in wait] for that one's heel until the day of Judgment."		[44](26):4 I have set enmity between you and Adam's seed. You will lie in wait for his heel and he for your head, until the day upon which you will be punished.'	[44](26):4 And I will set enmity between you and the offspring of the woman: she will lay in wait for your head and you will lay in wait for her heel until the day of judgment.'	

Pericope 26 EVE'S TALE: *Adam's Plea* (Gen 3:22-24)

GREEK	LATIN	ARMENIAN	GEORGIAN	SLAVONIC
27:1 Ταῦτα εἰπὼν κελεύει τοῖς ἀγγέλοις αὐτοῦ ἐκβληθῆναι ἡμᾶς ἐκ τοῦ παραδείσου.		[44](27):1 Զայս իբրեւ ասաց Աստուած, հրամայեաց հանել զմեզ ի դրախտէն.	[44](27):1 ესე თქუა უფალმან და ბრძანა ჩუენი ორთავე გამოჴდებაჲ სამოთხით.	25-27.1 И тако сьтвори насъ отʘждєны отъ рая,
27:2 Ἐλαυνομένων δὲ ἡμῶν καὶ ὀδυρομένων, παρεκάλεσεν ὁ πατὴρ ὑμῶν Ἀδὰμ τοὺς ἀγγέλους λέγων· Ἐάσατέ με μικρὸν ὅπως παρακαλέσω τὸν θεὸν καὶ σπλαγχνισθῇ καὶ ἐλεήσῃ με, ὅτι ἐγὼ μόνος ἥμαρτον.		[44](27):2 Եւ վարեցին հրեշտակքն հանել զմեզ: Ապաշաւս առաւ Ադամ ազգեստակաւ եւ ասէ. Թողացուցէ՛ք ինձ սակաւիկ մի, զի աղաչեցից զԱստուած ՛ի ման յանցանաց իմոց, թերեւս ողորմեսցի ինձ իմ եմ ոք ի ձեռն իմ միայն եմ մեղուցեալ, եւ ոչ հանէ ի դրախտէն:	[44](27):2 ევედრებოდა ადამ ანგელოზთა და ჰრქუა: "დაცადეთ მე, რაჲ- თა გევედრო უფალსა, ვინ უწყის, თუ სიბრძნითი მისი მე შემიწყალოს ადამი- თვის, რომელი-ესე ვჰყავ მე და არა გამოვჴედ სამოთხით".	25-27.2 мы же моляхомь сε аггєломь и глаголахомь имь · потрьп ѣтε насъ мало, да помолимь сε богʘ .
27:3 Αὐτοὶ δὲ ἐπαύσαντο τοῦ ἐλαύνειν αὐτόν, ἐβόησε δὲ Ἀδὰμ μετὰ κλαυθμοῦ λέγων· Συγχώρησόν μοι, κύριε, ὃ ἐποίησα.		[44](27):3 Թողուցին նմա հրեշտակքն ի հանելոյ ի դրախտէ աստի. եւ ասէ Ադամ. Շնորհեա ինձ Տէր Աստուած, զի մեղայ քեզ:	[44](27):3 მაშინ დაცადეს ანგელოზთა გამოდევნაჲ ჩუენი, ევედრებოდა ადამ უფალსა და თქუა: "გევედრებ ო, მომიტევე მე, უფალო, რომელი-ესე ვჰყავ".	25-27.3 и кличε Адамъ гласомь вεликмь · помилʘи ны, владыко, яко сьгрѣшихомь . ʘмилосрьди сε о насъ, владыко .
27:4 Τότε λέγει ὁ κύριος τοῖς ἀγγέλοις αὐτοῦ· Τί ἐπαύσασθε ἐκβάλλοντες τὸν Ἀδὰμ ἐκ τοῦ παραδείσου; Μὴ ἐμόν ἐστι τὸ ἁμάρτημα, ἢ κακῶς ἔκρινα;		[44](27):4 Ժամնեալ ասէ Տէր [զհրեշտակն]. Մի՛ տայք դմա առնուլ զտեղի, այլ հանէ՛ք ի դրախտէն. միթէ իմ մեղանք իցեն կամ ի դուր ինչ զատիմ:	[44](27):4 მაშინ ჰრქუა უფალმან ანგელოზთა: "რაისა დაცადეთ გა- მოჴადებაჲ ადამისი სამოთხით, ნუუკუე ჩემი ბრალი არსა, ანუ თუ არა მართალი ვსაჯე?"	

Pericope 26 EVE'S TALE: *Adam's Plea* (Gen 3:22-24)

GREEK	LATIN	ARMENIAN	GEORGIAN	SLAVONIC
27:1 After saying these things he commanded the angels to cast us out of the Garden: 27:2 and as we were being driven out amid our loud lamentations, your father Adam besought the angels and said: "Leave me a little (space) that I may entreat the Lord that he have compassion on me and pity me, for I only have sinned." 27:3 And they left off driving him and Adam cried aloud and wept saying: "Pardon me, O Lord, my deed." 27:4 Then the Lord said to the angels, "Why have you ceased from driving Adam from the Garden? Is it I who have done wrong? Or have I judged badly?"		[44](27):1 When God had said this, he commanded our expulsion from the Garden, [44](27):2 and the angels set about expelling us. Adam beseeched the angels and said, 'Let me be for a little, so that I may beseech God about my sins. Perhaps he will grant me penitence and not expel (me) from the Garden.' [44](27):3 The angels let him be from expelling (him) from the Garden, and Adam said, 'Be gracious to me, Lord God, for I have sinned against you.' [44](27):4 Then the Lord said [to the angels], 'Do not let him stand still, but expel (him) from the Garden. Were the sins mine? Do I pronounce judgement in vain?'	[44](27):1 Thus God said, and he ordered both of us to be expelled from the Garden. [44](27):2 Adam beseeched the angels and told them, 'Wait for me to beseech the Lord; who knows, perhaps the Lord will grant me a penance for that which I have done and I will not go out of the Garden.' [44](27):3 Then the angels waited for us to ask. Adam beseeched the Lord and said, 'I beseech you, Lord, pardon me for what I have done.' [44](27):4 Then the Lord told the angels, 'Why have you been waiting (before) separating Adam from the Garden? Is the blame mine (Am I to blame) or have I not judged justly?'	25-27.1 And so he exiled us from Paradise. 25-27.2 We, however, bid the angel saying to him, 'Be a little patient with us, so that we may entreat God.' 25-27.3 And Adam cried out in a loud voice, 'Have mercy on our sin, O Master, be merciful with us, O Lord.' *see 25-27.10 in pericope 27 for parallel material*

Pericope 26 EVE'S TALE: *Adam's Plea* (Gen 3:22-24)

GREEK	LATIN	ARMENIAN	GEORGIAN	SLAVONIC
27:5 Τότε οἱ ἄγγελοι πεσόντες ἐπὶ τὴν γῆν προσεκύνησαν τῷ κυρίῳ λέγοντες· Δίκαιος εἶ, κύριε, καὶ εὐθύτητας κρίνεις.	[44](27):5 [Armenian text]	[44](27):5 [Armenian text]	[44](27):5 [Georgian text]	
28:1 Στραφεὶς δὲ πρὸς τὸν Ἀδὰμ εἶπεν· Οὐκ ἀφήσω σε ἀπὸ τοῦ νῦν εἶναι ἐν τῷ παραδείσῳ.			[44](28):1 [Georgian text]	
28:2 Καὶ ἀποκριθεὶς ὁ Ἀδὰμ εἶπεν· Κύριε, δός μοι ἐκ τοῦ φυτοῦ τῆς ζωῆς ἵνα φάγω πρὶν ἢ ἐκβληθῆναί με.	[44](28):2 [Armenian text]	[44](28):2 [Armenian text]	[44](28):2 [Georgian text]	
28:3 Τότε ὁ κύριος ἐλάλησεν πρὸς τὸν Ἀδάμ· Οὐ λήψει νῦν ἀπ' αὐτοῦ· ὡρίσθη γὰρ τῷ χερουβὶμ καὶ τῇ φλογίνῃ ῥομφαίᾳ τῇ στρεφομένῃ φυλάσσειν αὐτὸ διὰ σέ, ὅπως μὴ γεύσῃ ἀπ' αὐτοῦ καὶ ἀθάνατος ἔσῃ εἰς τὸν αἰῶνα, ἔχεις δὲ τὸν πόλεμον ὃν ἔθετο ὁ ἐχθρὸς ἐν σοί.	[44](28):3 [Armenian text]	[44](28):3 [Armenian text]	[44](28):3 [Georgian text]	

Pericope 26 **EVE'S TALE:** *Adam's Plea* (Gen 3:22-24)   70E

GREEK	LATIN	ARMENIAN	GEORGIAN	SLAVONIC
27:5 Then the angels fell down on the ground and worshipped the Lord saying, "You are just, O Lord, and you judge righteously."		[44](27):5 Then the angels worshipped God and said, You are just, O Lord, and your judgements are upright.	[44](27):5 Then the angels fell to the ground and told him, bowing before the Lord, "You are just, Lord, and your sentence is upright."	
28:1 But the Lord turned to Adam and said: "I will not suffer you henceforward to be in the Garden."			[44](28):1 The Lord turned and told Adam, 'You are not to remain in the Garden.'	
28:2 And Adam answered and said, "Grant me, O Lord, of the Tree of Life that I may eat of it, before I be cast out."		[44](28):2 Adam said again to God, 'My Lord, I beseech you, give me of the Tree of Life, so that I may eat before I shall have gone forth from the Garden.'	[44](28):2 Adam replied to the Lord and told him, 'I beseech you, Lord, give me of the Tree of Life so that I may eat before I shall have gone forth.'	
28:3 Then the Lord said to Adam, "You shall not take of it now, for the Cherubim with the flaming sword that turns (every way) has been stationed to guard it from you that you taste not of it and live without death forever, but you have the war which the adversary has put into you.		[44](28):3 God said to Adam, 'You cannot take of it in your lifetime, because I have given an order to the Seraphs to guard it round about with weapons because of you, lest you should eat more of it and become immortal and say, "Behold, I shall not die;" and you will be boastful of it and be victorious in the war which the enemy has made with you.	[44](28):3 Then the Lord addressed a speech to Adam and told him, 'You will not take of it anymore in your lifetime. I have posted burning Cherubim and a turning sword to keep it from you, lest you should taste it and become immortal and boast saying, "I shall not die ever;" and you should conduct the fight which the enemy has conducted against you.	

Pericope 26 **EVE'S TALE:** *Adam's Plea* (Gen 3:22-24)

GREEK	LATIN	ARMENIAN	GEORGIAN	SLAVONIC
28:4 Ἀλλ' ἐξερχομένου σου ἐκ τοῦ παραδείσου, ἐὰν φυλάξεις ἑαυτὸν ἀπὸ παντὸς κακοῦ ὡς βουλόμενος ἀποθανεῖν, ἀναστάσεως πάλιν γενομένης, ἀναστήσω σε καὶ δοθήσεταί σοι ἐκ τοῦ ξύλου τῆς ζωῆς καὶ ἀθάνατος ἔσει εἰς τὸν αἰῶνα.		[44](28):4 այլ իբրև ելանիցես դու ի դրախտէ աստի, եւ պահեսցես զանձն քո ի չարախառնութենէ, ի սրբնկութենէ, ի շնութենէ, ի կախարդութենէ, յարծաթսիրութենէ, ի ագահութենէ, եւ յամենայն մեղաց. եւ ապա յարիցես ի մահուանէ աստի, որ լինելոց է յարութիւն. եւ յայնժամ տացից քեզ ի ծառոյն կենաց եւ լինիս դու անմահ մինչեւ յաւիտեան:	[44](28):4 ეკუეთუ განხვიდე სამოთხით და დაიცვა ყოვლისაგან ბოროტისა, მოჰკუდე და შემდგომად სიკუდილისა აღსდგე მერმესა მას აღდგომასა. მაშინ-ღა მიგცეს შენსა მისგან ცხორებისა და ეკუეთავ იყო ეკუთნისამდე".	

Pericope 26 EVE'S TALE: *Adam's Plea* (Gen 3:22-24) 71E

GREEK	LATIN	ARMENIAN	GEORGIAN	SLAVONIC
28:4 Yet when you have gone out of the Garden, if you keep yourself from all evil, as one wishing to die, when again the Resurrection has come to pass, I will raise you up and then there shall be given to you from the Tree of Life and you will be without death forever."		[44](28):4 Rather, when you go out of the Garden, guard yourself from slander, from harlotry, from adultery, from sorcery, from the love of money, from avarice and from all sins. Then, you shall arise from death, (in the) resurrection which is going to take place. At that time, I will give you of the Tree of Life and you will be eternally undying.'	[44](28):4 If you go out of the Garden and guard yourself from every evil, [you will die and after death you will arise in the future resurrection. Then, indeed,] I will give you of the Tree of Life and you will be undying for ever.'	

Pericope 27 **EVE'S TALE:** *Expulsion (Gen 3:22-24)*

GREEK	LATIN	ARMENIAN	GEORGIAN	SLAVONIC
29:1 Ταῦτα εἰπὼν ὁ κύριος ἐκέλευσεν τοῖς ἀγγέλοις αὐτοῦ ἐκβληθῆναι ἡμᾶς ἐκ τοῦ παραδείσου.		[44](29):1 Զայս իբրև ասաց Աստուած, Հրամայեաց հանել զմեզ ի դրախտէ անտի.	[44](29):1 ესე რა თქუა უფალმან, ბრძანა გამძებაი ჩუენი სამოთხით.	
29:2 Ἔκλαυσε δὲ ὁ πατὴρ ὑμῶν ἔμπροσθεν τῶν ἀγγέλων ἀπέναντι τοῦ παραδείσου καὶ λέγουσιν οἱ ἄγγελοι αὐτῷ· Τί θέλεις ποιήσωμέν σοι, Ἀδάμ;		[44](29):2 լալ սկսաւ Արամ առաջի Հրեշտակացն. և ասեն ցնա Հրեշտակքն. Զի՞նչ կամիս և ասեմք քեզ:	[44](29):2 და ტიროდა მამაი თქუენი წინაშე ანგელოზთა. ხოლო მათ ჰრქუეს მას:" რაი არს, ანუ რაი გიყოთ შენ?"	25-27.4 тогда послабише аггєли, гонєщєи ны .
29:3 Ἀποκρθεὶς δὲ ὁ πατὴρ ὑμῶν εἶπεν τοῖς ἀγγέλοις· Ἰδοὺ ἐκβάλλετέ με· δέομαι ὑμῶν, ἄφετέ με ἆραι εὐωδίας ἐκ τοῦ παραδείσου, ἵνα μετὰ τὸ ἐξελθεῖν με ἀνενέγκω θυσίαν τῷ θεῷ ὅπως εἰσακούσεταί μου ὁ θεός.		[44](29):3 Պատասխանի ետ Արամ և ասէ զՀրեշտակսն. Արդէն գնեց ՔՈղացուցէք սակայնիկ մի. զի առից ընդ իս խունկս անուշս ի դրախտէ անտի. զի իբրև ելանիցեմ անտի. մատուցանեմ Աստուծոյ խունկս անուշս. և պատրաստ. զի թերևս լուիցէ մեզ Աստուած:	[44](29):3 მაშინ მიუგო მამამან თქუენმან და ჰრქუა:" აჰა ესერა მე განვალ, აწ გევედრები თქუენ, რაითა განსლვასა ამას ჩემსა აღვლო საკუმ-მევლი სამოთხისაგან, რაითა ოდეს განვიდე, შევწირო საკუმეველი სულ-ნელებისაი და ისმინოს ჩემი ღმერთმან".	25-27.5 Адамь же помоли сѧ и речє · госп оди, пирпѹсти мьнє хранѹ, како живѹ азь. 25-27.6 Извєдоше ны аггєли изь рая и затворише раи оть насъ . 25-27.7 тогда Адамъ вьпия ше, глаголѧ · помилѹи ны, владыко, и припѹсти ми благоѹхание, ѥгда хощѹ сьтворити жрьтвѹ богѹ, да принєсѹ кадило .
29:4 Καὶ προσελθόντες εἶπον οἱ ἄγγελοι τῷ κυρίῳ· Ἰαήλ, αἰώνιε Βασιλεῦ, κέλευσον δοθῆναι τῷ Ἀδὰμ θυμιάματα εὐωδίας ἐκ τοῦ παραδείσου.				25-27.8 аггєль Иоиль нєп рѣстаньно молє сѧ глаголаше · помилѹи, владыко, прьво сьзданиѥ твоѥ. 25-27.9 и рєкоше аггєли вьси тѹ жє рѣчь кь богѹ о Адамѣ · помилѹи, владыко, прьвоѥ сьзданиѥ твоѥ .

Pericope 27 EVE'S TALE: *Expulsion (Gen 3:22-24)* 72E

GREEK	LATIN	ARMENIAN	GEORGIAN	SLAVONIC
29:1 When the Lord had said these things he ordered us to be cast out of the Garden. 29:2 But your father Adam wept before the angels opposite the Garden and the angels said to him: "What would you have us to do, Adam?" 29:3 And your father said to them, "Behold, you cast me out. I pray you, allow me to take away fragrant herbs from the Garden, so that I may offer an offering to God after I have gone out of the Garden that he hear me." 29:4 And the angels approached God and said: "Jael, Eternal King, command, my Lord, that there be given to Adam incense of sweet odor from the Garden."		[44](29):1 When God had said this, he commanded to expel us from the Garden. [44](29):2 Adam began to cry before the angels, and the angels said to him, 'What do you want us to do for you?' [44](29):3 Adam replied and said to the angels, 'I beseech you, let (me) be a little, so that I may take sweet incenses with me from the Garden, so that when I go out of here, I may offer sweet incenses to God, and offerings, so that, perhaps, God will hearken to us.'	[44](29):1 When the Lord had said that [he ordered us to be chased out of the Garden.] [44](29):2 And your father wept before the angels, but they told him, 'What is this or what shall we do for you?' [44](29):3 Then your father replied to them and told them, 'Behold, I am going out. Now I beseech you that at the very moment of my leaving the Garden I may take incense from the Garden so that, when I go out, I may offer a sweet-odored incense and God will be willing to hearken to me.'	25-27.4 Then the angels driving us forth relented a little, 25-27.5 and Adam prayed and said, 'O Lord, furnish me with nourishment, that I might live.' 25-27.6 The angel guided us out of Paradise and barricaded it off from us. 25-27.7 Then Adam prayed and said, 'Have mercy on us, O Master, let me have pleasing aromas, that whenever I make an offering to God, I may bring incense to him.' 25-27.8 Angel Joel prayed unceasingly and said, 'Have mercy, O Master, on your first creation.' 25-27.9 And all the angels spoke the same word to God concerning Adam, 'Have mercy, O Master, on your first creation.'

Pericope 27 EVE'S TALE: *Expulsion (Gen 3:22-24)*

GREEK	LATIN	ARMENIAN	GEORGIAN	SLAVONIC
29:5 Καὶ ἐκέλευσεν ὁ θεὸς ἐαθῆναι τὸν Ἀδὰμ ἵνα λάβῃ εὐωδίας καὶ σπέρματα εἰς διατροφὴν αὐτοῦ.				25-27.10 и рече господь кь аггеломь своимь · право ли ѥсть тако патити Адамоу, како моу ѥсть соуждено, или неправедьно ѥсть тако; 25-27.11 аггели неп рѣстаньно глаголахоу · праведьнь ѥсть соудь твои, госп оди, вь истиноу праведьнь .
29:6 Καὶ ἀφέντες αὐτὸν οἱ ἄγγελοι, ἔλαβε τέσσαρα γένη, κρόκον καὶ νάρδον καὶ κάλαμον καὶ κινάμωμον, καὶ ἕτερα σπέρματα εἰς διατροφὴν αὐτοῦ. Καὶ λαβὼν ταῦτα ἐξῆλθεν ἐκ τοῦ παραδείσου · καὶ ἐγενόμεθα ἐπὶ τῆς γῆς. *[two manuscripts from Nagel's family II have an epitome of the penitence narrative; see pericopes 2 and 4]*		[44](29):6 Թողացուցին նմա հրեշտակք և առ նինչ իւր խնկս անուշից. Շիրիկս և սպրանս. Առար զայն և եկաք ի դրախտէ ասորի յերկիրս այս.	[44](29):6 და მიუტევეს ანგელოზთა. და მორთ საკუმეველი სურნელი თბი: ნარდი, კროკნი, ლერწამი და იამოღო - ესე გამორთ სამოთხით აღამ ჴუეყნად.	25-27.12 тогда господь прип оусти ѥмоу благооухание · тьмиянь, ладань и ливань.

[Penitence narrative follows; see pericopes 2-4] |

Pericope 27 **EVE'S TALE:** *Expulsion (Gen 3:22-24)* 73E

GREEK	LATIN	ARMENIAN	GEORGIAN	SLAVONIC
29:5 And God commanded it to be so for Adam that he might take sweet spices and seeds for his food.				25-27.10 And the Lord said to his angels, 'Is it right, that Adam suffers thus, just as the verdict was pronounced on him, or is it unjust?' 25-27.11 The angels spoke in one accord, 'Just is your judgment, O Lord, in truth it is just.'
29:6 And as the angels let him go he took four kinds: crocus and nard and calamus and cinnamon and the other seeds for his food: and, after taking these, he went out of the Garden. And we were on the earth.		[44](29):6 The angels let him be, and he took sweet incenses with him, iris and balsam. We took them and went forth from the Garden to this land.	[44](29):6 And the angels let him and he took four sweet-odored kinds of incense: nard, saffron, reed, cinnamon; that is what Adam brought from the Garden onto the earth.	25-27.12 Then God allowed him to provide the pleasing aromas: incense, laudanum, and libanum.
[two manuscripts from Nagel's family II have an epitome of the penitence narrative; see pericopes 2 and 4]				*[Penitence narrative follows; see pericopes 2-4]*

Pericope 28 *Death of Adam*

GREEK	LATIN	ARMENIAN	GEORGIAN	SLAVONIC
30:1 Νῦν οὖν, τεκνία μου, ἐδήλωσα ὑμῖν τὸν τρόπον ἐν ᾧ ἠπατήθημεν. Ὑμεῖς δὲ φυλάξατε ἑαυτοὺς μὴ ἐγκαταλιπεῖν τὸ ἀγαθόν.		[44](30):1 Արդ [որդեակ] իմ, ՄԷԲ. [ցուցի] ձեզ զտասկս զայս, որպէս զիա՞րդ խաբեաք: բայց դուք զգուշացարուք զբարիս գործել. մի՛ թողուք ի բաց զպատուիրանն Աստուծոյ, եւ մի՛ մերժիք լուսորմութենէ նորա: Ասա զամենայն արրնակ հաստուցման զբարոյ եւ գշարի գուցէց ձեզ:	[44](30):1 "ხოლო აწ, შვილნო ჩემნო, გაუწყე თქუენ ესე საბე ყუელი, რომელთა შევიტყუენით და ამას გეეჯერები, რაითა დაიცვნეთ თავნი თქუენნი და ნუ დააცადებთ კეთილის ყოფასა".	
31:1 Ταῦτα δὲ εἰποῦσα ἐν μέσῳ τῶν υἱῶν αὐτῆς, κοιμωμένου τοῦ Ἀδὰμ ἐν τῇ νόσῳ αὐτοῦ, ἄλλην δὲ εἶχεν μίαν ἡμέραν ἐξελθεῖν ἐκ τοῦ σώματος αὐτοῦ. Καὶ λέγει τῷ Ἀδὰμ ἡ Εὔα·	45:1 Et sicut praedixit Michahel archangelus, post sex dies venit mors Adae.	[45](31):1 Ի ժամանակին յորժամ կայր Աադամ ի հիւանդութեանն եւ նորա շուրջ կային զմոկա, քանզի այլ մի մնաց նա կայր ի կենաց նորա, եւ եւանէր ոզին Ադամայ ի մարմնոյն. Պատմեաց նա զայս ամենայն, եւ դարձեալ նա ասէ ցԱդամ.	[45](31):1 ესე და თქუა ევა შორის შვილთა თვისთა, ოდეს ეძინა ადამს სნეულებასა მისსა. და მერეცსა დღესა გამოსლვად იყო სული გუამისაგან მისისა. ჰრქუა ევა ადამს:	
31:2 Διὰ τί ἀποθνήσκεις κἀγὼ ζῶ; ἢ πόσον χρόνον ἔχω ποιῆσαι μετὰ θάνατόν σου; Ἀνάγγειλόν μοι.	45:2 Cum cognovisset Adam, quia hora venit mortis suae, dixit ad omnes filios suos: ecce sum annorum DCCCCXXX, et si mortuus fuero, sepelite me contra ortum dei magnum (contra ortum dei in agrum habitationis illius?) habitationibus.	[45](31):2 Ընդէ՞ր մեռանիս դու եւ ես կեամ. զի՞նչ աանեմ քեզ կամ որչա՞փ ժամանակս կենցող եմ յերկրի յետ մահու քո պատմեսցես ինձ:	[45](31):2 "რად-მე შენ ხოლო მომჰკუდები და მე ცოცხალ ვარ, ანუ რა- ოდენ ჟამადმდე ვიყო, ანუ რაი ყოფად არს ჩემდა შემდგომად სიკუდილისა შენისა? მაუწყე მე".	

Pericope 28 **Death of Adam**

GREEK	LATIN	ARMENIAN	GEORGIAN	SLAVONIC
30:1 Now then, my children, I have shown you the way in which we were deceived; and do guard yourselves from transgressing against the good."		[44](30):1 Now, my son, Seth, I [have] shown you the way, how we sinned. But you, take care to do the good things. Do not abandon God's command and do not depart from his mercy. Behold, I will show you every sort of recompense, both of good and of evil."	[44](30):1 Now, therefore, my children I have taught you the whole way in which we were tricked and I beseech you to watch yourselves and not to stop doing good."	
31:1 And Eve said this in the midst of her sons, while Adam was lying ill and had but one more day before he would depart from his body. Eve said to Adam:	45:1 Just as Michael had predicted, after six days the death of Adam came.	[45](31):1 At the time when Adam was ill and they were standing around him, because one more day remained of his life and Adam's soul was going forth from his body, Eve related all this. And again Eve said to Adam,	[45](31):1 That, then, is what Eve said in the midst of her children when Adam was lying ill. And on the second day his soul was about to go out of his body. Eve said to Adam,	
31:2 "How is it that you die and I live or how long have I to live after you are dead? Tell me."	45:2 When Adam knew that the hour of his death had come, he said to all his children: "Now I am 930 years old, and if I die, bury me opposite the great Garden of God near his dwelling (opposite the Garden of God in the field of his dwelling?)."	[45](31):2 "Why do you die and I live? Tell me, what shall I do for you? How long shall I be on the earth after your death?"	[45](31):2 "Why do you alone die and I live? Or, how long shall I exist? Or, what will become of me after your death? Let me know about that."	

Pericope 28 *Death of Adam*

GREEK	LATIN	ARMENIAN	GEORGIAN	SLAVONIC
31:3 Τότε λέγει ὁ Ἀδὰμ τῇ Εὔᾳ· Μὴ θέλε φροντίζειν περὶ πραγμάτων· οὐ γὰρ βραδυνεῖς ἀπ' ἐμοῦ, ἀλλ' ἴσα ἀποθνῄσκομεν ἀμφότεροι· καὶ αὐτῇ τεθήσει εἰς τὸν τόπον τὸν ἐμόν. Κἂν ἀποθανῶ, κατάλειψόν με καὶ μηδείς μου ἅψηται ἕως οὗ ἄγγελος λαλήσει τι περὶ ἐμοῦ.	45:3 Et factum est, cum finisset omnes sermones illius, tradidit spiritum.	[45](31):3 Ասէ զնա Ադամ. Մի՛թէ գրաւեցիս ինչ գերկրաւորս այլ վարկիր զի [զդա] մեռանիմք երկրաւան, և զքեզ դիցեն ուր իսկ կայցեմ. բայց իբրև մեռանիմ մի՛ ինչ մերձենայք առ իս շարժել ի տեղոջէ անտի, մինչև Աստուած խաւսեսցի ընդ ձեզ վասն իմ.	[45](31):3 მაშინ ჰრქუა ადამ ევას:" ნუჰრაი გჯონნ შენ, რაისა ჰყავ. ჰკადეთ მოვკუდეთ ორნივე, შენცა დაგებად ხარ ჰე თანა და მე ხოლო თუ მოვკუდე. ნუ შემრევენ ადგილით ჰედით, ვიდრე ოდეს ღმერთმან გიბრძა- ნოს ჰემთვის.	40-41.1 Тогда възьва Адамь великıемь гласомь оумлькии Евго, юже бо дꙋхь мои омалѣль ıєсть вь мьнѣ (ed. одолѣєть сє, read отьдѣлıа ıєть сє, оть тѣла моıєго). нь вьстани, изиди и помоли сє кь богꙋ, доньдеже прѣдамь дꙋхь мои кь богꙋ.
31:4 Οὐ γὰρ ἐπιλήσεταί μου ὁ θεός, ἀλλὰ ζητήσει τὸ ἴδιον σκεῦος ὃ ἔπλασεν. Ἀνάστα, μᾶλλον εὖξαι τῷ θεῷ ἕως οὗ ἀποδώσω τὸ πνεῦμά μου εἰς τὰς χεῖρας τοῦ δεδωκότος μοι αὐτὸ διότι οὐκ οἴδαμεν πῶς ἀπαντήσωμεν τοῦ ποιήσαντος ἡμᾶς, ἢ ὀργισθῇ ἡμῖν ἢ ἐπιστρέψῃ τοῦ ἐλεῆσαι ἡμᾶς.		[45](31):4 զի ոչ եթէ Աստուած մոռասցի զիս, այլ խնդրէ զանասթն զոր ինքն ստեղծաւ է: Արդ, արի կաց յաղաւթս առ Աստուած մինչև տամ զոգի իմ ի ձեռս նորա, որ ետ զնա զի ոչ գիտեմք որպէս զիարդ պատճէմք հաւրն ամենայնի, բարկացցի եթէ ողորմեսցի մեզ:	[45](31):4 რამეთუ არა დამივიწყოს მე ღმერთმან, არამედ მოიძიოს ჭურჭი, რომელი შექმნა. აღდეგ და ილოცე ღმრთისა მიმართ, რაითა შევვე- დრო სული ჰემი ხელთა შემქმელისა ჰემისათა. რამეთუ არა უწყი, ვითარ შევხუედვად ვარ მე შემქმელისა ყოველთაისა ანუ თუ მრისხავსა ანუ თუ შემიყნარებს?"	

Pericope 28 *Death of Adam*

GREEK	LATIN	ARMENIAN	GEORGIAN	SLAVONIC
31:3 And Adam said to her: "Give no thought to this, for you will not tarry long after me, but both of us are to die together. And (as to) this one he shall set (her) in my place. But when I die, leave me alone and let no man touch me till the angel shall says something concerning me. 31:4 For God will not forget me, but will seek the vessel he made. Now, arise, and pray to God until I give up my soul, which he gave me, into His hands. For we know not how we are to meet our Maker, whether He will be angry with us, or will turn to show mercy on us."	45:3 And it happened that, when he had finished all his words, he gave up his spirit.	[45](31):3 Adam said to her, "Do not concern yourself with earthly things, but consider that we will both die as a coup[le], and they will place you where I will be. But when I die, do not come near me to move me from the place, until God speaks with you about me. [45](31):4 For God will not forget me, but he seeks the vessel which he made. Now, arise, pray to God until I give up my soul, which he gave me, into his hands. For I do not know how we shall preserve for the Father of all, whether he will be angry or will be merciful to us."	[45](31):3 Then Adam told Eve, "Be not concerned, whatever you have done. If we must both die, you too will be set near me. And if I [alone] am to die, [do not move] me from my place until God gives you a command about me, [45](31):4 for the Lord will not [forget] me, but rather he will seek out the vessel which he has made. Arise and pray a prayer to God that my soul be commended into the hands of my Creator. For I do not know how I am going to reach the Creator of all, or whether he is angry with me or whether he will accept me."	40-41.1 Then Adam called in a loud voice, "Stop talking, Eve, my spirit is already diminished in me (ed. lit. "is being overcome." Read instead "my spirit is departing from my body"), but arise, go out and pray to God, until I have given my spirit to God."

Pericope 29 EVE'S TALE: *Eve's Confession*

GREEK	LATIN	ARMENIAN	GEORGIAN	SLAVONIC
32:1 Τότε ἀνέστη ἡ Εὔα καὶ ἐξῆλθεν ἔξω· καὶ πεσοῦσα ἐπὶ τὴν γῆν ἔλεγεν·		[45](32):1 Յայնժամ յարեաւ նա, արտաքաց զԱստուած եւ ասէ.	[45](32):1 მაშინ აღდგა ევა და გამოვიდა ადამისაგან და იბნა და თქუა:	40-41.2 тогда въставь Евьга изиде вьнь и прилеже образомь кь земли, и помоли се кь богу и рече ·
32:2 Ἥμαρτον, ὁ θεός, ἥμαρτον, ὁ πατὴρ τῶν ἁπάντων, ἥμαρτόν σοι, ἥμαρτον εἰς τοὺς ἐκλεκτούς σου ἀγγέλους, ἥμαρτον εἰς τὰ χερουβίμ, ἥμαρτον εἰς τὸν ἀσάλευτόν σου θρόνον, ἥμαρτον, κύριε, ἥμαρτον πολλά, ἥμαρτον ἐναντίον σοῦ καὶ πᾶσα ἁμαρτία δι' ἐμὲ γέγονεν ἐν τῇ κτίσει.		[45](32):2 Մեղայ Աստուած. մեղայ քեզ. Տէր իմ սիրելի, մեղայ ընտրելո[ց] քո[յ] հրեշտակաց, մեղայ քերովբէիցն մեղայ սերովբէիցն, մեղայ առաջի քո Տէր. աղաչեմ զամենեսեան զոր ստացեալ է Աստուծոյ յերկինս եւ յերկրի, զի բարեխաաաաաաաաաաա ար Հայր ի յերկինս։	[45](32):2 " შეგცოდე, ღერთო, შეგცოდე და ვცოდე წინაშე შენსა, ვცოდე წინაშე რჩეულთა ანგელოზთა შენთა, ვცოდე წინაშე ქერობინთა, ვცოდე წინაშე საყდრთხევლსა სიმდიდრისა შენისასა, ვცოდე წინაშე ნათესავთა ცისათა, ვცოდე წინაშე მფრინველთა ცისათა, ვცოდე წინაშე მხეცთა ქუეყა-ნისათა. შეგცოდე, ღერთო, ყოვლითა ანგარებითა ჩემთა ყოველთა დაბადებულთა შენთა, გევედრები, თქუენ ყოველთა დაბადებულთა ცისათა და ქუეყანისათა, ევედრებოდეთ ჩემთვის უფალსა ყოველთასა".	40-41.3 сьгрѣшихь ти, господи, сьгрѣшихь ти, владыко, прѣдь аггелы твоими и серафими шестокрилатн- ыми . сьгрѣшихь ти прѣдь страшьнымь прѣстоломь . сьгрѣшихь ти, господи, сьгрѣшихь . вьсакь бо грѣхь мене ради сьтвори се.

Pericope 29 EVE'S TALE: *Eve's Confession* 76E

GREEK	LATIN	ARMENIAN	GEORGIAN	SLAVONIC
32:1 And Eve rose up and went outside and fell on the ground and said:		[45](32):1 Then Eve arose, beseeched God and said,	[45](32):1 Then Eve arose and went out from Adam('s place). She did penitence and said,	40-41.2 Then Eve stood up, went out and fell with her face to the ground, and prayed to God and said,
32:2 "I have sinned, O God, I have sinned, O Father of All, I have sinned against You. I have sinned against your elect angels. I have sinned against the Cherubim. I have sinned against Your unshakable Throne. I have sinned, o Lord, I have greatly sinned, I have sinned before You and all sin has begun through my doing in the creation."		[45](32):2 "I have sinned, God; I have sinned against you, my beloved Lord; I have sinned against your elect angels; I have sinned against the Cherubim; I have sinned against the Seraphs; I have sinned before you, Lord. I beseech all (you) whom God created in the heavens and on the earth, that you intercede with the Father in heaven."	[45](32):2 "I have sinned against you, God; I have sinned against you and I have sinned before you. I have sinned before your elect angels. I have sinned before the Cherubim. I have sinned before the altar of your holiness. I have sinned before the generations of the heavens. I have sinned before the birds of heavens. I have sinned before the beasts of the earth. I have sinned against you, God, by all my greed, among all your creatures. I beseech you all, you creatures of heaven and earth, beseech the Lord of all for me."	40-41.3 "I have sinned before you, O Lord, sinned, O Master, before the angels and six-winged Seraphim, sinned before your awesome throne, sinned, O Lord, sinned; for each and every sin occurs through me."

Pericope 29 EVE'S TALE: *Eve's Confession*

GREEK	LATIN	ARMENIAN	GEORGIAN	SLAVONIC
32:3 Ἔτι δὲ εὐχομένης τῆς Εὔας [ἐπὶ τὰ γόνατα αὐτῆς οὔσης] ἰδού, ἦλθεν πρὸς αὐτὴν ὁ ἄγγελος τῆς ἀνθρωπότητος καὶ ἀνέστησεν αὐτὴν λέγων·		[45](32):3 եւ մինչդեռ կայր աղաւթս նա. ի ծունր իջեալ. աՃա եկն առ նա Մքրայէլ հրեշտակապետն կանգնէլ զնա, եւ ասէ.	[45](32):3 ილოცვიდა ოდენ ევა მუხლთა თვისთა ზედა და მეყსეულად მოვიდა მიქაელ ანგელოზი კაცებისა და აღადგინა ევა და ჰრქვა:	40-41.4а и прииде аггелъ господьнь къ Євьзѣ и рече·
32:4 Ἀνάστα, Εὔα, ἐκ τῆς μετανοίας σου· ἰδοὺ γὰρ ὁ Ἀδὰμ ὁ ἀνήρ σου ἐξῆλθεν ἀπὸ τοῦ σώματος αὐτοῦ· Ἀνάστα καὶ ἰδὲ τὸ πνεῦμα αὐτοῦ ἀναφερόμενον εἰς τὸν ποιήσαντα αὐτὸν τοῦ ἀπαντῆσαι αὐτῷ.		[45](32):4 Արի նա յապաշխարութենէ քումդէ, աՃա Աղամայ առն քո ել Հոգին ի մարմնոյ անտի:	[45](32):4 აღდეგ სინანულისაგან მაგის შენისა, რამეთუ ადამ, ქმარი შე-ნი, გამოსრულ არს ხორცთაგან. აღდეგ და იხილე სული მისი, ვითარ-ა ჰყავს შემოქმედსა თვისსა".	40-41.4b въстани, Євьго, оть покаянния, юже бо Адамь изиде оть тѣла своюго и доухъ юго изиде и прииде прѣдъ господа.

Pericope 29 EVE'S TALE: *Eve's Confession*

GREEK	LATIN	ARMENIAN	GEORGIAN	SLAVONIC
32:3 Even as Eve prayed [on her knees] behold, the angel of mankind came to her, and raised her up and said:		[45](32):3 While Eve was praying on bended knee, behold, the archangel Michael came to her, stood her up and said,	[45](32):3 While Eve was praying on her [[knees]], suddenly Michael came, the angel of mankind, he stood Eve up, and told her,	40-41.4a And the angel of the Lord came to Eve and said,
32:4 "Rise up, Eve, from your penitence, for behold, Adam your husband has gone out of his body. Rise up and behold his spirit borne aloft to meet his Maker."		[45](32):4 "Arise, Eve, from your penitence. Behold, the soul of your husband Adam has gone forth from the body."	[45](32):4 "Arise from that penitence, for Adam your spouse has gone forth from the body. Arise and see his soul, how his Creator has already (got) it."	40-41.4b "Rise up, Eve, from your repentance, for Adam has already departed out of his body and his spirit is separated and gone before God."

Pericope 30 *Angelic Liturgy*

GREEK	LATIN	ARMENIAN	GEORGIAN	SLAVONIC
33:1 Ἀναστᾶσα δὲ Εὕα ἐπέβαλεν τὴν χεῖρα αὐτῆς ἐπὶ τὸ πρόσωπον αὐτοῦ. [Καὶ λέγει αὐτῇ ὁ ἄγγελος· ἆρον καὶ αὐτὴν ἀπὸ τῶν γηίνων.]		[45](33):1 Կանգնեցաւ եւա,	[45](33):1 აღდგა ევა და დაიდვა ხელი პირსა ზედა თვისსა და ამაღლდა ანგელოზი იგი და ჰრქუა ევას:" აღიხილენ თუალნი შენნი და განეშორე ზრუნვათაგან ქუეყანისათა".	
33:2 Καὶ ἀτενίσασα εἰς τὸν οὐρανὸν ἰδεν ἅρμα φωτὸς ἐρχόμενον ὑπὸ τεσσάρων ἀετῶν λαμπρῶν ὃ οὐκ ἦν δυνατὸν γεννηθῆναι ἀπὸ κοιλίας ἢ εἰπεῖν τὴν δόξαν αὐτῶν ἢ ἰδεῖν τὸ πρόσωπον αὐτῶν, καὶ ἀγγέλους προάγοντας τὸ ἅρμα.			[45](33):2 ხოლო ევა, ვითარცა აღიხილნა თვალნი თვისნი ზეცად და იხილნა ეტლნი ცეცხლისანი და ნათელი აღმავალი ოთხთა ქართა ზედა, ეგრე ბრწყინვალე იყვნეს, ვითარცა ვერარაი ემსგავსების თქუმად, ვერ შემძლებელ იყო განცდად ვერცა მუცლით, ვერცა ზურგით, და ანგელოზნი წინა უძღოდეს ეტლთა მათ,	
33:3 Ὅτε δὲ ἦλθεν ὅπου ἔκειτο ὁ πατὴρ ὑμῶν Ἀδάμ, ἔστη τὸ ἅρμα καὶ τὰ Σεραφὶμ ἀνὰ μέσον τοῦ πατρὸς καὶ τοῦ ἅρματος.			[45](33):3 და ვითარცა მივიდეს, საღცა-იგი იყო მამაი, დადგა ეტლი იგი და სერაბინნი დგეს შორის მისსა და შორის ეტლთა.	

Pericope 30 *Angelic Liturgy*

GREEK	LATIN	ARMENIAN	GEORGIAN	SLAVONIC
33:1 And Eve rose up and put her hand on the face (of Adam), [and the angel said to her, "Lift up your hand from that which is of the earth."]		[45](33):1 Eve arose,	[45](33):1 Eve arose and put her hand on her face and the angel went up again, and he told Eve, "Raise you eyes and abandon earthly concerns."	
33:2 And she gazed steadfastly into heaven, and beheld a chariot of light, borne by four bright eagles, (and) it was impossible for any man born of woman to tell the glory of them or behold their face—and angels going before the chariot.			[45](33):2 As for Eve, when she had raised her eyes towards the heavens, she saw chariots of fire and a light which went up, (borne) by four [[winds]]: they were so resplendent that no word could express it, and it was impossible to sound them out, neither from the front nor from the back. And angels were proceeding before these chariots.	
33:3 But when they came to the place where your father Adam was, the chariot halted and the Seraphim were between the father and the chariot.			[45](33):3 And when they had arrived (at the place) where the father was, the chariot stopped and the Seraphs stood between him and the chariots.	

Pericope 30 *Angelic Liturgy*

GREEK	LATIN	ARMENIAN	GEORGIAN	SLAVONIC
33:4 Ἴδον δὲ ἐγὼ θυμιατήρια χρυσᾶ καὶ τρεῖς φιάλας· καὶ ἰδοὺ πάντες οἱ ἄγγελοι μετὰ λίβανον καὶ θυμιατήρια ἦλθον ἐν σπουδῇ ἐπὶ τὸ θυσιαστήριον καὶ ἐνεφύσων αὐτά· καὶ ἡ ἀτμὶς τοῦ θυμιάματος ἐκάλυψεν τὰ στερεώματα.			[45](33):4 და ვიხილე მე, ევა, სასაკუმევლე სამი ოქროისაი და ფიალები და სამი ანგელოზნი მოვიდეს სწრაფით საკურთხეველსა ზედა. მოილეს ნა-კუერცხალი და შთაასხეს საკუმეველი ანგელოზთა მათ მას ზედა. და ვითარცა ჰბერვიდეს, აღვიდოდა კუამლი და დაფარნა სამყარონი ცისანი.	40-41.5 И възврата се Євга гдѣ лежить тѣло отьца нашего Адама и видѣ кадильницѫ златѫ и .г. свѣтильницє горѫще и .г. аггєлы, дрьжєщє тѣхь, кадєщє тѣло адамово, и воня благоѹхания възидѣ до нєбєсь .
33:5 Καὶ προσέπεσαν οἱ ἄγγελοι τῷ θεῷ βοῶντες καὶ λέγοντες· Ἰαὴλ ἅγιε, συγχώρησον, ὅτι εἰκὼν σοῦ ἐστιν καὶ ποίημα τῶν χειρῶν σου τῶν ἁγίων.			[45](33):5 აკუედეს ანგელოზნი იგი და თაყუანის-სცემდეს, ღაღადებდეს და იტყოდეს: "ღმერთო, მოუტევენ ადამს, რამეთუ ხატი შენი და ქმნული ხელთა შენთა არს და დაბადებული შენი არს".	40-41.6 и сьшьдьшємь сє аггєломь поклонишє сє прѣдь прѣстоломь, глаголющє архаггєль Иоиль · свєть свєтымь, владыко прости тварь свою, яко тварь рѫкѹ твоєю ѥсть .
34:1 [καὶ αὖθις] ἴδον ἐγὼ Εὔα δύο μεγάλα καὶ φοβερὰ μυστήρια ἐνώπιον τοῦ θεοῦ· καὶ ἔκλαυσα ἐκ τοῦ φόβου καὶ ἐβόησα πρὸς τὸν υἱόν μου Σὴθ λέγουσα·	46:1 Obtenebratus est sol et luna et stellae per dies VII. et cum esset Seth amplexans corpus patris sui lugens desuper et Eva cum esset respiciens in terram intextas manus super caput eius habens et caput super genua imponens et omnes filii eius fletibus amaris simis lacrimassent:		[46](34):1 და ვიხილეს მე, ევა, ორნი საოცელნი დიდნი შიშით დაცვმულნი წინაშე ღმრთისა, და ვტიროდე და ვარქუ ძესა ჩემსა სეითს:	42-44.1a Євга же видѣ вєлия чюдєса, строєща сє прѣдь богомь, и плака сє сь страхомь вєликымь и възва сына своєго Сида, и рєчє ємѹ ·

Pericope 30 *Angelic Liturgy* 79E

GREEK	LATIN	ARMENIAN	GEORGIAN	SLAVONIC
33:4 And I beheld golden censers and three bowls, and beheld all the angels with censers and frankincense came in haste to the incense-offering and blew upon it and the smoke of the incense veiled the firmament.			[45](33):4 And I, Eve, saw three gold censers, and (three) [cups] and three angels come quickly upon the altar. These angels took a burning coal and put it in the censer and set the censer upon the (altar). And while they blew, the smoke went up and veiled the firmaments of the heavens.	40-41.5 And Eve returned again to where the corpse of our father Adam lay, and she saw a golden incense pot and three burning flares and three angels attending them, and the corpse of Adam anointed and the scent of fragrance ascending to Heaven.
33:5 And the angels fell down to God, crying aloud and saying, "Jael, Holy One, have pardon, for he is Your image, and the work of Your holy hands."			[45](33):5 The angels were praising (God), they were bowing before him, crying out and saying, "God, forgive Adam for he is your image and the work of your hands: he is your creature."	40-41.6 And as the angels assembled, they bowed before the throne and the archangel Joel said, "Holy above holy, O Lord, forgive your creature, for it is the creation of your hands."
34:1 [And then] I Eve beheld two great and fearful mysteries before the presence of God and I wept for fear, and I cried aloud to my son Seth and said,	46:1 The sun, moon and stars grew dark for seven days. Seth embraced the body of his father and mourned over it. Eve cast her eyes upon the ground with her hands clasped above her head and her head placed on her knees. All her children wept with very bitter tears.		[46](34):1 And I, Eve, saw two great lights prostrated in fear before [God] and I wept and told my son Seth,	42-44.1a Eve saw great marvels, which were being performed before God and cried in great distress and called her son Seth and said to him,

Pericope 30 *Angelic Liturgy*

GREEK	LATIN	ARMENIAN	GEORGIAN	SLAVONIC
34:2 Ἀνάστα, Σήθ, ἐκ τοῦ σώματος τοῦ πατρός σου καὶ ἐλθὲ πρός με καὶ ἴδε ἃ οὐκ εἶδεν ὀφθαλμὸς ποτε τινὸς καὶ πῶς δέονται ὑπὲρ τοῦ πατρός σου Ἀδάμ.	46:2 Et ecce Michahel angelus apparuit stans ad caput Adae et dixit ad Seth: exurge desuper corpus patris tui et veni ad me et vide, quid de eo disponat dominus deus. plasma eius est et misertus est ei.		[46](34):2 აღდეგ ჴორცისაგან მამისა შენისა და მოვედ ჩემდა და იხილე რომელი თუალთა შენთა არა უხილავს ადამისთჳს მამისა შენისა".	42-44.1b въстани, Сиде, отъ тѣла отьца твоѥго и прииди, да видиши чюдо, ѥже не видѣль ѥси николиже.
35:1 Τότε ἀνέστη Σὴθ καὶ ἦλθεν πρὸς τὴν μητέρα αὐτοῦ καὶ λέγει αὐτῇ· Διὰ τί κλαίεις·			[46](35):1 მაშინ აღდგა სეთ და მოვიდა ევასა, დედისა თჳსისა, და ჰრქუა:"რად სტირ?	42-44.2a въставъ же Сидь прииде къ матери своѥи, и рече ѥмоу.
35:2 Καὶ λέγει αὐτῷ· Ἀνάβλεψον τοῖς ὀφθαλμοῖς σου καὶ ἴδε τὰ ἑπτὰ στερεώματα ἀνεῳγμένα καὶ πῶς κεῖται τὸ σῶμα τοῦ πατρὸς ἐπὶ πρόσωπον, καὶ πάντες οἱ ἄγγελοι μετ᾽ αὐτοῦ εὐχόμενοι ὑπὲρ αὐτοῦ καὶ λέγοντες· Συγχώρησον αὐτῷ, ὁ πατὴρ τῶν ὅλων, ὅτι εἰκών σού ἐστιν.			[46](35):2 აღიხილენ თუალნი შენნი და იხილენ შჳდნი სამყარონი განჴსნულნი და იხილე ანგელებნი მამისა ადამის, ვითარ დცს იგი ჶონავზე ღმრთისა. და ყოველნი ანგელოზნი ევედრებიან მისთჳს და იტყვიან: მოჳტევე, ღმერთო, ადამს, რამეთუ ხატი შენი არს და მსგავსი, რამეთუ შენ შეჰქმენ".	42-44.2b възри сыноу на небо. 42-44.3 и възрѣвъ и видѣ Сидь вьсе воиньство аггель, стоѥще прѣдъ прѣстоломь господьнимь и молеще се глаголахоу · помилоуи, владыко, тварь свою .
35:3 Ἆρα δέ, τέκνον μου Σὴθ τί ἐστίν μοι; πότε παραδοθήσεται εἰς τὰς χεῖρας τοῦ ἀοράτου θεοῦ ἡμῶν;			[46](35):3 "ჵო შჳლო ჩემო, სეთ,	
35:4 Τίνες δέ εἰσιν, υἱέ μου Σήθ, οἱ δύο Αἰθίοπες οἱ παριστάμενοι ἐπὶ τὴν προσευχὴν τοῦ πατρός σου;			[46](35):4a ანუმცა ვინღათა ამათ მისცემენ სისხლსა ქრმისა ჩემისასა, რამეთუ ouცნ ოვნი ჶონავზე ღმრთისა".	

Pericope 30 *Angelic Liturgy* 80E

GREEK	LATIN	ARMENIAN	GEORGIAN	SLAVONIC
34:2 "Rise up, Seth, from the body of your father Adam, and come to me, and see a spectacle which no man's eye has yet beheld and how they supplicate on behalf of your father, Adam."	46:2 Then Michael the angel appeared, standing at Adam's head, and said to Seth: "Arise from the body of your father, and come with me and see what the Lord God has arranged for him. He is his creature and he has taken pity on him.		[46](34):2 "Rise up from beside your father's body, come towards me and see that which your eyes have not seen, concerning Adam your father."	42-44.1b "Arise, Seth, from the corpse of your father and come to see a marvelous thing, such as you have never seen before."
35:1 Then Seth arose and came to his mother and said to her: "Why do you weep?"			[46](35):1 Then Seth arose and went close to his mother Eve and told her, "Why are you weeping?	42-44.2a Seth arose and came to his mother and she said to him,
35:2 And she said to him: "Look up and see with your eyes the seven heavens opened, and see how the body of your father lies on its face and all the holy angels are praying on his behalf and saying: 'Pardon him, Father of All, for he is Your image.'"			[46](35):2 Raise your eyes and see the seven firmaments open and see the likeness of father Adam, as he lies before God and all the angels are beseeching him and saying, 'God, forgive Adam, for he is your image and your likeness, because it is you who have created him.'"	42-44.2b "Look, my son, toward heaven." 42-44.3 And looking up Seth saw the whole angelic host standing before the throne of the Lord, saying in prayer, "Pity your creation O Master."
35:3 Pray, my child Seth, what shall this mean? And will he one day be delivered into the hands of our Invisible God?			[46](35):3 "What is this, then, my son Seth?	

Pericope 30 *Angelic Liturgy*

GREEK	LATIN	ARMENIAN	GEORGIAN	SLAVONIC
			[46](35):4b მიუ-გო ევას სეთ და ჰრქუა:" არა ევრე. დედაო, არა იცან ესე, რომელთა იღო-ებაი სოჳლ სისხლისფერთაი მათ". [46](35):4c მიუგო ევა და ჰრქუა:" არა იცჳნო, შვილო ჩემო".	
36:1 Λέγει δὲ Σὴθ τῇ μητρὶ αὐτοῦ· ὅτι εἰσὶν ὁ ἥλιος καὶ ἡ σελήνη, καὶ αὐτοὶ προσπίπτοντες καὶ εὐχόμενοι ὑπὲρ τοῦ πατρός μου Ἀδάμ.			[46](36):1 მიუგო სეთ და ჰრქუა:" ესე არიან მზე და მთოვარე და იგინი დავრდომილ არიან და ევედრებიან ადამისთჳს, მამისა ჩემისა".	42-44.4 пакы Сиδь рече кь матєри своюи · възьри, яко слиньцє и луна покланяютасѧ прѣстолу и молеще сѧ за отьца нашєго Адама .
36:2 Λέγει αὐτῷ ἡ Εὔα· Καὶ ποῦ ἐστιν τὸ φῶς αὐτῶν καὶ διὰ τί γεγόνασι μελανοειδεῖς;	*see 46.1*		[46](36):2 "სადა არს ნათელი იგი მზისაი, რამეთუ არლა რაი არს მის თანა. ანუ რაჲდე დაშავებულ არს ევრე?"	42-44.5 и рече Євьга · гдє єсть свѣть тѣмь;
36:3 Καὶ λέγει αὐτῇ Σήθ· Οὐκ ἀπέστη τὸ φῶς αὐτῶν, ἀλλ' οὐ δύνανται φαίνειν ἐνώπιον τοῦ φωτὸς τῶν ὅλων, τοῦ πατρὸς τῶν φώτων, καὶ διὰ τοῦτο ἐκρύβη τὸ φῶς ἀπ' αὐτῶν.			[46](36):3 მიუგო სეთ და ჰრქუა ევას:" რამეთუ განჴდა ნათელი მისი წინაშე ღმრთისა ყოველთაისა და შევა ნათელი მისი ბოშისაგან ღმრთისა".	42-44.6 рече Сидь матєри своюи · єгда въста архаггель Михаиль молити сѧ, и умлькошє вьсє силы аггєльскыє прѣдь госп одомь,

Pericope 30 *Angelic Liturgy* 81E

GREEK	LATIN	ARMENIAN	GEORGIAN	SLAVONIC
35:4 But who are, my son Seth, the two Ethiopians who stand by at the prayers for your father?"			[46](35):4a Do they deliver [the blood of my spouse] to these Indians, for they were before God?" [46](35):4b Seth replied to Eve and told her, "No, mother, [did you not recognize those whom you called Indians in these colors of blood]?" [46](35):4c Eve replied to him and told him, "I do not know them, my son."	
36:1 And Seth said to his mother, "They are the sun and moon and themselves fall down and pray on behalf of my father Adam."			[46](36):1 Seth replied to her and told her, "These are the sun and the moon: they are prostrated and they are beseeching for Adam, my father."	42-44.4 Again Seth spoke to his mother, "Look there, how the sun and moon bow down to the throne, praying for our father Adam."
36:2 Eve said to him: "And where is their light and why have they taken on such a black appearance?"	*see 46.1*		[46](36):2 Where is the light of the sun, for it is no more with it, or why is it darkened thus?"	42-44.5 And Eve said, "Where is their light?"
36:3 And Seth answered her, "The light has not left them, but they cannot shine before the Light of all things, the Father of Light; and on this account their light has been hidden."			[46](36):3 Seth replied to her and told Eve, "Because its light has been eclipsed before the God of all and its light had become darkened by fear of God."	42-44.6 Seth said to his mother, "When the archangel Michael himself arose in order to pray, all the power of the angels before throne of the Lord ceased."

Pericope 31 *Assumption of Adam to Paradise*

GREEK	LATIN	ARMENIAN	GEORGIAN	SLAVONIC
37:1 Λέγοντος δὲ τοῦ Σὴθ ταῦτα πρὸς τὴν μητέρα αὐτοῦ Εὔαν, ἰδοὺ ἐσάλπισεν ὁ ἄγγελος· καὶ ἀνέστησαν πάντες οἱ ἄγγελοι οἱ ἐπ' ὄψεσιν κείμενοι καὶ ἐβόησαν φωνὴν φοβερὰν λέγοντες·	47:1 Et omnes angeli canentes tubis dixerunt:		[47](37):1 ამას ჰრაო ეტყოდა სეთი ევას, მეყსეულად დიდსა ანგელოზსან დაჰბერა საყვირსა და აღმართნეს ანგელოზნი, რომელნი დაცუემულ იყვნეს პირსა ზედა თვისსა. ევედრებოდეს ადმისათვის, ხმა-ყვეს ხმითა დიდითა და თქუეს:	42-44.7a и пакы аггели велиемь гласомь възьваше, глюще ·
37:2 Εὐλογημένη ἡ δόξα κυρίου ἀπὸ ποιημάτων αὐτοῦ, ὅτι ἠλέησεν τὸ πλάσμα τῶν χειρῶν αὐτοῦ Ἀδάμ.	benedictus es, domine, quia misertus es plasmae tuae.		[47](37):2 "კურთხეულ არს ღმერთი ყოვლითა კურთხევითა. შეიწყალე პირველი დაბადებული".	42-44.7b благословена слава госп одьня, помиловавыи тварь свою Адама.
37:3 Ὅτε δὲ εἶπον τὰς φωνὰς ταύτας οἱ ἄγγελοι, ἰδοὺ ἦλθεν ἓν τῶν Σεραφὶμ ἑξαπτερύγων· καὶ ἥρπασε τὸν Ἀδὰμ καὶ ἀπήγαγεν αὐτὸν εἰς τὴν Ἀχερουσίαν λίμνην καὶ ἀπέλουσεν αὐτὸν τρίτον καὶ ἤγαγεν αὐτὸν ἐνώπιον τοῦ θεοῦ.			[47](37):3 და ოდეს თქუეს ანგელოზთა ხმაი ესე, მოვლინა მისა ერთი სერაბინთაგანი ექუსფრთე და მიიტაცა ადამი ტბასა მას ქერუანისასა	45-46.1 Тогда прииде множьство аггель, херувими и серафими, и възеше тѣло Адамово и поставише к вь Герусие блато и прославивьше его ту омываху .г.- щи .

Pericope 31 *Assumption of Adam to Paradise* 82E

GREEK	LATIN	ARMENIAN	GEORGIAN	SLAVONIC
37:1 Now while Seth was saying this to his mother, behold, an angel blew the trumpet, and all the angels who were lying on their faces rose up, and they cried aloud in an fearsome voice and said:	47:1 Then all the angels, playing trumpets, said:		[47](37):1 As Seth was telling that to Eve, at once a great angel blew the trumpet and all the angels who were prostrated on their faces stood up again. They prayed for Adam and cried out in a loud voice, and said,	42-44.7a And again the angels cried out in a loud voice saying,
37:2 "Blessed (be) the glory of the Lord from the works of His making, for He has pitied Adam, the creature of His hands."	"Blessed are you, Lord, for you have taken pity on your creature."		[47](37):2 "Blessed [is God, by all blessing. You] pardoned the protoplast."	42-44.7b "Blessed is the glory of the Lord, who has reprieved his creature Adam."
37:3 But when the angels had said these words, behold, there came one of the Seraphim with six wings and snatched up Adam and carried him off to the Acherusian lake, and washed him thrice, and led him before God.			[47](37):3 And when the angels had said these words, one of the six-winged Seraphim was sent towards him (Adam). He took Adam to the lake of (A)cheron,	45-46.1 Then came a multitude of angels, Cherubim and Seraphim, and they took the corpse of Adam and laid him in the Sea of Gerusia and honoring him, they washed him three times.

Pericope 31 *Assumption of Adam to Paradise*

GREEK	LATIN	ARMENIAN	GEORGIAN	SLAVONIC
37:4 Ἐποίησεν δὲ τρεῖς ὥρας κείμενος. Καὶ μετὰ ταῦτα ἐξέτεινεν τὴν χεῖρα αὐτοῦ ὁ πατὴρ τῶν ὅλων καθήμενος ἐπὶ τοῦ θρόνου αὐτοῦ καὶ ἦρεν τὸν Ἀδὰμ καὶ παρέδωκεν αὐτὸν τῷ ἀρχαγγέλῳ Μιχαὴλ λέγων·	47:2 Tunc vidit Seth manum domini extensam tenentem Adam; et tradidit Michaheli dicens:		[47](37):4 და განბანა სამჯერ, მოუვანა ოგ ჭონაშე ღმრთისა და ოდეა ოგ ვინხა ზედა თვისსა ვიდრე სამ ჟამ ოდენ. და შემდგომად მისსა მოყო ხელი თვისი ღმერთმან საყრთით თვისით და აღადგინა ადამი და მისცა მი- ქაელს და ჰრქვა მას:	45-46.2a въ .г.-тии же часъ прострѣ господь роукоу свою, сєдєщи на прѣстолѣ, и възєть Адама, и прѣдасть кго архаггєлоу Михаилоу, и речє кмоу господь ·
37:5 Ἆρον αὐτὸν εἰς τὸν παράδεισον ἕως τρίτου οὐρανοῦ καὶ ἄφες αὐτὸν ἐκεῖ ἕως τῆς ἡμέρας ἐκείνης τῆς μεγάλης τῆς οἰκονομίας ἧς ποιήσω εἰς τὸν κόσμον.	47:3 sit in custodia tua usque in diem dispensationis in suppliciis ad annos novissimos, quando convertam luctum eius in gaudium. Tunc sedebit in throno eius, qui eum supplantavit.		[47](37):5 "მოუვანე ეგე მესამესა ცასა სამოთხეს და დაუტევე ჭონაშე საკურთხეველსა ვიდრე დღედმდე გაბებისა, რომელი მევულვებოს ყოველ- თა თანა ხორციელთა საყუარელისა მისა ჩემისა თანა".	42-44.2b вънєси тѣло кго вь раи, доухь же кго да прѣбываєть вь трєтиємь нєбєси . тѣло же кго тоу да прѣбываєть до въскрьсєния мокго .
37:6 Τότε ὁ Μιχαὴλ ἦρεν τὸν Ἀδὰμ καὶ ἀφῆκεν αὐτὸν ὅπου εἶπεν αὐτῷ ὁ θεός· καὶ πάντες οἱ ἄγγελοι ὕμνουν ὕμνον ἀγγελικὸν θαυμάζοντες ἐπὶ τῇ συγχωρήσει τοῦ Ἀδάμ.			[47](37):6 მაშინ მიჰყვანა ჭარყუანა ადამი ადგილსა მას, რომელსა უბრძანა ღმერთმან, და ყოველნი ანგელოზნი ფსალმუნებდეს ფსალმუნსა ანგელოზისა. აქებდე საკვირველებასა ადამისსა და ალთქუმასა მას მერ- მისსა.	45-46.3 тогда архаггєль покмь Адама и принєсє кго идєже речє кмоу господь .

Pericope 31 *Assumption of Adam to Paradise*

GREEK	LATIN	ARMENIAN	GEORGIAN	SLAVONIC
37:4 And he stayed there three hours, lying down, and thereafter the Father of all, sitting on his holy throne stretched out his hand, and took Adam and handed him over to the archangel Michael saying:	47:2 Then Seth saw the hand of the Lord outstretched, holding Adam. He handed him over to Michael, saying:		[47](37):4 and he dipped him in it three times. Then he led him back before God and (Adam) remained (prostrate) on his face for three hours. And after that, God stretched out his hand from his throne, raised Adam up and gave him to Michael, and he told him,	45-46.2a In the third hour, however, the Lord, seated on the throne, stretched forth his hand and took Adam and gave him to the archangel Michael and said to him,
37:5 "Lift him up into the Garden unto the third Heaven, and leave him there until that fearful day of my reckoning, which I will make in the world."	47:3 "Let him be in your care until the day of retribution, in supplication until the last years when I shall change his mourning into joy. Then he will sit on the throne of him who beguiled him."		[47](37):5 "Take him to the third heaven, to the Garden, and leave him before the altar until the day of the 'oikonomia' which I contemplate concerning all the fleshly (beings) with my well-beloved Son."	42-44.2b "Carry his corpse into Paradise; his spirit shall tarry in the third Heaven, but his corpse shall remain here until my resurrection."
37:6 Then Michael took Adam and left him where God told him. And all the angels sang an angelic hymn being amazed at the pardoning of Adam.			[47](37):6 Then Michael took Adam to the place which God had ordered and all the angels were chanting angelic psalms. They were praising this wonder: the forgiveness of Adam and the promise of a future (life).	45-46.3 Then the archangel took Adam and carried him there, to the place God had commanded him.

Pericope 32 *Adam and Abel's Funerary Rites*

GREEK	LATIN	ARMENIAN	GEORGIAN	SLAVONIC
38:1 Μετὰ δὲ τὴν γεγενομένην χαρὰν τοῦ Ἀδὰμ ἐβόησεν πρὸς τὸν πατέρα ὁ ἀρχάγγελος Μιχαὴλ διὰ τὸν Ἀδάμ. 38:2 Καὶ ἐλάλησεν ὁ πατὴρ πρὸς αὐτὸν ἵνα συναχθῶσιν πάντες οἱ ἄγγελοι ἐνώπιον τοῦ θεοῦ, ἕκαστος κατὰ τὴν τάξιν αὐτοῦ, τινὲς μὲν ἔχοντες θυμιατήρια ἐν χερσὶν αὐτῶν, ἄλλοι δὲ κιθάρας καὶ φιάλας καὶ σάλπιγγας.		[47](38):2 եւ ժողովեցան Հրեշտակք ամենայն առաջի նորա ըստ իւրաքանչիւր կարգի. ոմանք ունէին բուրվառս ի ձեռս իւրեանց, ոմանք ունէին փողս, եւ ոմանք ունէին արհնութիւս։	[47](38):1 შემდგომად ადმისა ლადად-ყო მოკალე ღმრთისა მთავარ [47](38):2 და ღმერთმან ბრძანა დაცემად საყვირისა და შეკრებაჲ ყოველთა ანგელოზთა წინაშე ღმრთისა თითოეულად შესტა მათ, რომელთა აქუნდა სასაკუმევლე და რომელთამე აქუნდა საგალობელი და რომელნი- მე საყვირსა სცემდეს.	
38:3 Καὶ ἰδοὺ κύριος στρατιῶν ἐπέβη καὶ τέσσαρες ἄνεμοι εἷλκον αὐτόν, καὶ τὰ χερουβὶμ ἐπέχοντα τοῖς ἀνέμοις καὶ οἱ ἄγγελοι ἐκ τοῦ οὐρανοῦ προάγοντες αὐτόν. Καὶ ἐλθόντες ἐπὶ τὴν γῆν ὅπου ἦν τὸ σῶμα τοῦ Ἀδάμ.		[47](38):3 եւ ահա Տէր զաւրութեանց ի կառս բերրրէից. եւ չորք հողմք ձգէին զնա, եւ բերրրէքն սպասէին հողմոցն այն. եւ Հրեշտակքն գնային առաջի նորա. եկն Աստուած յերկիր ի տեղի ուր կայր մարմինն Ադամայ, եւ ամենայն Հրեշտակք արհնութեամբ առաջի նորա։	[47](38):3 და აჰა უფალი საბაოთისა აჰხდა ქერობინთა ქართა ზედა და ანგელოზნი შვიდით ცით წინა ფდღოლეს მას, და მოვიდეს ქუეყანად, სადაცა ისხნეს ხორცნი ადამისი. და ყოველნი ანგელოზნი ფგალობდეს.	

Pericope 32 *Adam and Abel's Funerary Rites* 84E

GREEK	LATIN	ARMENIAN	GEORGIAN	SLAVONIC
38:1 But after this joyous event of Adam, the archangel Michael cried to the Father concerning Adam. 38:2 And the Father commanded him that all the angels should assemble before God, each in his order, some having censers in their hands, and others lyres, bowls and trumpets. 38:3 And behold, the Lord of Hosts entered and four winds drew Him and Cherubim mounted on the winds and the angels from heaven escorting Him and they came on the earth, where was the body of Adam.		[47](38):2 and all the angels assembled before her, each according to his rank. Some of them bore censers in their hands, others bore trumpets and others bore blessings. [47](38):3 Behold, the Lord of hosts upon a Cherub chariot and four wind[s] were drawing him, and Cherubim were serving those winds and the angels were proceeding before him: God came to the earth, to the place where Adam's body lay, and all of the angels (were) before him with praises.	[47](38):1 After which Michael cried out towards God, [47](38):2 and God ordered that the trumpet be sounded and that all the angels assemble before God, each one in his rank: those who held a censer; those who held a psaltery; and those who sounded the trumpet. [47](38):3 And behold, the Lord of Sabaoth rose upon the winds of the Cherubim, and from the seven heavens angels were proceeding before him, and they came to the earth to the place where the fleshly (remains) of Adam had been put, and all the angels were sing-ing his (praises).	

Pericope 32 *Adam and Abel's Funerary Rites*

GREEK	LATIN	ARMENIAN	GEORGIAN	SLAVONIC
38:4 Καὶ ἦλθον εἰς τὸν παράδεισον· καὶ ἐκινήθησαν πάντα τὰ φυτὰ τοῦ παραδείσου, ὡς πάντας ἀνθρώπους γεγεννημένους ἐκ τοῦ Ἀδὰμ νυστάξαι ἀπὸ τῆς εὐωδίας, χωρὶς τοῦ Σὴθ μόνου, ὅτι ἐγένετο καθορῶν τοῦ θεοῦ.		[47](38):4 եկն Աստուած ի դրախտն եւ [շարժեցան] ամենայն տունկքն եւ ամենայն մարդ որ առ Ադամ էին քուն էառ զնոսա, բայց միայն Սէթ առաքինն արթուն էր քան տեսու[չ]ութեանն Աստուծոյ։	[47](38):4 და მოჰყვა პირველად სამოთხესა თჳსსა, და შეიძრნეს ყუავილნი სამოთხისანი სულნელებითა თჳსითა, სულნელებისაგა ნ დიდებულისა ღმრთისა დასულებეს ყუველნი ნაშობნი ადამისნი, გარნა სეით ხოლო არა, რამეთუ ნაშობი იყო სიმდიდრისა ღმრთისაო.	
39:1 [καὶ ἦλθεν ὁ θεὸς] πρὸς τὸ σῶμα τοῦ Ἀδὰμ καὶ ἐλυπήθη σφόδρα ἐπ᾿ αὐτῷ· καὶ λέγει αὐτῷ ὁ θεός· Ἀδάμ, τί τοῦτο ἐποίησας; Εἰ ἐφύλαξας τὴν ἐντολήν μου, οὐκ ἂν ἐχαίροντο οἱ καταγαγόντες σε εἰς τὸν τόπον τοῦτον.		[47](39):1 եկն Աստուած առ մարմինն Ադամայ ուր կայր մեռեալ, տրտմեցաւ Աստուած յոյժ եւ ասէ ի ձայն բարձրութեան. Ո՛ Ադամ. զի՞նչ արարեր դու. եթէ պահեալ էր քո զպատուիրանն իմ, ոչ ուրախ լինէին ի վերայ քո, ոյք իջուցին զքեզ յայդ տեղիդ.	[47](39):1 და ოდეს მოვიდა უფალი დავრდომილსა მას ზედა გუამსა ადამისსა, შეჭუენა მას ზედა უფალი და ჰრქუა ხმითა მჴურვალებისაით ა: "უკუეთუმცა დავემარხნეს მცნებანი ჩემნი, არამცა დავრდომილ იყავ მაგას ადგილსა, არამცა ითხა მტერმან შენმან შენი, რომელ გამოვედ მე შენ მაგას ადგილსა,	

Pericope 32 *Adam and Abel's Funerary Rites* 85E

GREEK	LATIN	ARMENIAN	GEORGIAN	SLAVONIC
38:4 And they came to the Garden and all the leaves of the Garden were stirred so that all men begotten of Adam slept from the fragrance save Seth alone, because he was born according to the appointment of God.		[47](38):4 God came to the Garden and all the plants [moved], and all the people who were with Adam fell asleep. Only Seth alone, the virtuous one, was awake, according to God's dire[c]tion.	[47](38):4 And (God) first reached his Garden, and the flowers of the Garden, with their sweet odors, were moved at the sweet odor of the glorious God. All the children of Adam grew numb, except only for Seth, for he was son of the greatness of God.	
39:1 [And God came] to the body of Adam and grieved greatly over him and God said to him: "Adam, what is this you have done? Had you kept my commandment, those who born you down to this place would not have rejoiced.		[47](39):1 God came to Adam's body, where he was lying dead. God mourned greatly and said in a sweet voice, "Oh, Adam. Why did you do that? If you had observed my commandment, those who brought you down to this place would not have rejoiced over you.	[47](39):1 And when the Lord had come to the body of Adam which had fallen (on the earth), the Lord was sorrowful for him and told him in a sad voice, "If you had kept my commandments, you would not have fallen in that place and your enemy would not have been able to see that he had caused you to be expelled in that place.	

Pericope 32 *Adam and Abel's Funerary Rites*

GREEK	LATIN	ARMENIAN	GEORGIAN	SLAVONIC
39:2 Πλὴν λέγω σοι ὅτι τὴν χαρὰν αὐτῶν ἐπιστρέψω εἰς λύπην, τὴν δὲ λύπην σου ἐπιστρέψω εἰς χαράν· καὶ ἐπιστρέψω σε εἰς τὴν ἀρχήν σου καὶ καθίσω σε εἰς τὸν θρόνον τοῦ ἀπατήσαντός σε.		[47](39):2 *բայց զուրախութիւն նոցա դարձուցից ի տրտմութիւն. եւ զտրտմութիւն քո դարձուցից յուրախութիւն. արարից զքեզ սկիզբն ուրախութեան եւ նստեցուցից զքեզ յաթոռ նորա, որ խաբեացն զքեզ*	[47](39):2 არამედ სიხარული მისი ჯუელად გარდავაკციო და მოგა- ჯციო მას მთავრობასა და დაგსუა შენ საყდართა ზედა მტერისა შენისათა, რომელ იგი ჯდა მას ზედა, რომლისა თანა იმოვა ამართავანებაი იგი.	
39:3 Ἐκεῖνος δὲ [τὸν καθίσαντα ἐπ᾽ αὐτῷ πρὶν γένεσθαι αὐτὸν ἐν ὑπερηφανίᾳ] εἰσβληθήσεται εἰς τὸν τόπον τοῦτον, ἵνα ἴδῃ σε καθήμενον ἐπάνω αὐτοῦ· τότε κατακριθήσεται αὐτὸς καὶ οἱ ἀκούσαντες αὐτοῦ, καὶ λυπηθήσεται ὁρῶν σε καθήμενον ἐπὶ τοῦ θρόνου αὐτοῦ.		[47](39):3 *եւ արկցի զնոսա ի տեղի խաւարի եւ մահու*	[47](39):3 გამოვარდეს მავან ადგილსა და შენ გიხილოს მავან ადგილსა მჯდომარე საყდართა ზედა".	
40:1 Μετὰ ταῦτα εἶπεν ὁ θεὸς τῷ ἀρχαγγέλῳ Μιχαήλ· "Ἄπελθε εἰς τὸν παράδεισον ἐν τῷ τρίτῳ οὐρανῷ καὶ ἔνεγκε τρεῖς σινδόνας βυσσίνας καὶ σηρικάς.	48:1 Et dixit iterum dominus ad Michahel et Urihel angelos: afferte mihi tres sindones bissinas	[48](40):1 *Եւ ապարիկ խաւսեցաւ Աստուած զՄիքայէլ եւ ասէ. երթ դու ի դրախտն [երրորդ] երկինս եւ բեր [ինձ] կտաւս երիս.*	[48](40):1 და ამისა შემდგომად უბრძანა ღმერთმან მიქაელს	

Pericope 32 *Adam and Abel's Funerary Rites*

GREEK	LATIN	ARMENIAN	GEORGIAN	SLAVONIC
39:2 Yet, I tell you that I will turn their joy to grief and your grief will I turn to joy, and I will return you to your rule, and seat you on the throne of your deceiver.		[47](39):2 But I will turn their rejoicing into sorrow, and I will turn your sorrow into rejoicing. I shall make you the beginning of rejoicing and I shall set you on the throne of him who deceived you,	[47](39):2 But I will change his joy into sorrow and I will lead you back towards this realm and I will set you upon your enemy's throne, where he was seated, close (by the place) where his rebellion was discovered.	
39:3 But that one [the one who sat on it prior to his becoming arrogant] shall be cast into this place that he may see you seated upon it. Then he himself shall be condemned along with those who obeyed him and he shall grieve when he see you sitting upon his throne.		[47](39):3 and I shall cast them into a place of darkness and death."	[47](39):3 He will fall in the place (where) you (are) and he will see you in that (other) place sitting upon a throne."	
40:1 Then God said to the archangel Michael: "Go away to Paradise in the third heaven, and carry away three fine linen clothes."	48:1a Again the Lord said to the angels Michael and Uriel: "Bring me 3 linen shrouds	[48](40):1 After this, God spoke to Michael and said, "Go to the Garden of the [third] heaven and bring [me] three linen cloths".	48(40):1 And after that, God gave an order to Michael who took (Adam) back to the Garden, which is in the third heaven.	

Pericope 32 *Adam and Abel's Funerary Rites*

GREEK	LATIN	ARMENIAN	GEORGIAN	SLAVONIC
40:2 Καὶ εἶπεν ὁ θεὸς τῷ Μιχαὴλ καὶ τῷ Γαβριὴλ καὶ τῷ Οὐριήλ· Στρώσατε σινδόνας καὶ σκεπάσατε τὸ σῶμα τοῦ 'Αδάμ· καὶ ἐνεγκόντες ἔλαιον ἐκ τοῦ ἐλαίου τῆς εὐωδίας ἐκχέατε ἐπ'αὐτόν. Καὶ ἐκήδευσαν αὐτὸν οἱ τρεῖς μεγάλοι ἄγγελοι.	48:1b et expandite super Adam. et alias sindones super Abel filium eius, et sepelite Adam et filium eius.	[48](40):2 իբրև իբեր, ասէ Աստուած զՄիքայէլ եւ զՈւիէլ եւ գԳաբրիէլ. տարածեցէք զկտաւսն եւ ծածկեցէք զմարմինն Ադամայ. եւ բերէք իւղ անուշի. բերէն եւ արկին զնովաւ. եւ <պատուեցին> զնա նովին հանդերձիւն։	[48](40):2 და მიავლინა სამოთხეს, რომელ არს მელამესა ცასა. მოიღებელ სამნო არძნაკნო სობღოსანო წარგრაკნოლებო და პრკუა ღმერთმან მიკაელს: "განა არტენოთ არძნაკნო ეკო და შეგრანებო გუამი ადამისა და მორელთ საცხებელო ზეთის სოლოსაკან და დაასხთო მაკას ზედა. და შე- მოსნე ივო სამთა ანგელოზთა. და ოდეს შემოსნე გუამი ივო ადამოსი,	45-46.4 Пакы господь рече кь архаггелоу · вьниди вь раи и вьзьми плащаницоу порфироу и покрыи тѣло Адамово, и прими маслиньно масло и прѣлѣи его .
40:3 Ὅτε δὲ ἐτέλεσαν κηδεύοντες τὸν 'Αδάμ, εἶπεν ὁ θεὸς ἐνεχθῆναι καὶ τὸ σῶμα τοῦ "Αβελ· καὶ ἐνεγκόντες ἄλλας σινδόνας ἐκήδευσαν αὐτόν.		[48](40):3 եւ իբրև կատարեցին զամենայն, հրամայեաց Աստուած բերել զԱբելի մարմինն. բերին եւ այլ կտաւս եւ հանդերձեցին զնա.	[48](40):3 და პრკუა ღმერთმან:"მოღ ეთ გუამი ივო აბელისაცა და ამო-ხუენოთ სხუენცა არძნაკნო და შემონეთ ივოცა,	45-46.5 такожде и тѣло Авелово сьтвори при нѥмь .

Pericope 32 *Adam and Abel's Funerary Rites*

GREEK	LATIN	ARMENIAN	GEORGIAN	SLAVONIC
40:2 And God said to Michael and to Gabriel and Uriel: "Spread out the clothes and cover the body of Adam." And they bore the sweet olive oil and poured it upon him. And the three great angels prepared him for burial.	48:1b and stretch them over Adam. Bring other shrouds and stretch them over Abel, his son. Then bury Adam and his son."	[48](40):2 When he had brought them, God said to Michael and to Ozel and to Gabriel, 'Bring these linen cloths and cover Adam's body, and bring sweet oil." They brought them and set them around him and wound him in that garment.	48(40):2 They seized three folded shrouds of [[cloth]] and God told Michael and Gabriel, "Unfold these shrouds and envelop Adam's body and take the ointment from the olive tree and pour it upon him." And three angels dressed him (in it) and when they had dressed Adam's body (in it),	45-46.4 Once again the Lord spoke to the archangel, "Go into Paradise and take the purple cloth and cover the corpse of Adam and take the olive oil and pour it over him."
40:3 When they finished preparing Adam, God said they should bear the body of Abel also. And they brought more linen and prepared him for burial.		[48](40):3 When they had finished everything, God ordered them to bring Abel's body. They brought still other linen cloths and dressed him.	48(40):3 God told them, "Take Abel's body as well, seize other shrouds and dress him in them also	45-46.5 The same was done to Abel's body.

GREEK	LATIN	ARMENIAN	GEORGIAN	SLAVONIC
40:4 Ἐπειδὴ ἀκήδευτος ἦν ἀφ' ἧς ἡμέρας ἐφόνευσεν αὐτὸν Κάϊν ὁ ἀδελφὸς αὐτοῦ. Καὶ πολλὰ ἐθέλησε κρύψαι αὐτὸν ὁ Κάϊν, ἀλλ'οὐκ ἐδυνήθη, ὅτι ἀνεπήδα τὸ σῶμα αὐτοῦ ἀπὸ τῆς γῆς, καὶ ἐξήρχετο φωνὴ ἀπὸ τῆς γῆς λέγουσα·	48:2 Et processerunt omnes virtutes angelorum ante Adam. et sanctificata est dormitatio mortuorum.	[48](40):4 ըանդի կայր յայրէ յայնմանէ[է] իաս յորում սպան զնա կային անարէնն, եւ կամեցաւ ծածկել զնա եւ ոչ կարաց. ըանդի վարվառ էրն մարմինը նորա ի հողոյ անտի. ձայն եղեւ երկնից եւ ասէ.	[48](40):4 რამეთუ შეუმსილო იდვა მიერ დღითგან, ვინაიცა მოკლა იგი კაენმან უკეთურმან და უნდა დაფლვად ქუეყანასა და ვერ უძლო, რამეთუ აღმოვარდის ქუეყანით გუამი იგი მისი. და ხმაი ესმა ზეცით. და ჰრქუა მას:	
40:5a Οὐ κρυβήσεται εἰς τὴν γῆν ἔτερον πλάσμα ἕως οὗ ἀφιέναι μοι τὸ πρῶτον πλάσμα τὸ ἀρθὲν ἀπ' ἐμοῦ, τὸν χοῦν ἐξ ἧς ἐλήφθη.		[48](40):5a ոչ է արէն ծածկել զդա [յ] երկրի, եթէ ոչ [խախ] առաջին ստեղծուածն դառնայ [յ] երկիր ուստի եկն.	[48](40):5a "ვერ დაეფლას ეგე ქუეყანასა, არა თუ პირველად ქმნილი მიექცეს ქუეყანად, რომლისაგან შეექმნა".	
40:5b Ἔλαβον δὲ οἱ ἄγγελοι ἐν τῷ καιρῷ ἐκείνῳ καὶ ἔθεντο αὐτὸν ἐπὶ τὴν πέτραν ἕως οὗ ἐτάφη Ἀδὰμ ὁ πατὴρ αὐτοῦ.	48:3 Sepelierunt Adam et Abel Michahel et Urihel angeli in partibus paradisi videntibus Seth et matre eius et alio nemine. et dixerunt Michahel et Urihel: sicut vidistis, similiter sepelite mortuos vestros. [III+***legenda de ligno crucis***]III	[48](40):5b Առին զնա այնուհետեւ ի սմին ժամանակի որ էրն, մինչեւ մեռաւ Ադամ. ապա յետ այնորիկ թերին զնա եւ արարին նմա զոր արհամարհ արարին Ադամայ հայր նորա.	[48](40):5b მას ჟამსა მორტ იგი რომელსაცა კლდესა ზედა და იდვა იგი მუნ, ვიდრემდის მოკუდა ადამ. მაშინ მოიღეს და შემოსეს იგი ვითარცა მამაი თვისი.	

Pericope 32 *Adam and Abel's Funerary Rites* 88E

GREEK	LATIN	ARMENIAN	GEORGIAN	SLAVONIC
40:4 For he was unburied since the day when Cain his brother slew him; for Cain took great pains to conceal (him) but could not, for the body sprang up from the earth and a voice went out of the earth saying:	48:2 And all the virtues of the angels processed before Adam, and thus was the dormition of the dead sanctified.	[48](40):4 For he had remained [from] that day upon which Cain the lawless one had killed him and had wished to hide him, and had been unable. For, as soon as his body was in the dust, a heavenly voice came and said,	48(40):4 for he had remained lying naked since the day when wicked Cain killed him. And he wished to bury him in the earth and he was unable (to do so), because his body came back out of the earth. For a voice made itself heard from heaven and said to him,	
40:5a "No other body can be covered until --with respect to the first creature who was taken from me -- the earth from which he was taken is returned to me."		[48](40):5a "It is not permitted to hide him [in] the earth [before] the first creature has returned to the earth from which he came."	48(40):5a "He will not be able to be buried in the earth before he who was created first has returned to the earth from which he was created."	
40:5b And the angels took at that moment and put him upon a rock until Adam, his father, was buried.	48:3 The angels Michael and Uriel buried Adam and Abel in the regions of paradise which Seth and his mother saw, but no one else. Michael and Uriel: "Just as you see us doing, likewise bury your dead." [III+***Legend of the Wood of the Cross***]III	[48](40):5b Thenceforth, they took him into that same cave where he was until Adam died. Then, after this, they brought him and treated him just as they had treated his father Adam.	48[40]:5b Then he took it to a rock and it remained spread out there until the death of Adam. Thus (the angels) took him and dressed him like his father.	

Pericope 32 *Adam and Abel's Funerary Rites*

GREEK	LATIN	ARMENIAN	GEORGIAN	SLAVONIC
40:6 Καὶ προσέταξεν ὁ θεὸς μετὰ τὸ κηδεῦσαι καὶ τὸν Ἄβελ ἆραι αὐτοὺς εἰς τὰ μέρη τοῦ παραδείσου, εἰς τὸν τόπον ὅπου ἧρεν χοῦν ὁ θεὸς καὶ ἔπλασεν τὸν Ἀδάμ. Καὶ ἐποίησεν ὀρυγῆναι εἰς δύο τὸν τόπον.		[48](40):6 *[Armenian text]*	[48](40):6 *[Georgian text]*	
40:7 Καὶ ἀπέστειλεν ὁ θεὸς ἑπτὰ ἀγγέλους εἰς τὸν παράδεισον· καὶ ἤγαγον εὐωδίας πολλὰς καὶ ἔθεντο αὐτὰς ἐν τῇ γῇ. Καὶ μετὰ ταῦτα ἔλαβον τὰ δύο σώματα καὶ ἔθαψαν αὐτὰ εἰς τὸν τόπον εἰς ὃν ὤρυξαν καὶ ᾠκοδόμησαν αὐτοί.		[48](40):7 *[Armenian text]*	[48](40):7 *[Georgian text]*	
41:1 ἐκάλεσεν δὲ ὁ θεὸς τὸν Ἀδὰμ καὶ εἶπεν· Ἀδὰμ Ἀδάμ. ἀπεκρίθη τὸ σῶμα ἐκ τῆς γῆς καὶ εἶπεν· ἰδοὺ ἐγώ, κύριε.		[48](41):1 *[Armenian text]*	[48](41):1 *[Georgian text]*	47.1 И призва господь Адама и рече · Адаме, Адаме, где еси;
41:2 Καὶ εἶπεν αὐτῷ ὁ θεὸς ὅτι εἶπόν σοι ὅτι γῆ εἶ καὶ εἰς γῆν ἀπελεύσει.		[48](41):2 *[Armenian text]*	[48](41):2 *[Georgian text]*	47.2 тѣло же отвѣща · се, азъ господи .

Pericope 32 *Adam and Abel's Funerary Rites*

GREEK	LATIN	ARMENIAN	GEORGIAN	SLAVONIC
40:6 And God commanded that after they had prepared the body of Abel for burial that they bear Abel up also to the area of the Garden, to the spot where God had taken the earth and fashioned Adam. And God made them dig the spot for two.		[48](40):6 After the dressing, God commanded that both of them be taken [to the region of the Garden] and be brought to the place from which the dust had been taken and Adam created. God caused them to dig	48(40):6 God ordered that both of them should be taken up to the Garden, on the eastern part, in the place from which God had taken some soil and created Adam. And God ordered Michael to dig.	
40:7 And God sent seven angels to the Garden and they brought many fragrant spices and placed them in the earth, and afterward they took the two bodies and placed them in the spot which they had dug and built (a sepulcher).		[48](40):7 in that place and sent them to bring sweet incenses and iris incense and he caused them to put oils upon the dust and to cover the spices. Then after this, they took the bodies of both of them and put them in the place in which he had fashioned them. They [dug] and made a sepulchre over them.	48(40):7 And God sent seven angels to the Garden: they gathered many kinds of incense from the Garden and they brought it to them. Then they took both bodies, put them into the grave and covered them (with earth).	
41:1 And God called and said, "Adam, Adam." And the body answered from the earth and said: "Here am I, Lord."		[48](41):1 God called to Adam's body through the dust and said, "Adam, Adam." Adam's body said to the dust, "Answer and say, 'Here (I am), Lord.'"	[48](41):1 Then God turned and called Adam. Adam's body answered him from the soil and said, "Here I am, [[Lord]].	47.1 And the Lord called Adam to himself and said, "Adam, Adam, where are you?"
41:2 And God said to him: "I told you (that) earth you are and to earth shall you return.		[48](41):2 The Lord said to him, "Behold, just as I said to you, 'Adam, you are dust and you return to dust;'	[48](41):2 And the Lord told him, "Behold, as I told you, you are soil and you have returned to the soil,	47.2 And his body answered, "I am here, O Lord."

Pericope 32 *Adam and Abel's Funerary Rites*

GREEK	LATIN	ARMENIAN	GEORGIAN	SLAVONIC
41:3 Πάλιν τὴν ἀνάστασιν ἐπαγγέλλομαί σοι· ἀναστήσω σε ἐν τῇ ἀναστάσει μετὰ παντὸς γένους ἀνθρώπων τοῦ ἐκ τοῦ σπέρματός σου..		[48](41):3 բայց յարութիւն գոր [խոստացայ] յարուցից զքեզ ի նմէն:	[48](41):3 ხოლო აღდგომაო, ნომელ აღვთოქჳ, ა ღვაღვინო ქამსა აღდგომისასა".	47.3a господь рече · тако рѣхь тебѣ · ꙁємлѧ ѥси и вь тождє ꙁємлю пакы поидєши .
42:1 Μετὰ δὲ τὰ ῥήματα ταῦτα ἐποίησεν ὁ θεὸς σφραγῖδα τρίγωνον καὶ ἐσφράγισεν τὸ μνημεῖον ἵνα μηδείς τι ποιήσῃ αὐτῷ ἐν ταῖς ἓξ ἡμέραις, ἕως οὗ ἀποστραφῇ ἡ πλευρὰ αὐτοῦ πρὸς αὐτόν.		[48](42):1 եւ յետ խաւսելոյն զայս Աստուծոյ, առ կնիք երեքկնի եւ կնքեաց զգերեզմանն Արամայ, եւ ասէ. Մի ոք ինչ մերձեսցի յաւուրս յայսմիկ մինչեւ դարձին մարմինք դորա ի դա:	[48](42):1 ხოლო შემდგომად ამის მოღო ღმერთმან ბეჭედი ოჳი სამ-კაჲელო და ღაბეჭა სამარეჲ ოჳი აღამისი და ჰრქუა:" ნუმცა ვინ შეეხების ექუსთა ამათ ღღეთა, ვიღრემდე მოიქცეს გუერდი შენი შენღავე".	47.3b и пакы на вьскрьсєниѥ вьскрьснєши и сь вьсѣмь родомь чловѣчьскымь .
42:2 Τότε ὁ κύριος καὶ οἱ ἄγγελοι ἐπορεύθησαν εἰς τὸν τόπον αὐτῶν.		[48](42):2 եւ ապա յայժմամ վերացաւ Տէր հրեշտակօք Հանդերձ Հրեշտակապարք իւրովք սերովբէիւք եւ լուածողէն կառաւք իւրաքանչիւր կայանս.	[48](42):2 მაშინ-ღა ღუერთი აღხღა ზეცად ღა ანგელოზნი თვითო-ფლად წჲსთა თვისთა ზღა.	47.4 и прѣкрьсти господь гробь на .д. страны и вьложи ѥго вь гробь, и прѣлиѧ и рєчє · твоѧ оть твоихь тєбѣ приносить сє.

Pericope 32 *Adam and Abel's Funerary Rites* 90E

GREEK	LATIN	ARMENIAN	GEORGIAN	SLAVONIC
41:3 Again I promise to you the Resurrection; I will raise you up in the Resurrection with every man, who is of your seed."		[48](41):3 but I will raise you in the resurrection which [I] promised you."	[48](41):3 but I will raise you up in the resurrection which I have promised you, at the time of resurrection.	47.3a The Lord said, "So I told you, 'You are earth and to the same earth you will return again.'
42:1 After these words, God made a three-fold seal and sealed the tomb, that no one might do anything to him for six days till his rib should return to him.		[48](42):1 After God had said this, he took a three-fold seal and sealed Adam's tomb and said, "Let none approach in these days, until their bodies return to it."	[48](42):1 Then, after that, God took the triangular seal and sealed the tomb of Adam and he said, "Let no person touch it during these six days, until your rib returns to you."	47.3b And at the resurrection, you will rise with all of mankind."
42:2 Then the Lord and his angels went to their place.		[48](42):2 Then, at that time, the Lord ascended to the heavens with his angels, Seraphim and chariot of light, each to his station.	[48](42):2 Then God ascended to the upper heaven and each of the angels to his office.	47.4 And the Lord made on four sides the sign of the cross over his grave, and one laid him in the grave, and he anointed it and said, "What is yours, taken from you, is again returned to you."

33 LATIN 49:1 Post sex dies vero quod mortuus est Adam, cognoscens Eva mortem suam, congregavit omnes filios suos et filias suas, qui fuerunt Seth cum XXX fratribus et XXX sororibus, et dixit ad omnes Eva:
49:2 Audite me, filii mei, ut referam vobis, quod ego et pater vester transgressi sumus praeceptum dei et dixit nobis Michahel archangelus:
49:3 propter praevaricationes vestras generi vestro superinducet dominus noster iram iudicii sui primum per aquam secundum per ignem: his duobus iudicabit dominus omne humanum genus.
50:1 Sed audite me, filii mei! facite ergo tabulas lapideas et alias tabulas luttea et scribite in his omnem vitam meam et patris vestri quae a nobis audistis et vidistis.
50:2 Si per aquam iudicabit genus nostrum, tabulae de terra solventur et tabulae lapideae perma nebunt. si autem per ignem iudicabit genus nostrum, tabulae lapideae solventur et de terra luteae decoquentur.
50:3 haec omnia cum dixisset Eva filiis suis expandit manus in caelum orans et inclinans genua in terram et adorans dominum et gratias agens tradidit spiritum.

33 LATIN 49:1 Six days after Adam's death, Eve knew her own death [was near], so she gathered together all her sons and daughters, who were Seth along with his thirty brothers and thirty sisters. Eve said to them all:
49:2 "'Hear me, my children, that I might recount for you how I and your father transgressed the precept of God. Michael the archangel said to us:
49:3 'On account of your conspiracies, our Lord will bring upon your race the wrath of his judgment, first by water, and second by fire. By these two will the Lord judge all the human race.'
50:1 But hear me, my children! Make, therefore, tablets of stone, and other tablets of earth, and write on them my whole life, and that of your father, which you have heard from us and seen.
50:2 If he judges our race by water, the tablets of earth will dissolve, but the tablets of stone will endure. If, however, he judges our race by fire, the tablets of stone will be destroyed, but the tablets of earth will be fired."
50:3 When she had said all these things to her children, she stretched out her hand toward heaven, knelt upon the earth, worshipped God, and giving thanks, gave up her spirit.

Pericope 34 *Eve's Prayer to Join Adam*

GREEK	LATIN	ARMENIAN	GEORGIAN	SLAVONIC
42:3 Εὔα δὲ καὶ αὐτή, πληρωθέντων τῶν ἓξ ἡμερῶν, ἐκοιμήθη. Ἔτι δὲ ζώσης αὐτῆς, ἔκλαυσεν περὶ τῆς κοιμήσεως τοῦ Ἀδάμ· οὐ γὰρ ἐγίνωσκεν ποῦ ἐτέθη. Ἐπειδὴ ἐν τῷ ἐλθεῖν τὸν κύριον ἐπὶ τὸν παράδει-σον πρὸς τὸ κηδεῦσαι τὸν Ἀδάμ, ἐκοιμήθησαν ἅπαντες, ἕως οὗ ἐτέλεσεν τοῦ κηδεῦσαι τὸν Ἀδάμ, πλὴν τοῦ Σὴθ μόνου· καὶ οὐδεὶς ἐγίνωσκεν ἐπὶ τῆς γῆς, πλὴν τοῦ υἱοῦ αὐτοῦ Σήθ.		[48](42):3 լցան եւ կատարեցան ժամանակք նաժի եւ մեռանէր․ Սկսաւ լալ եւ խնդրէր ճանաչել զտեղին որ թաղեցաւ Ադամ, քանզի անտեղեակ էր․ զի ի ժամանակին իրրեւ եկն Աստուած ի մարն Ադամայ շարժեցան ամենայն տունակք դրախտին, եւ ի սուրբ հոգւյն քուն էառ զամենայն որ էին ի վերայ երկրի մինչեւ հանդերձեցին զԱդամ, եւ ոչ ոք գիտաց ի վերայ երկրի բայց միայն Սէթ.	[48](42):3 ხოლო ევა დასულებულ იყო ექვსი ოყო ესე ექსი ყუეელი იგი დღე. ტიროდა ევა და უწყდა შესვგან, სადა დაეეუდვეს ადამო, რამეთუ არა უწყოდა. ოდეს გარდამოხდა უფალი ჰურეუებად, ადგეეტა არა ყოველთა ხეთა სამოთხისათა სულელებაი მისა, რამეთუ სულებელებისა მისგან ყოველნო დასულებდეს. ვიდრე შემსნადმდე და დამარხვად ადამისა არავინ აჩნდა სეთისა ხოლო;	48.1a Евга же пребысть по Адамѣ .s. дьнеи, молещи се глаголаше плачющи се
42:4 Καὶ προσηύξατο Εὔα κλαίουσα ἵνα ταφῇ εἰς τὸν τόπον ὅπου ἦν Ἀδὰμ ὁ ἀνὴρ αὐτῆς. Μετὰ δὲ τὸ τελέσαι αὐτὴν τὴν εὐχὴν λέγει·		[48](42):4 Ցաղիաց ադաղակեր սկսաւ եւա աղաչել զԱստուած զի տարցեն զնա ի տեղին որ թաղեցաւ Ադամ․ Իրրեւ կատարեաց զաղաթան ասէ.	[48](42):4 და ილოცვიდა ევა, ტიროდა, რაითამცა მიეყვანეს და ჰქუე- ნეს, სადა დაევეს ადამ. და ოდეს ადასრულა ლოცვაი იგი, თქუა:	
42:5 Κύριε δέσποτα, θεὲ πάσης ἀρετῆς, μὴ ἀπαλλοτριώσης με τοῦ σώματος Ἀδὰμ ἐξ οὗ ᾖρες με ἐκ τῶν μελῶν αὐτοῦ,		[48](42):5 Աստուած իմ Աստուած արուստից. մի ստրաջուցաներ զիս ի տեղոջէն Ադամայ.	[48](42):5 "უფალო, ნუ უცხო მყოფ მე ადგილისა მისგან ადამისა,	

Pericope 34 *Eve's Prayer to Join Adam* 92E

GREEK	LATIN	ARMENIAN	GEORGIAN	SLAVONIC
42:3 And Eve also, when the six days were fulfilled, fell asleep. But while she was living, she wept bitterly about Adam's falling asleep, for she knew not where he was laid. For when the Lord came to the Garden to bury Adam all were asleep until he finished the burial of Adam except Seth alone. And no one knew (this) on the earth, except her son Seth.		[48](42):3 The times of Eve were filled and completed and she was dying. She began to weep and sought to know the place where Adam was buried, because she was ignorant (of it). For, at the time when God came for the death of Adam, all the plants of the Garden were moved and, through the Holy Spirit, sleep overcame all those who were upon the earth, until they had dressed Adam, and none upon the earth knew, except Seth alone.	[48](42):3 But Eve grew numb [[when]] she saw all [[that]]. Eve wept and wished to see where they had put Adam, for she did not know. When the Lord had descended upon the earth, the sweet odor of all the trees of the Garden did not {...} because of his sweet odor all had grown numb. Until the wrapping and the burial of Adam, nobody understood anything except Seth.	48.1a Eve lived six days beyond Adam; she prayed and said crying,
42:4 And Eve prayed while weeping that she might be buried in the place where her husband Adam was. And after she had finished her prayer, she said:		[48](42):4 Again Eve began to cry out, to beseech God that they should bring her to the place where Adam was buried. When she had completed that prayer, she said,	[48](42):4 Then Eve begged (and) wept so that (God) might lead her off, show her the place where they had put Adam. And when she had completed her prayer, she said,	
42:5 "Lord, Master, God of all virtue, do not alienate me from the body of Adam, from whose members you made me.		[48](42):5 "My God, God of miracles, do not alienate me from Adam's place,	[48](42):5 "Lord, do not alienate me from Adam's place,	

Pericope 34 Eve's Prayer to Join Adam

GREEK	LATIN	ARMENIAN	GEORGIAN	SLAVONIC
42:6 ἀλλ' ἀξίωσον κἀμὲ τὴν ἀναξίαν καὶ ἁμαρτωλὴν εἰσελθεῖν μετὰ τοῦ σκηνώματος αὐτοῦ. Ὥσπερ ἤμην μετ'αὐτοῦ ἐν τῷ παραδείσῳ ἀμφότεροι μὴ χωρισθέντες ἀπ'ἀλλήλων,		[48](42):6 *այլ հաամայեա դնել զիս ի գերեզմա(ն)[ի] նորա.*	[48](42):6 არამედ ღირსმეც ჩემიცა მის თანა,	
42:7 ὥσπερ ἐν τῇ παραβάσει πλανηθέντες παρέβημεν τὴν ἐντολήν σου μὴ χωρισθέντες, οὕτως καὶ νῦν, κύριε, μὴ χωρίσῃς ἡμᾶς.		[48](42):7 *որպէս էաք ի միասին ի դրախտին եւ չէաք մեկուսի ի միմեանց. որպէս ի կենսատուութեանն մոլեալ յանցեա[ք]. յորում տեղիս թաղեցաւ Ադամ, թաղեցայց եւ ես ընդ նմա:*	[48](42):7 ვითარცა ორნივე ვიყვენით სამოთხესა შინა განუშორებ-ელად ურთიერთას,	48.1b господи боже, якоже ме ѥси сътвориль отъ ребра Адамова, тако и сь нимь да боудоу.
42:8 Μετὰ δὲ τὸ εὔξασθαι αὐτὴν ἀναβλέψασα εἰς τὸν οὐρανὸν ἀνεστέναξε τύπτουσα τὸ στῆθος αὐτῆς καὶ λέγουσα· Θεὲ τῶν ἁπάντων, δέξαι τὸ πνεῦμά μου. Καὶ ἀπέδωκεν τὴν ψυχὴν αὐτῆς.		[48](42):8 *Զայս իբրեւ ասաց աղաչելով, եւ հայեցի ի նմանէ:*	[48](42):8 სიტყუელსა მას ჩუენსა ზე განვამრებ, არამედ სადაცა ოდენ დასდვე, მუნცა მე და შემდგომად ლოცვისა მისისა აღმოუტევა სული.	48.2 и приниче на гроудехь своихь глаголющи · господи, боже, приими доухь мои. 48.3 и тоу прѣдасть доухь свои кь богоу.

Pericope 34 *Eve's Prayer to Join Adam* 93E

GREEK	LATIN	ARMENIAN	GEORGIAN	SLAVONIC
42:6 But deem me worthy, even me who is unworthy and a sinner, to enter into his tabernacle. Just as I was with him in the Garden, both of us not being separated from the other;		[48](42):6 but command to place me in his tomb.	[48](42):6 but command me, me also, (to be) with him,	
42:7 just as in our transgression, we were (both) led astray and transgressed your command, but were not separated, even so now, o Lord, do not separate us."		[48](42):7 Just as we were together in the Garden, and were not separate from one another, just as in life, so in ou[r] death. In the place in which Adam was buried let me, too, be buried with him."	[48](42):7 as we both were in the Garden, inseparable from one another.	48.1b "Lord God, as you created me from the rib of Adam, so I want to be with him." 48.2 And she lowered her head onto her breast, saying, "Lord God, receive my spirit."
42.8. But after she had prayed, she gazed heavenwards and groaned aloud and smote her breast and said: "God of All, receive my spirit," and she delivered up her spirit.		[48](42):8 When, beseeching, she had said this, her soul left her.	[48](42):8 Do not separate us in our death, but place me where you have placed him." And after this prayer she gave up her soul.	48.3 And so she gave her spirit to God.

Pericope 35 *Eve's Funeral and Epilogue*

GREEK	LATIN	ARMENIAN	GEORGIAN	SLAVONIC
43:1 Καὶ ἦλθε Μιχαὴλ καὶ ἐδίδαξεν τὸν Σὴθ πῶς κηδεύσῃ τὴν Εὔαν. Καὶ ἦλθαν τρεῖς ἄγγελοι· καὶ ἦραν τὸ σῶμα αὐτῆς καὶ ἔθαψαν αὐτὸ ὅπου ἦν τὸ σῶμα τοῦ Ἀδὰμ καὶ τοῦ Ἀβελ.	51:1 Postea cum magno fletu sepelierunt eam omnes filii eius. cum essent lugentes quattuor dies, tunc apparuit eis Michahel archangelus dicens ad Seth:	[51](43):1 եւ եկն Մրքայէլ հրեշտակապետն խաանեաւ առ Սէթ եւ ուսոյց նմա թէ որպէս հանդերձեսցէ զնա։ եկին երեք հրեշտակք եւ առին զմարմինն նաբի, եւ տարան եղին ուր կայր մարմինն Ադամայ եւ Աբելի։	[51](43):1 და მოვიდა მიქელ ანგელოზი და ასწავა სეთის, ვითარ შემომსენოს ევას. მოვიდეს სამნი ანგელოზნი და აღღეს გუამი ადამისა.	49-50.1 и прииде архаггель Михаиль кь Сидѹ и наѹчи Сида, како да съхранить матерь свою . 49-50.2 и приидоше .г. аггели, вьзѥвьше тѣло Ѥвьжино и погребоше ѥ, где и тѣло Адамово и Авелово, сына ѥю .
43:2 Καὶ μετὰ ταῦτα ἐλάλησεν ὁ Μιχαὴλ τῷ Σὴθ λέγων· Οὕτως κήδευσον πάντα ἄνθρωπον ἀποθνῄσκοντα ἕως ἡμέρας τῆς ἀναστάσεως.	see 48.3	[51](43):2 Եւ ապարիկ խաանեաւ Մրքայէլ առ Սէթայ եւ ասէ. Այսպէս հանդերձեսցիր զամենայն մարդ որ մեռանի մինչեւ յաւր կատարածի յարութեանն։	[51](43):2 და შემდგომად ამის ეტყოდა მიქელ ანგელოზი:" შემოსედ ყოველი მკუდარი, რომელი მოკუდეს, ესრეთ, ვიდრე აღსასრულადმდე ყოველთა კაცთასა".	49-50.3 и рече архаггель кь Сидѹ · тако да съхранишь вьсакого чловѣка ѹмирающаго до дьне вьскрьсения .
43:3 Μετὰ δὲ τὸ δοῦναι αὐτὸν νόμον εἶπεν· Παρ' ἓξ ἡμερῶν μὴ πενθήσητε· τῇ δὲ ἑβδόμῃ ἡμέρᾳ κατάπαυσον καὶ εὐφράνθητι ἐν αὐτῇ ὅτι ἐν αὐτῇ ὁ θεὸς καὶ οἱ ἄγγελοι ἡμεῖς εὐφραινόμεθα μετὰ τῆς δικαίας ψυχῆς τῆς μεταστάσης ἀπὸ τῆς γῆς.	51:2 homo dei, ne amplius lugeas mortuos tuos quam sex dies quia septimo die signum resurrectionis est futuri seculi requies, et in die septimo requievit dominus ab omnibus operibus suis. [III+omni opere suo. Octavus vero dies futurae et aeternae beatitudinis est, in qua omnes sancti cum ipso creatore et salvatore simul cum anima et corpore nunquam de cetero morituri regnabunt per infinita secula seculorum. Amen] III. 51:3 tunc Seth fecit tabulas.	[51](43):3 Զայս իբրեւ ասաց հրեշտակն առ Սէթայ, վեցերգաւ լերկիրն փառաւորելով զՏայր եւ զորդի եւ զորդին Հոգին սյդմ եւ միշտ։	[51](43):3 ოდეს ასწავა სეთის ესე ყოველი, ამცნება ზეცა ლოცოსაგან და ჰრქვა მას:" ყუფლის ხუთისა დღისა არა ოვლოდეთ მკუდართა ზედა, ხოლო დღესა მას მეშვიდესა განისუენე რამეთუ ამას დღესა განისუენა ღმერთმან ყუველთაგან მისთა, რომელ ქმნა ყუფალმან".	49-50.4 пакы рече ѥмѹ · творите паметь и вь .г. дьнь, и вь .д. и вь .к. и вь .м., и вьсе по чинѹ, ѩкоже аггели веселимь се сь праведьнами дѹшами .

Pericope 35 *Eve's Funeral and Epilogue* 94E

GREEK	LATIN	ARMENIAN	GEORGIAN	SLAVONIC
43:1 And Michael came and taught Seth how to prepare Eve for burial. And there came three angels and they bore her body and buried it where Adam and Abel's bodies were.	51:1 Afterwards, all her children buried her with great weeping. After they had mourned her for four days, Michael appeared to them and said to Seth:	[51](43):1 Michael, the archangel, came and spoke to Seth and taught him how to dress her. Three angels came and took Eve's body and brought it and placed it where Adam's and Abel's bodies were.	[51](43):1 And the angel Michael came and taught Seth how to dress Eve. Three angels came and took Eve's body and placed it where they had placed Adam's body.	49-50.1 And the archangel Michael came to Seth and instructed him as to how he should bury his mother. 49-50.2 And three angels came, took Eve's corpse and buried it, where also the corpse of Adam and their son Abel were buried.
43:2 And afterwards Michael spoke to Seth saying; "Lay out in this manner every man that dies until the day of the Resurrection."	see 48.3	[51](43):2 After this, Michael spoke to Seth and said, 'Thus shall you dress every human being who dies, until the day of the end, through the resurrection."	[51](43):2 And after that, the angel Michael told him, "Thus dress every dead person who dies, until the death of all human beings."	49-50.3 And the archangel said to Seth, "So shall you bury every person who dies until the resurrection."
43:3 And after giving him this rule he said: "Mourn not beyond six days, but on the seventh day, rest and rejoice on it, because on that very day, God and we the angels rejoice with the righteous soul, who has passed away from the earth."	51.2 "Man of God, mourn no longer than 6 days, for the 7th day is the sign of the resurrection, the repose of the coming age, and on the 7th day the Lord rested from all his works. [III+ all his work. Indeed, the 8th day is (the sign) of the future and eternal blessedness, in which all the holy will reign throughout endless ages with the Creator and Savior himself, in both soul and body, never again to die Amen.] III 51:3 Then Seth made tablets.	[51](43):3 When the angel had said this to Seth, he ascended to heaven, praising the Father and the Son and the Holy Spirit, now and forever.	[51](43):3 When he had taught Seth all that, he ascended to the uppermost heaven, far from Seth, and he told him, "Do not mourn for the dead more than five days and on the seventh day rejoice, for on that day God rested from all his (works) which the Lord had made."	49-50.4 Again he said to him, "Arrange a memorial ceremony on the third day and on the ninth and on the twentieth and on the fortieth, and arrange everything in proper order, so that we angels might take joy in it along with the souls of the righteous."

Pericope 35 *Eve's Funeral and Epilogue*

GREEK	LATIN	ARMENIAN	GEORGIAN	SLAVONIC
43:4 Ταῦτα εἰπὼν ὁ ἄγγελος ἀνῆλθεν εἰς τὸν οὐρανὸν δοξάζων καὶ λέγων· Ἀλληλούϊα. Ἅγιος, ἅγιος, ἅγιος, κύριος. Εἰς δόξαν θεοῦ πατρός. Ἀμήν.			[51](43):4 რომლისაი არს დიდებაი და პატივი და თაყუანის-ცემაი თანა მამით და სულით წმიდით აწ და მარადის და უკუნითი უკუნისამდე. ამინ.	49-50.5 Тогда архаггель Иоиль прослави бога, глаголюще · свєть, свєть, свєть, алилюиа, 49-50.6 свєть господь, испльнь нєбо и зємля славы юго.

Pericope 35 *Eve's Funeral and Epilogue*

GREEK	LATIN	ARMENIAN	GEORGIAN	SLAVONIC
43:4 After the angel said these things he ascended into heaven, glorifying (God) and saying: "Allelujah, Holy, holy, holy is the Lord, to the glory of God the Father, Amen."			[51](43):4 To him is glory and honor and adoration, with the Father and the Holy Spirit, now and for ever and for ever and ever. Amen.	49-50.5 Then the archangel Joel glorified God with words, "Holy, Holy, Holy, Allelulia. 49-50.6 Holy is the Lord, heaven and earth are full of His glory."

36 (following Mozley) [52] Tunc Seth fecit (duas?) tabulas lapideas et (duas?) luteas, (et composuit apices literarum?) et scripsit in eis vitam patris sui Adae et matris sue Evae quam ab eis audivit et oculis suis vidit et posuit tabulas in medio domus patris sui in oratorio ubi orabat dominum. et post diluvium a multis videbantur hominibus tabulae illae scriptae (lapides illi scripti?) et a nemine legebantur.
Salomon autem sapiens vidit scripturam et deprecatus est dominum et apparuit ei angelus domini dicens: ego sum qui tenui manum Seth, ut scriberet cum digito suo (ferreo digito?, ferreo stilo?) lapides istos, et eris sciens scripturam, ut cognoscas et intelligas (ubi sint) quid contineant lapides isti omnes et ubi fuerit oratorium, ubi Adam et Eva adorabant dominum deum. et oportet te ibi aedificare templum domini id est domum orationis. Tunc Salomon supplevit templum domini dei et vocavit literas illas achiliacas hoc est sine verborum doctrina scriptas (achilicas quod est latine lapideas id est sine labiis doctrina scripta?, achiliacas quod est latine sillabicas hoc est sine librorum doctrina scriptas ?) digito Seth, tenens manum eius angelus domini.
[53] et in ipsis lapidibus inventum est, quod prophetavit septimus ab Adam Enoch dicens ante diluvium de adventu Christi: ecce veniet dominus in sanctis suis (in sanctis milibus suis?, in milibus suis?, in sanctis nubibus suis?) facere iudicium de omnibus et arguere impios de omnibus operibus suis quibus locuti sunt de eo peccatores et impii murmuratores et irreligiosi qui secundum concupiscentias suas ingrediuntur et os eorum locutum est superbiam. [IV+et os illorum locuntur superbiam ibunt in orcum, iusti vero plaudentes in regnum caelorum. [54] (Adam vero post quadraginta dies introivit in paradisum et Eva post octoginta et fuit Adam in paradisum annos septem et sub die moverunt omnem bestiarum)]IV.

37[55] Sciendum est quod de octo partibus plasmatum fuit corpus Ade. Una pars erat de limo terre unde facta est caro eius et inde piger erit. Alia pars erat de mari unde factus est sanguis eius et inde erat uagus et profugus. Tertia pars erat de lapidibus terre unde sunt ossa eius et inde erat durus et auarus. Quarta pars erat de nubibus, inde facte sunt cogitaciones eius et inde factus est luxuriosus. Quinta pars erat de uento unde factus est anelitus et inde factus est leuis. Sexta pars erat de sole unde facti sunt oculi eius et inde erat bellus et preclarus. Septima pars est de luce mundi unde factus est gratus et inde habet scienciam. Octaua pars est de spiritu sancto unde facta est anima et inde sunt episcopi et sacerdotes et omnes sancti et electi dei.

38 [56] Et sciendum quod deus fecit et plasmauit Adam in eo loco in quo natus est Iesus scilicet in ciuitate Bedleem que est in medio mundi, et ibi de quatuor angulis terre corpus Ade factum est, deferentibus angelis de limo terre de partibus illis, uidelicet Micaele Gabriele Raphaele et Uriele. Et erat illa terra candida et munda sicut sol, et conspersa est illa terra de quatuor fluminibus id est Geon Phison Tigris et Euphrates, et factus est homo ad imaginem dei, et insufflauit in faciem eius spiraculum uite scilicet animam. Sicut enim a quatuor fluminibus conspersus sic a quatuor uentis accepit flatus.

39 [57] Cum factus fuisset Adam et non erat ei nomen impositum adhuc, dixit dominus ad quatuor angelos ut quererent ei nomen, et exiuit Micael ad orientem et uidit stellam orientalem Ancolim nomine et sumpsit primam literam ab illa, et exiuit Gabriel ad meridiem et uidit stellam meridianam nomine disis et tulit primam literam ab illa; exiuit Raphael ad aquilonem et uidit stellam aquilonarem Arthos nomine et tulit primam literam ab ipsa; exiuit Uriel ad occidentem et uidit stellam occidentalem Mencembrion nomine et attulit primam literam ab eadem; quibus literis adductis dixit dominus ad Urielam, Lege literas istas, et legit et dixit, Adam, et dixit dominus, Sic uocetur nomen eius. Explicit uita protoplasti nostri Ade et Eue uxoris eius.

36 (following Mozley) [52] Then Seth made (two?) tablets of stone and (two?) of earth, (and he devised the caps of letters?) and wrote on them the life of this father, Adam, and his mother, Eve, which he had heard from them and seen with his own eyes. He placed the tablets in the middle of his father's house in the oratory where he prayed to the Lord. After the flood, these written tablets were seen by many men (these written stones?) but were legible to no one.
Solomon, however, being wise, saw the writing and prayed to the Lord. There appeared to him an angel of the Lord, saying: "I am he who held the hand of Seth, that he might write these stones with his finger (with an iron finger/ with an iron stylus?). You will be knowledgeable of these writings, so that you might know and understand (whence they are) what all these stone contain, and where the oratory was where Adam and Eve worshipped the Lord God. You must build there the temple of the Lord, which is the house of prayer.
Then Solomon completed the temple of the Lord God, and called these letters 'achiliacae,' that is, written without the teaching of words' ('achiliacae' stones, which is in Latin, teaching written without lips' / achiliacae' which is in Latin, parchments 'written without the teaching of books' ?) by the finger of Seth, while the angel of the Lord held his hand.
[53] On these stones was found what Enoch, the seventh from Adam, prophesied before the flood about the coming of Christ: "Behold the Lord will come in his sanctuary (in his holy soldiers, in his soldiers, in his holy clouds ?) to render judgment on all and to accuse the impious of all their works by which they have spoken concerning him — sinners, impious murmurers, and the irreligious who have lived according to their feelings of desire, and whose mouths have spoken pridefully. [IV+Those whose mouths have spoken pridefully will go to Hades, but the just will surely go rejoicing into the kingdom of heaven.
[54] (Adam entered the Garden after forty days, and Eve after eighty. Adam was in the Garden for seven years and in one day they moved every beast]IV.

37 [55]. It must be known that the body of Adam was formed of eight parts. The first part was of the dust of the earth, from which was made his flesh, and thereby he was sluggish. The next part was of the sea, from which was made his blood, and thereby he was aimless and fleeing. The third part was of the stones of the earth, from which his bones were made, and thereby he was hard and covetous. The fourth part was of the clouds, from which were made his thoughts, and thereby he was immoderate. The fifth part was of the wind, from which was made his breath, and thereby he was fickle. The sixth part was of the sun, from which were made his eyes, and thereby he was handsome and beautiful. The seventh part was of the light of the world, from which he was made pleasing, and thereby he had knowledge. The eight part was of the Holy Spirit, from which was made his soul, and thereby are the bishops, priests, and all the saints and elect of God.

38 [56]. It must also be known that God made and formed Adam in that place where Jesus was born, that is, in the city of Bethlehem, which is in the center of the earth. There Adam was made from the four corners of the earth, when angels brought some of the dust of the earth from its parts, viz. Michael, Gabriel, Raphael, and Uriel. This earth was white and pure like the sun and it was gathered together from the four rivers, that is, the Geon, Phison, Tigris, and Euphrates. Man was made in the image of God, and he blew into his face the breath of life, which is the soul. For just as he was gathers from the four rivers, thus from the four winds he received his breath.

39 [57] When Adam was made, and there was no name assigned to him yet, the Lord said to the four angels to seek a name for him. Michael went out to the east and saw the eastern star, named Ancolim, and took its first letter from it. Gabriel went out to the south, and saw the southern star, named Disis, and took its first letter from it. Raphael went out to the north, and saw the northern star, named Arthos, and took its first latter from it. Uriel went out to the west, and saw the western star, named Mencembrion, and took its first letter from it. When the letter were brought together, the Lord said to Uriel: "read these letters." He read them and said, "Adam." The Lord said: "Thus shall his name be called. "Here ends the life of our protoplast, Adam, and his wife, Eve."

Index

In this index are included the proper names to be found in the Synopsis, except for "Adam" and "Eve," which occur on virtually every page. The numbers are the page numbers of the Synopsis. If the page number is followed by letters, they indicate the versions on that page in which the name is found. If no letters are found, the name occurs in all the versions found on that page. G = Greek and Ge = Georgian

Abel	26GLAGe 27 28GLAS 29LGe 30 31 87 89G 94GAS
Acherusian Lake	82GGe
Amilabes	26G 27G
Angels	4Ge 5 10GGeS 11GLS 15L 16 17 23 24AGe 25A 27S 28GAS 29 32 35GLGeS 36GAGeS 37LAGeS 40GLAGe 46GAGe 51 53S 54S 62 69LAGe 70 72 73 74G 76 77 78 79 80 81 82 83GGeS 84 87S 88 89GGe 90GAGe 94S 96
Beliar	18S
Bethlehem	96
Cain	19AGe 25 26GL 27 28 30 31 88GAGe
Cherub	11A 15AGe 57 62 70LGe 76GAGe 82S 84 88GAGe
Christ	45AGe
demons	30
Devil, Satan	6 7S 11 12LAGeS 13LAGe 15 18LA 19A 36AS 37LAS 43A 48 49LAGe 50LAGe 51 52GAGe 54AS 58 GAGe 60GS
Diophotos	26G
enemy	12G 18Ge 36GGe 48G 49S 70AGe 85S 86S
enoch	96
ethiopians	81G
euphrates, river	96
Gabriel, angel	28Ge 62A 87GAGe 96

Index of Names

Gap'at'	26
Geon, river	96
Gerusia, sea of	82G
Indians	81Ge
Jael	72G 78G
Jehovah	16L
Jesus	96
Joel, angel	6 72S 79S 95S
Jordan, river	9 10LAGe 12S 20AGe 45LAGe
King, of God	45L
Michael, archangel	1G 6 16 17LA 21Ge 24L 27S 28GAS 32 44 45A 46L 62GS 74L 77AGe 81S 82L 83GGeS 84G 86 87GAGe 89Ge 91 92GAGe 94 96
Mongrel, beast	41S
Moses	1G
Ozel	87A
Pison, river	96
powers(s)	23 24AGe 25Ge
Raphael, angel	96
Satan	see Devil
seraph	70A 76AS 78 82GGeS 90A
Seth	29AGe 31 34 35 36A 37S 39 41 43 44 46 59A 74A 79LS 81 82GLGe 85 91 94 96
Solomon	96
son, of God	45L 68AGe
Tigris, river	8 9 11GLAGe 96
Uriel	86L 87L 96
Virtues	32 see also power(s)

www.ingramcontent.com/pod-product-compliance
Lightning Source LLC
Chambersburg PA
CBHW030343240426
43661CB00052B/1728